IMAGES
of America

PHARR

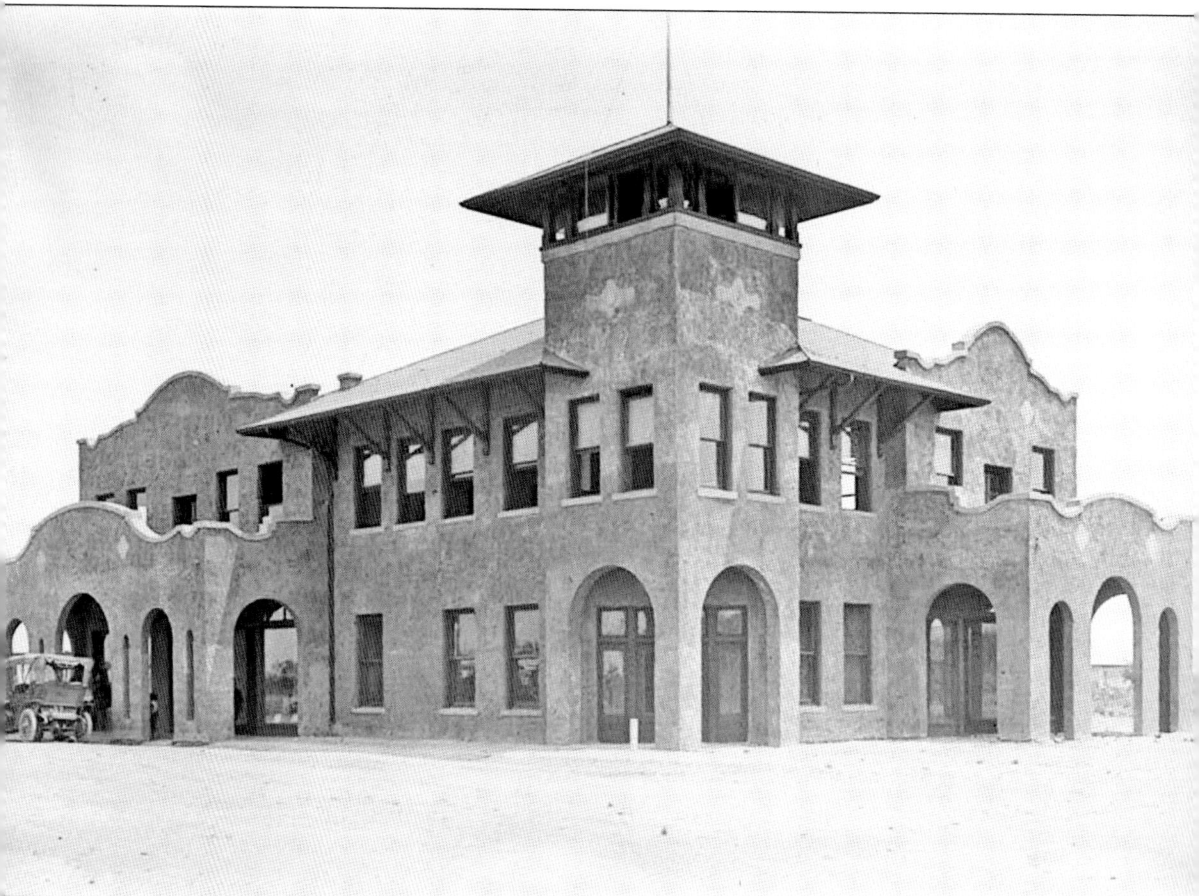

This photograph of the first building in Pharr was taken sometime between 1915 and 1920. It was made right after the building's completion and is the first picture ever taken of it. Eventually, it would become the home of First National Bank, Pharr City Hall, and Pharr Drug, and is considered the trademark of the entire city. The structure, although having taken on renovations, appears almost identical and still stands today. (Courtesy of the Library of Congress.)

On the Cover: The Humble gas station was located at the southeast corner of Cage Boulevard and Business 83. The first full-service gas station in downtown Pharr that offered quality service to all its customers, it was flanked by a service garage and a neighboring café for the convenience of those customers traveling through the Hub City. (Courtesy of the University of Texas–Pan American Library and Special Collections Department.)

IMAGES
of America

PHARR

Romeo Rosales Jr.

ARCADIA
PUBLISHING

ISBN 978-1-4671-3137-7

Published by Arcadia Publishing
Charleston, South Carolina

Printed in the United States of America

Library of Congress Control Number: 2013952332

For all general information, please contact Arcadia Publishing:
Telephone 843-853-2070
Fax 843-853-0044
E-mail sales@arcadiapublishing.com
For customer service and orders:
Toll-Free 1-888-313-2665

Visit us on the Internet at www.arcadiapublishing.com

To my wife, Claudia, who has always supported me and loved me, to all my family, and to my late beloved uncle Juan Ramon Garcia

Contents

ACKNOWLEDGMENTS

The city of Pharr's history is fascinating and unique, and so I am happy that I was given the opportunity to write its first history book. There are so many people that I want to thank for helping make this book possible. First of all, I would like to thank my wife, Claudia, and my son, Azariah, for sacrificing so much so that I could complete this book. Both of you have supported me and loved me through this entire journey. I love you both so much. I would also like to thank all of my family, especially my mother and father for always supporting me and pushing me in the right direction. I love you both dearly. Next, I would like to thank my grandfather Ruben "Sepi" Rosales and my grandmother Emma Rosales for sitting with me and staying up late at night many times to analyze photographs and discuss the history of Pharr. I had so much fun learning from you both. I would also like to thank the Pharr Memorial Library director, Adolfo Garcia, not only for giving me a job but also for going with me to the University of Texas–Pan American Special Collections Department and the Museum of South Texas History to hunt down numerous photographs for this book. Your guidance really helped me. I definitely cannot forget to thank Julio Enriquez, a coworker and friend of mine, for constantly helping me with all the photographs that are in this book. You sacrificed a lot of your time to help make my dream come true, and I am forever grateful for your help. I also cannot forget to thank Reyes and Anita Vela for believing in what I was doing and also helping me understand the history of the city. Your help was greatly appreciated. Finally, I would like to thank several other contributors to the book. Thanks go to Tony Villegas, for allowing me to use some of your photographs; Raquel Salinas, for helping understand the history of the city; Aida Escobar, for donating several great photographs of the city to the library that were used in this book; the Museum of South Texas History staff, for all the photographs you contributed; and Janette Garcia, archivist and librarian at the University of Texas–Pan American, for all your help as well. And a thank-you goes to the entire city of Pharr—council members, community leaders, and community members—for your support and for making this the best mid-sized city in South Texas.

INTRODUCTION

Pharr, Texas, is named after one of its founding fathers, Henry Newton Pharr, and is located in South Texas about eight miles north of the Rio Grande. Henry Newton Pharr belonged to a Louisiana family that was most notably known for its members' abilities in business matters and public affairs. He was a sugar planter, mechanical engineer, and businessman who made good use of his education from Centenary College and Vanderbilt University. Before he ventured off into the Rio Grande Valley to purchase land, he was in charge of dredge boats, digging canals and building drainage plants in Louisiana. At one point, sometime in the very early 1900s, he was also director of the State National Bank of New Iberia, Louisiana. In 1904, he paid a visit to the Rio Grande Valley and was hoping to invest in some land at that time but was unable to do so; this was a decision he later admitted he came to regret. Again, in 1909, he visited the Rio Grande Valley, determined to not return to Louisiana until he invested in some land. Where he would invest, he was unsure, but after visiting land where the current city of Pharr sits, he was positive that was the land for him. Several meetings between Pharr and his partner, John C. Kelly, were held at the Miller Hotel in Brownsville, Texas, to discuss the idea of investing in large tracts of land. That year, 1909, was when the city of Pharr was rightfully established. Pharr later became the president of the Louisiana-Rio Grande Sugar Company and the Louisiana-Rio Grande Canal Company, which owned 16,000 acres in 1910.

Pharr is situated within a Spanish land grant made in 1767 to Juan Jose Hinojosa. The Hinojosa family and heirs sold off portions of their lands to various groups in the late 19th century and occupied the area as late as 1882. In 1909, John C. Kelly and Henry Newton Pharr had aspirations of establishing a sugarcane empire in Deep South Texas. The two began their partnership by establishing the Pharr Townsite Company, the Louisiana-Rio Grande Sugar Company, and the Louisiana-Rio Grande Canal Company. The one problem that troubled them was how they were going to make the soil in Pharr agriculturally suitable to grow sugarcane. The job of figuring this enigma out was given to a civil engineer, a Mr. Gore. He was commissioned with the difficult task of constructing an irrigation system with a main canal that could supply water for at least 16,000 acres. Gore was not the type of man to settle for the bare minimum, and so he quickly drew up the plans to establish a pump house right near the Rio Grande so that water could be pumped directly from the river into the main canal and then to all the local farms. By the time his project was completed, Gore's pump house was capable of supplying water for up to 40,000 acres. Needless to say, Kelly and Pharr were more than impressed and pleased. The rapid growth of the city soon followed.

The city of Pharr's rapid growth was far from perfection, however. The city, like many others across the nation before the Civil Rights Act of 1964 and the Voting Rights Act of 1965, was segregated and divided up between Mexican Americans and whites. The railroad tracks that run east and west on Business 83 divided the city. The whites resided on the south side, and all the minorities resided on the north side of the tracks. On the grounds of language differences, geography, ethnic preferences, and economics, segregated schools in town continued to be the norm for the school district into the 1970s. Segregation in town was evident in 1971 during the Pharr police riots. Many residents in town claimed that law enforcement officials were wrongfully targeting minorities and using excessive force for no apparent reason other than racism. Ironically, many of these law enforcement officials were minorities themselves. Chief Alfredo Ramirez was relieved of his command during the riots and was replaced by Edinburg police chief Alfredo Gonzalez. It was under Gonzalez's command that the one and only casualty of the entire ordeal took place. A 20-year-old man named Alfonso Flores, who had just received a haircut at the Ramos Hair Salon, was shot and killed by Edinburg deputy Robert Johnson. A total of 31 adults and 8 juveniles were arrested and charged with various crimes. The riots made national news, and a portion can still be seen today on YouTube. It was a trying time for the city, and it was clear changes had to be made. Mayor R.S. Bowe resigned after relenting pressure from Pharr residents forced his resignation two months after the riots. Citizens of Pharr, both whites and Mexicans, were disgusted with Mayor Bowe's leadership. Many say his resignation, and the riots themselves, were the beginning of positive changes in Pharr and in the valley. It was the start of a period of more inclusion for Mexican Americans in the South Texas region. Since then, the city has exhibited positive changes and a large step forward in the right direction.

The city of Pharr holds precedence as the heart of the Rio Grande Valley, as all visitors to the valley who travel along former US Route 281, recently changed to Interstate 69, must first enter through Pharr before reaching their destinations. In 1920, Pharr had an estimated population of 1,560 residents. Today, the city has a population of nearly 74,000 people. It has come a long way since its incorporation in 1916 and continues to be a vital component of the major growth of the Rio Grande Valley. There have been many positive changes within the city that make it a wonderful place for vacationers and winter Texans to visit. Pharr's warm climate attracts residents from as far north as Canada during the wintertime because the winters here are not harsh and the number of inches of snow that has fallen in the city's recorded history can be counted on one hand. The future for Pharr looks bright, and continued growth is a sure thing. I hope the amazing story of the city of Pharr will delight readers, because the city has a unique and rich history that place it in a category of its own.

One

Foundation, Incorporation, and Pioneers

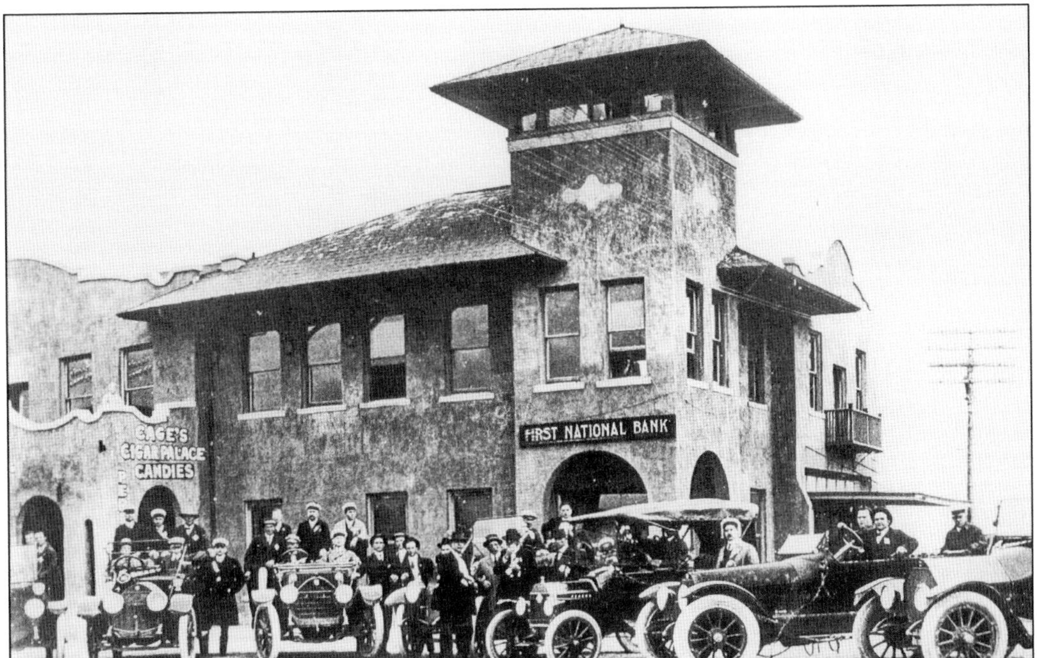

This early-1920s picture depicts the first official building in the city of Pharr. The First National Bank was created due to the need for the exchange of money and was housed in the city hall building. This picture also shows a delegation from the chamber of commerce from the city of Dallas. These men were prospectors who were lured into Pharr for its abundant land and potential for exponential growth. (Courtesy of the University of Texas–Pan American Library and Special Collections Department.)

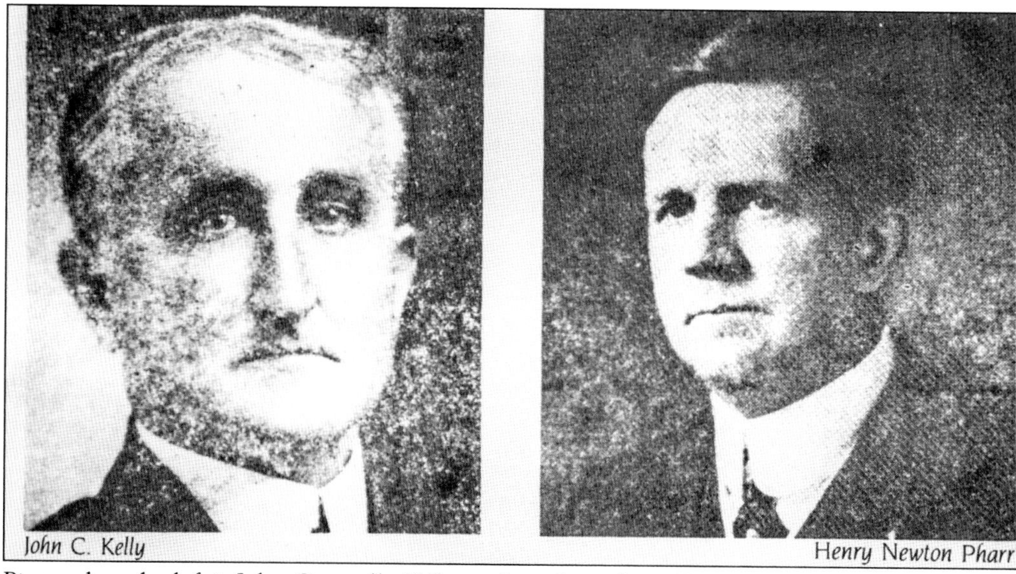

Pictured on the left is John Connally Kelly, and on the right is Henry Newton Pharr. These two men are the founding fathers of the city of Pharr and are responsible for the tremendous growth the city has experienced throughout its more than 100 years of existence. Their vision and dream propelled the city into the 20th century. Pharr has stood the test of time and continues to thrive today. (Courtesy of the Pharr Memorial Library Archives.)

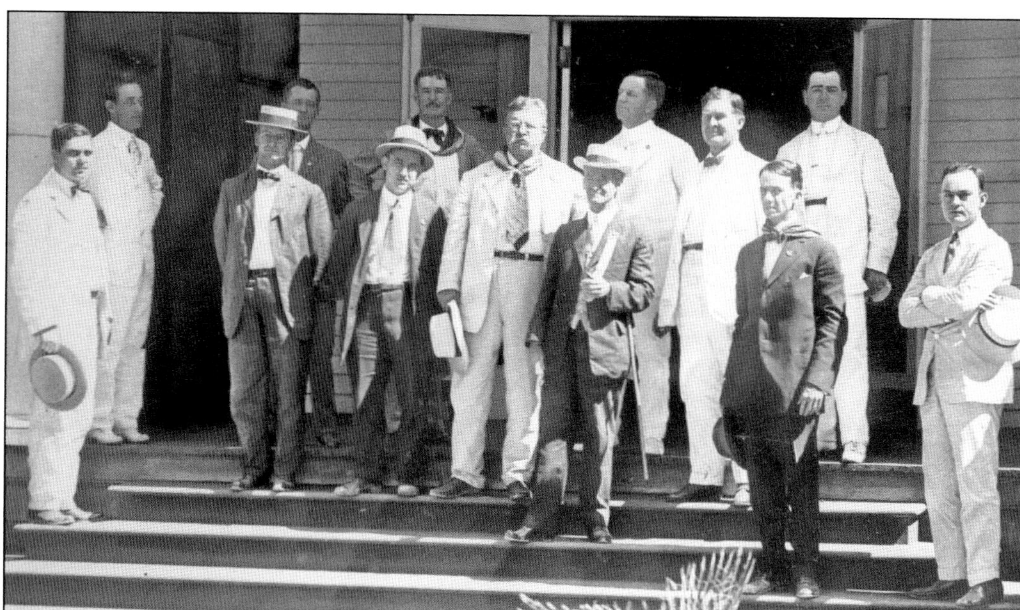

This early-1900s photograph shows the city's founding father, Henry Newton Pharr, with Pres. Theodore Roosevelt (center, in white suit and glasses). Pharr is standing to Roosevelt's left on the top step. Pharr was a very influential man in New Iberia, Louisiana, where he was a sugarcane grower. He established himself even more when he founded the Louisiana-Rio Grande Canal Company in Pharr where the town was named after him by his partner, John Connally Kelly. (Courtesy of the Pharr Memorial Library Archives.)

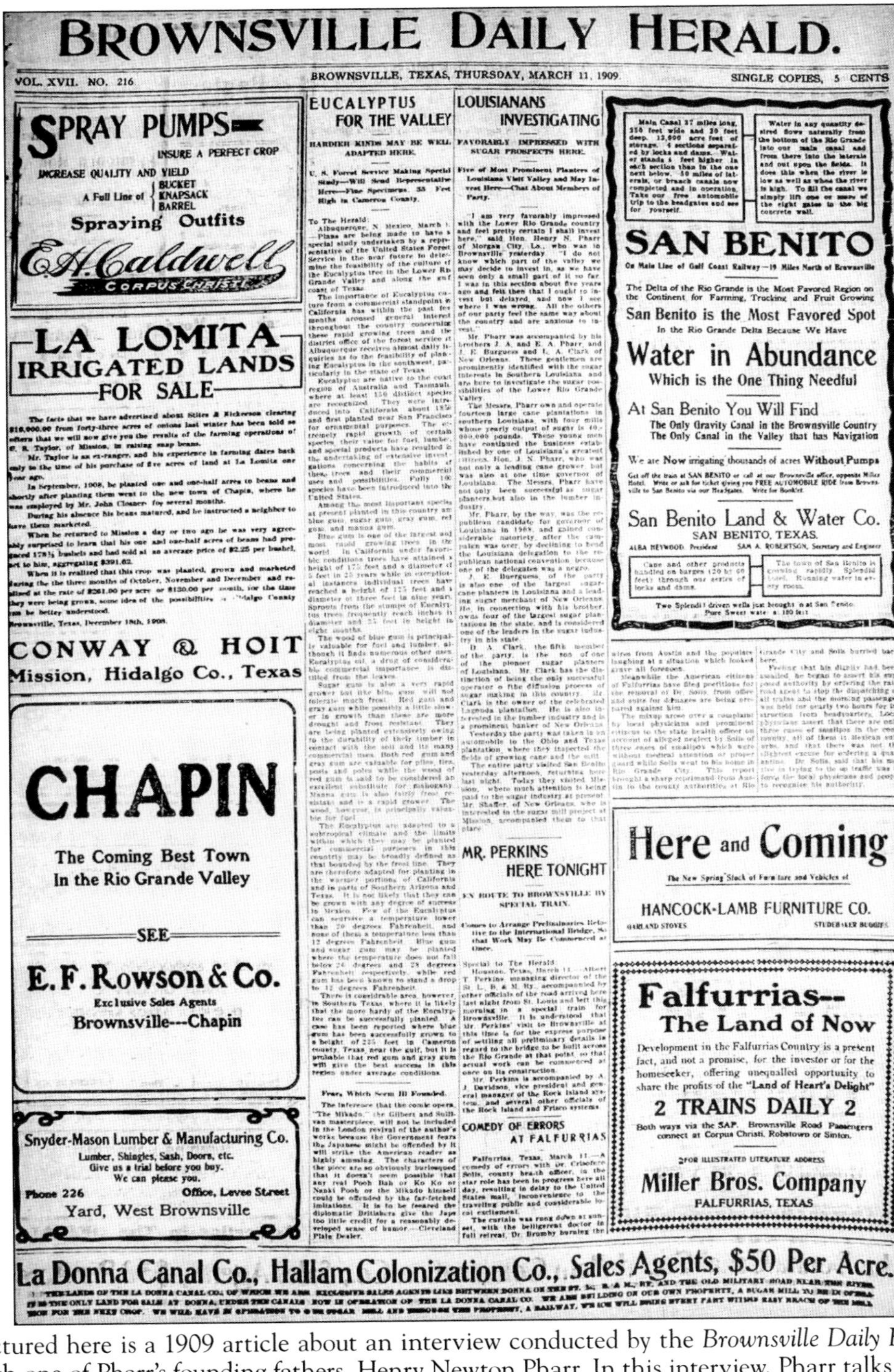

BROWNSVILLE DAILY HERALD.

VOL. XVII. NO. 216 — BROWNSVILLE, TEXAS, THURSDAY, MARCH 11, 1909. — SINGLE COPIES, 5 CENTS

SPRAY PUMPS — INSURE A PERFECT CROP

INCREASE QUALITY AND YIELD

A Full Line of BUCKET, KNAPSACK, BARREL Spraying Outfits

E. H. Caldwell, Corpus Christi

LA LOMITA IRRIGATED LANDS FOR SALE

The facts that we have advertised about Stites & Nickerson clearing $10,000.00 from forty-three acres of onions last winter has been sold so often that we will now give you the results of the farming operations of C. S. Taylor, of Mission, in raising snap beans.

Mr. Taylor is an ex-ranger, and his experience in farming dates back only to the time of his purchase of five acres of land at La Lomita one year ago.

In September, 1908, he planted one and one-half acres to beans and shortly after planting them went to the new town of Chapin, where he was employed by Mr. John Closner for several months.

During his absence his beans matured, and he instructed a neighbor to have them marketed.

When he returned to Mission a day or two ago he was very agreeably surprised to learn that his one and one-half acres of beans had produced 178½ bushels and had sold at an average price of $2.25 per bushel, net to him, aggregating $391.62.

When it is realized that this crop was planted, grown and marketed during the the three months of October, November and December and realized at the rate of $261.00 per acre or $130.00 per month, for the time they were being grown, some idea of the possibilities of Hidalgo County can be better understood.

Brownsville, Texas, December 18th, 1908.

CONWAY & HOIT, Mission, Hidalgo Co., Texas

CHAPIN — The Coming Best Town In the Rio Grande Valley — SEE E. F. Rowson & Co., Exclusive Sales Agents, Brownsville—Chapin

Snyder-Mason Lumber & Manufacturing Co. Lumber, Shingles, Sash, Doors, etc. Give us a trial before you buy. We can please you. Phone 226. Office, Levee Street. Yard, West Brownsville

EUCALYPTUS FOR THE VALLEY

HARDIER KINDS MAY BE WELL ADAPTED HERE.

U. S. Forest Service Making Special Study—Will Send Representative Here—Fine Specimens 35 Feet High in Cameron County.

To The Herald:

Albuquerque, N. Mexico, March 1.—Plans are being made to have a special study undertaken by a representative of the United States Forest Service in the near future to determine the feasibility of the culture of the Eucalyptus tree in the Lower Rio Grande Valley and along the gulf coast of Texas.

The importance of Eucalyptus culture from a commercial standpoint in California has within the past few months aroused general interest throughout the country concerning these rapid growing trees and the district office of the forest service at Albuquerque receives almost daily inquiries as to the feasibility of planting Eucalyptus in the southwest, particularly in the state of Texas.

Eucalyptus are native to the coast region of Australia and Tasmania where at least 150 distinct species are recognized. They were introduced into California about 1856 and first planted near San Francisco for ornamental purposes. The extremely rapid growth of certain species, their value for fuel, lumber, and special products have resulted in the undertaking of extensive investigations concerning the habits of these trees and their commercial uses and possibilities. Fully 100 species have been introduced into the United States.

Among the most important species at present planted in this country are blue gum, sugar gum, gray gum, red gum, and manna gum.

Blue gum is one of the largest and most rapid growing trees in the world. In California under favorable conditions trees have attained a height of 175 feet and a diameter of 5 feet in 25 years while in exceptional instances individual trees have reached a height of 175 feet and a diameter of three feet in nine years. Sprouts from the stumps of Eucalyptus trees frequently reach inches in diameter and 25 feet in height in eight months.

The wood of blue gum is principally valuable for fuel and lumber, although it finds numerous other uses. Eucalyptus oil, a drug of considerable commercial importance, is distilled from the leaves.

Sugar gum is also a very rapid grower but like blue gum will not tolerate much frost. Red gum and gray gum while possibly a little slower in growth than these are more drought and frost resistant. They are being planted extensively owing to the durability of their timber in contact with the soil and its many commercial uses. Both red gum and gray gum are valuable for piles, ties, posts and poles while the wood of red gum is said to be considered an excellent substitute for mahogany. Manna gum is also fairly frost resistant and is a rapid grower. The wood, however, is principally valuable for fuel.

The Eucalyptus are adapted to a subtropical climate and the limits within which they may be planted for commercial purposes in this country may be broadly defined as that bounded by the frost line. They are therefore adapted for planting in the warmer portions of California and in parts of Southern Arizona and Texas. It is not likely that they can be grown with any degree of success in Mexico. Few of the Eucalyptus can survive a temperature lower than 20 degrees Fahrenheit, and none of them a temperature less than 12 degrees Fahrenheit. Blue gum and sugar gum may be planted where the temperature does not fall below 24 degrees and 28 degrees Fahrenheit respectively, while red gum has been known to stand a drop to 12 degrees Fahrenheit.

There is considerable area, however, in Southern Texas, where it is likely that the more hardy of the Eucalyptus can be successfully planted. A case has been reported where blue gum has been successfully grown to a height of 225 feet in Cameron county, Texas, near the gulf, but it is probable that red gum and gray gum will give the best success in this region under average conditions.

Fears, Which Seem Ill Founded.

The inference that the comic opera, "The Mikado," the Gilbert and Sullivan masterpiece, will not be included in the London revival of the author's works because the Government fears the Japanese might be offended by it will strike the American reader as highly amusing. The characters of the piece are so obviously burlesqued that it doesn't seem possible that any real Pooh Bah or Ko Ko or Nanki Pooh or the Mikado himself could be offended by the far-fetched imitations. It is to be feared the diplomatic Britishers give the Japs too little credit for a reasonably developed sense of humor.—Cleveland Plain Dealer.

LOUISIANANS INVESTIGATING

FAVORABLY IMPRESSED WITH SUGAR PROSPECTS HERE.

Five of Most Prominent Planters of Louisiana Visit Valley and May Invest Here—Chat About Members of Party.

"I am very favorably impressed with the Lower Rio Grande country and feel pretty certain I shall invest here," said Hon. Henry N. Pharr of Morgan City, La., who was in Brownsville yesterday. "I do not know which part of the valley we may decide to invest in, as we have seen only a small part of it so far. I was in this section about five years ago and felt then that I ought to invest but delayed, and now I see where I was wrong. All the others of our party feel the same way about the country and are anxious to invest."

Mr. Pharr was accompanied by his brothers J. A. and E. A. Pharr, and J. E. Burguess and L. A. Clark of New Orleans. These gentlemen are prominently identified with the sugar interests in Southern Louisiana and are here to investigate the sugar possibilities of the Lower Rio Grande Valley.

The Messrs. Pharr own and operate fourteen large cane plantations in southern Louisiana, with four mills whose yearly output of sugar is 40,000,000 pounds. These young men have continued the business established by one of Louisiana's greatest citizens, Hon. J. N. Pharr, who was not only a leading cane grower, but was also at one time governor of Louisiana. The Messrs. Pharr have not only been successful as sugar planters but also in the lumber industry.

Mr. Pharr, by the way, was the republican candidate for governor of Louisiana in 1908, and gained considerable notoriety, after the campaign was over, by declining to head the Louisiana delegation to the republican national convention because one of the delegates was a negro.

J. E. Buerguess, of the party is also one of the largest sugar-cane planters in Louisiana and a leading sugar merchant of New Orleans. He, in connection with his brother, owns four of the largest sugar plantations in the state, and is considered one of the leaders in the sugar industry in his state.

D. A. Clark, the fifth member of the party, is the son of one of the pioneer sugar planters of Louisiana. Mr. Clark has the distinction of being the only successful operater o fthe diffusion process of sugar making in this country. Mr. Clark is the owner of the celebrated Lagonda plantation. He is also interested in the lumber industry and is a prominent banker of New Orleans.

Yesterday the party was taken in an automobile to the Ohio and Texas plantation, where they inspected the fields of growing cane and the mill.

The entire party visited San Benito yesterday afternoon, returning here last night. Today they visited Mission, where much attention is being paid to the sugar industry at present. Mr. Shaffer, of New Orleans, who is interested in the sugar mill project at Mission, accompanied them to that place.

MR. PERKINS HERE TONIGHT

EN ROUTE TO BROWNSVILLE BY SPECIAL TRAIN.

Comes to Arrange Preliminaries Relative to the International Bridge, So that Work May Be Commenced at Once.

Special to The Herald:

Houston, Texas, March 11.—Albert T. Perkins, managing director of the St. L., B. & M. Ry., accompanied by other officials of the road arrived here last night from St. Louis and left this morning in a special train for Brownsville. It is understood that Mr. Perkins' visit to Brownsville at this time is for the express purpose of settling all preliminary details in regard to the bridge to be built across the Rio Grande at that point, so that actual work can be commenced at once on its construction.

Mr. Perkins is accompanied by A. J. Davidson, vice president and general manager of the Rock Island system, and several other officials of the Rock Island and Frisco systems.

COMEDY OF ERRORS AT FALFURRIAS

Falfurrias, Texas, March 11.—A comedy of errors with Dr. Crisoforo Solis, county health officer, in the star role has been in progress here all day, resulting in delay to the United States mail, inconvenience to the traveling public and considerable local excitement.

The curtain was rung down at sunset, with the belligerent doctor in full retreat, Dr. Brumby burning the wires from Austin and the populace laughing at a situation which looked grave all forenoon.

Meanwhile the American citizens of Falfurrias have filed preetitions for the removal of Dr. Solis from office and suits for damages are being prepared against him.

The mixup arose over a complaint by local physicians and prominent citizens to the state health officer on account of alleged neglect by Solis of three cases of smallpox which were without medical attention or proper guard while Solis went to his home in Rio Grande City. This report brought a sharp reprimand from Austin to the county authorities at Rio Grande City and Solis hurried back here.

Feeling that his dignity had been assailed, he began to assert his supposed authority by ordering the railroad agent to stop the dispatching of all trains and the morning passenger was held for nearly two hours for instruction from headquarters. Local physicians assert that there are only three cases of smallpox in the community, all of them in Mexican suburbs, and that there was not the slightest excuse for ordering a quarantine. Dr. Solis, said that his motive in trying to tie up traffic was to force the local physicians and people to recognize his authority.

Main Canal 37 miles long, 150 feet wide and 20 feet deep. 12,000 acre feet of storage. 4 sections separated by locks and dams. Water stands 6 feet higher in each section than in the one next below. 50 miles of laterals, or branch canals now completed and in operation. Take our free automobile trip to the headgates and see for yourself.

Water in any quantity desired flows naturally from the bottom of the Rio Grande into our main canal and from there into the laterals and out upon the fields. It does this when the river is low as well as when the river is high. To fill the canal we simply lift one or more of the eight gates in the big concrete wall.

SAN BENITO

On Main Line of Gulf Coast Railway—19 Miles North of Brownsville

The Delta of the Rio Grande is the Most Favored Region on the Continent for Farming, Trucking and Fruit Growing

San Benito is the Most Favored Spot In the Rio Grande Delta Because We Have

Water in Abundance — Which is the One Thing Needful

At San Benito You Will Find — The Only Gravity Canal in the Brownsville Country — The Only Canal in the Valley that has Navigation

We are Now irrigating thousands of acres Without Pumps

Get off the train at SAN BENITO or call at our Brownsville office, opposite Miller Hotel. Write or ask for ticket giving you FREE AUTOMOBILE RIDE from Brownsville to San Benito via our Headgates. Write for Booklet.

San Benito Land & Water Co., SAN BENITO, TEXAS.

ALBA HEYWOOD, President — SAM A. ROBERTSON, Secretary and Engineer

Cane and other products handled on barges (20 by 60 feet) through our series of locks and dams.

The town of San Benito is growing rapidly. Splendid hotel. Running water in every room.

Two Splendid driven wells just brought in at San Benito. Pure Sweet water at 180 feet

Here and Coming — The New Spring Stock of Furniture and Vehicles of HANCOCK-LAMB FURNITURE CO. — GARLAND STOVES — STUDEBAKER BUGGIES

Falfurrias— The Land of Now

Development in the Falfurrias Country is a present fact, and not a promise, for the investor or for the homeseeker, offering unequalled opportunity to share the profits of the "Land of Heart's Delight"

2 TRAINS DAILY 2

Both ways via the SAP. Brownsville Road Passengers connect at Corpus Christi, Robstown or Sinton.

FOR ILLUSTRATED LITERATURE ADDRESS

Miller Bros. Company, FALFURRIAS, TEXAS

La Donna Canal Co., Hallam Colonization Co., Sales Agents, $50 Per Acre.

Pictured here is a 1909 article about an interview conducted by the *Brownsville Daily Herald* with one of Pharr's founding fathers, Henry Newton Pharr. In this interview, Pharr talks about investing in land in the Rio Grande Valley. At the time, he did not know where he would invest, but sometime that same year, he decided on the location of the city of Pharr. He also states that he was in the Rio Grande Valley five years prior to this interview, in 1904. (Courtesy of the University of North Texas Libraries.)

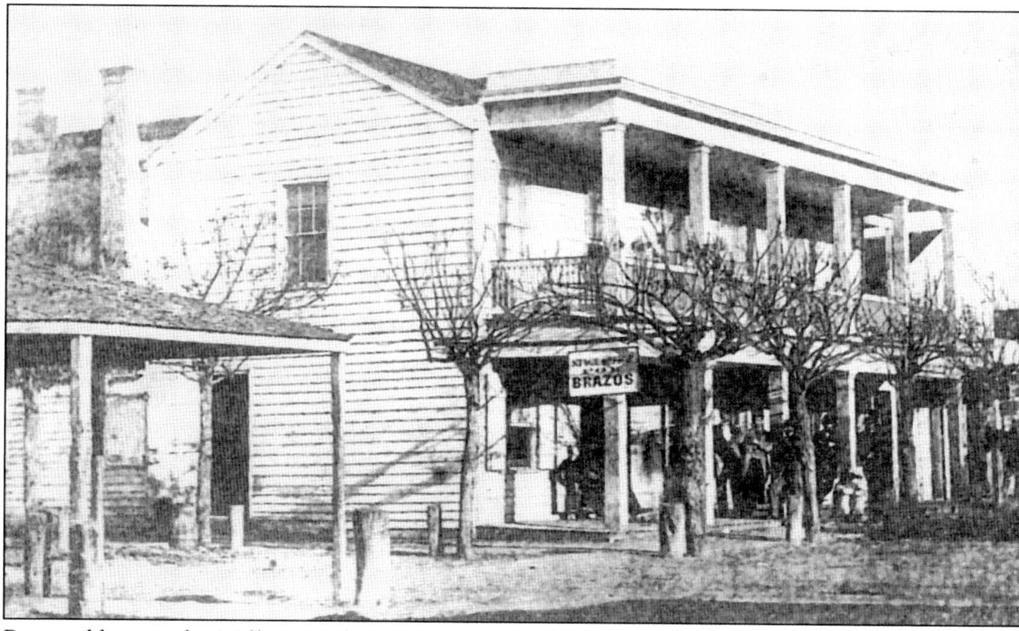

Pictured here is the Miller Hotel in the very early 1900s. The hotel was located in Brownsville, Texas, about 55 miles east of Pharr, but was instrumental in the founding of the city of Pharr. This was where Henry Newton Pharr and John C. Kelly met a few times to discuss their partnership and purchasing large tracts of land in the Rio Grande Valley. Their partnership would eventually lead to establishing the city of Pharr. (Courtesy of the Pharr Memorial Library Archives.)

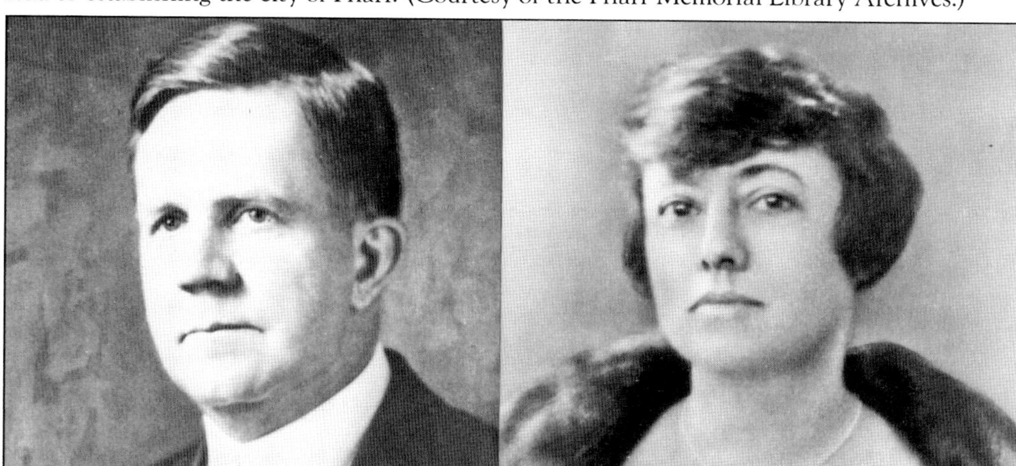

Pictured here are Henry Newton Pharr and his wife, Anna Jane Smith. They married at Jackson, Louisiana, on January 26, 1898. After their marriage, they were blessed with two children, John N. Pharr and Anna Jane Pharr. An interesting fact about the last name Pharr is that it was originally spelled "Farr." The Spelling of the Scottish name was changed when a scholarly member of the family who had a considerable knowledge of the Greek language substituted the Greek letter *phi* (in English, *ph*) for the initial *f*, and since then, the last name has been spelled Pharr. (Courtesy of the Pharr Memorial Library Archives.)

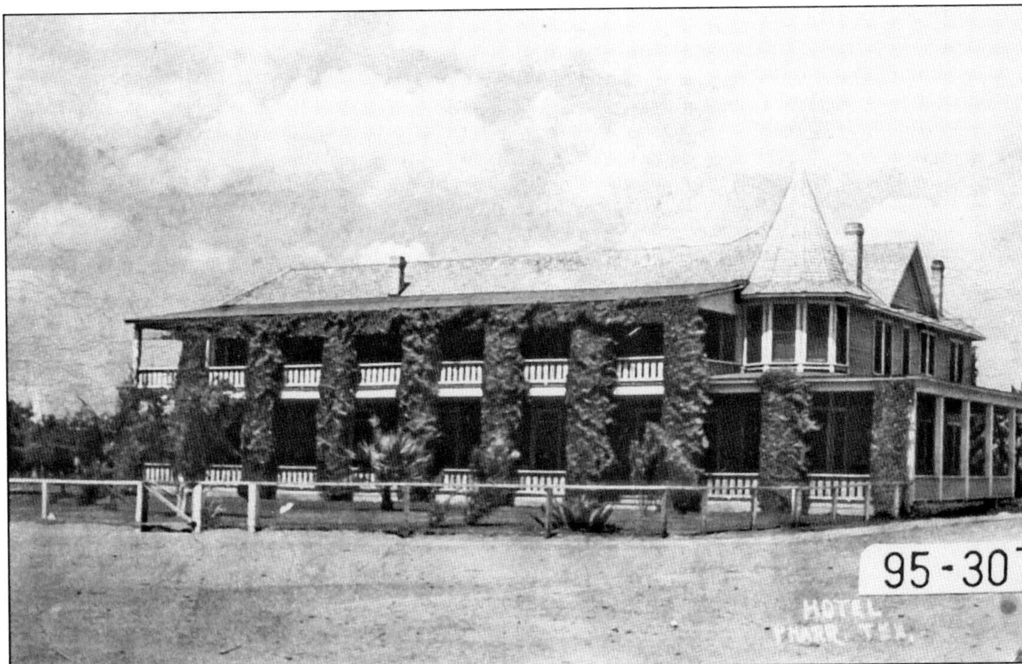

The Pharr Hotel was built in 1910 on Cage Boulevard and West Park Avenue and was considered the "gem of the valley," costing some $10,000. A Mr. and Mrs. Linesetter managed it until it burned down in 1934. This two-story hotel was a major social center for travelers and political leaders from all across South Texas. It also accommodated workers working on the irrigation system for the Kelly-Pharr tract. (Courtesy of the University of Texas–Pan American Library and Special Collections Department.)

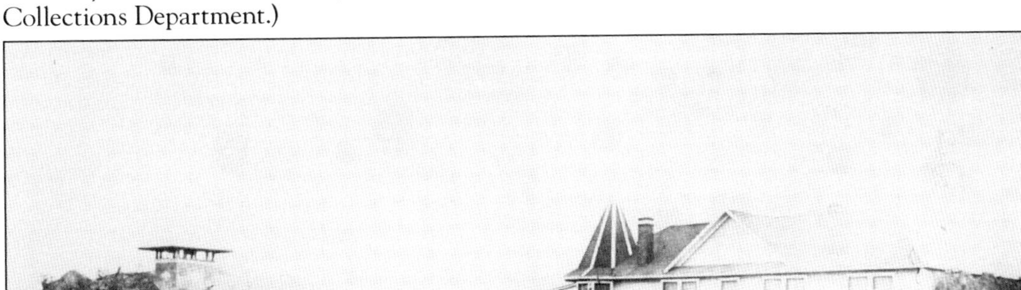

Photographer J.C. Murff took this 1920s photograph. It is one of the only, if not the only, photograph that exists that shows Pharr's first building and the Pharr Hotel pictured together. This photograph was taken north of Park Avenue, with the photographer facing southeast. (Courtesy of the Museum of South Texas History.)

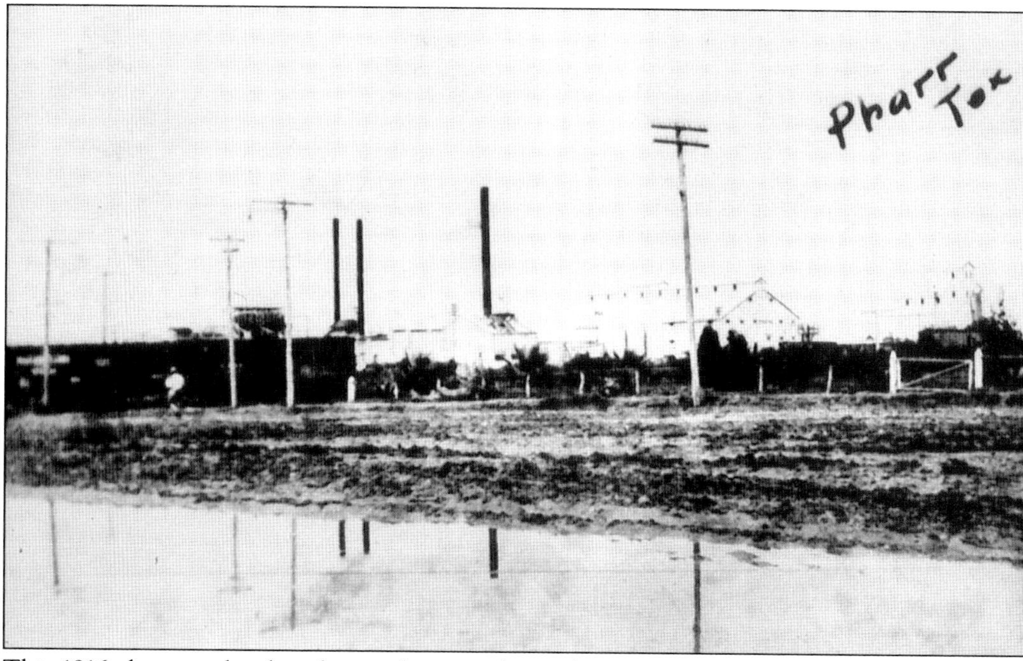

This 1916 photograph taken from a distance shows the city's alfalfa mill of the Pharr Mill and Elevator Company. Just one year later, in 1917, the alfalfa drier burned, entailing a loss of $70,000 not covered by insurance. The grain elevator for the company was saved, so the city was lucky enough not to lose it all. (Courtesy of the Museum of South Texas History.)

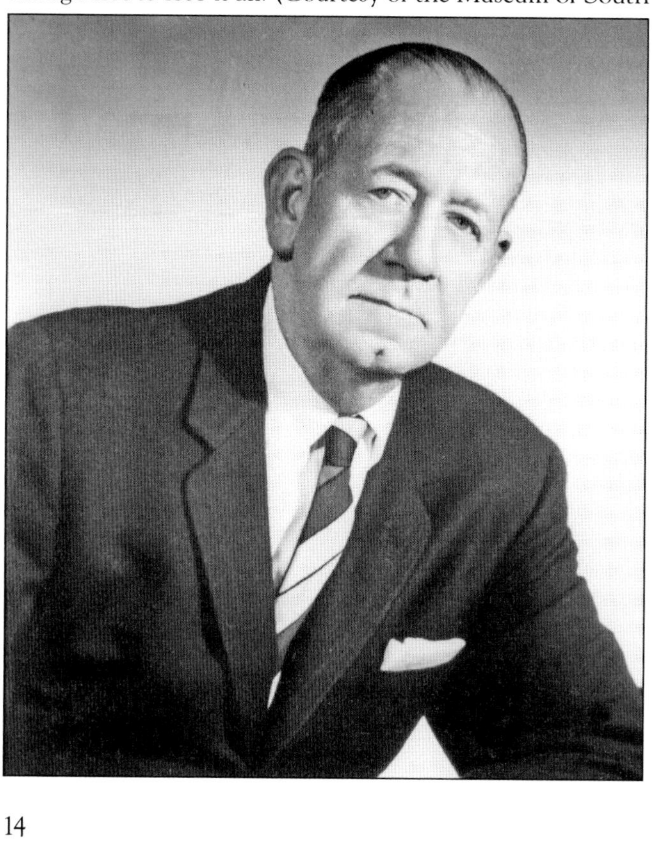

John N. Pharr was Henry Newton Pharr's only son. John graduated with a bachelor's of science degree from Yale University in 1923. During the Great War (World War I), he enlisted in the Aviation Corps, where he served for one year and was commissioned second lieutenant. He was his father's assistant in the sugar business. (Courtesy of the Pharr Memorial Library Archives.)

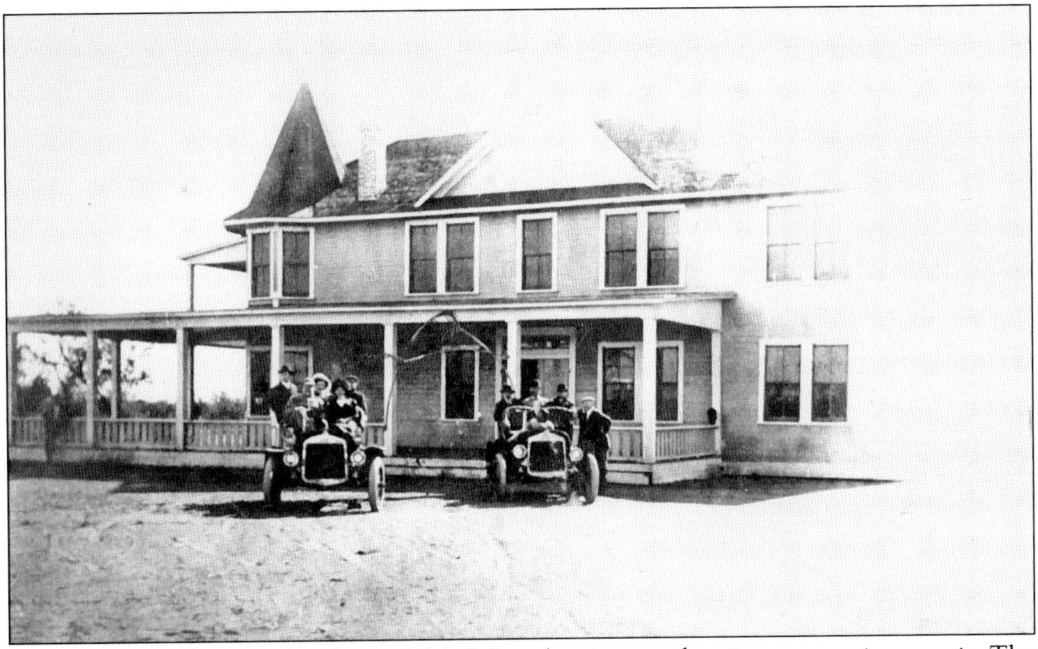

The Pharr Hotel was such a beautiful lodging that it gave the city some serious merit. The Linesetters ran the hotel in such a manner that it was mandatory to be dressed in formal attire while attending dinner. This 1912 photograph was taken immediately after construction and shows the Pharr Hotel prior to the additions seen in the photograph at the top of page 13 It is believed that this is the oldest surviving picture of the hotel. (Courtesy of the University of Texas–Pan American Library and Special Collections Department.)

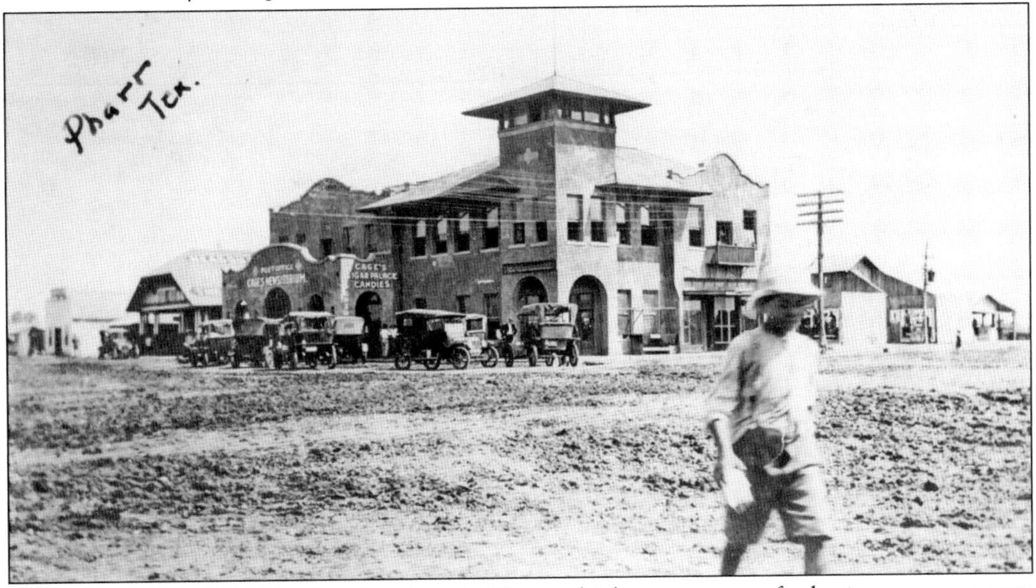

Pictured here in 1915 is the first building in Pharr, which was a mecca for businessmen, as seen by all the cars parked outside. The building housed Pharr's city hall, the First National Bank, a Mr. Cage's newsitorium, Pharr Drug, and the city post office for a short time when Cage was postmaster. This building was commonly referred to as "La Botica" (the drugstore) by locals. (Courtesy of the Museum of South Texas History.)

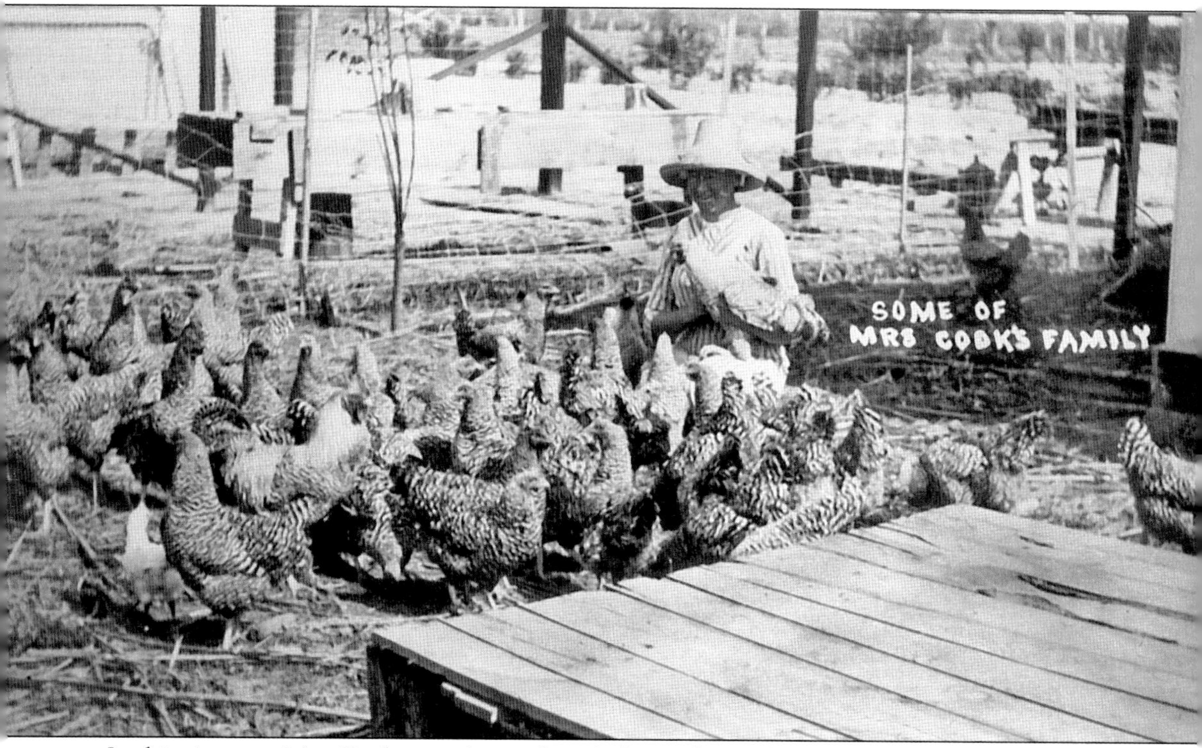

In this picture, a Mrs. Cook is tending to her plethora of Barred Rock chickens. The Cook family farm was located on the corner of I Road (Veterans Boulevard) and Sam Houston Street. To get to the Cook farm, one had to travel to the outskirts of Pharr's city limits. Today, the Cook home would have been well situated within the boundaries of the city. (Courtesy of the University of Texas–Pan American Library and Special Collections Department.)

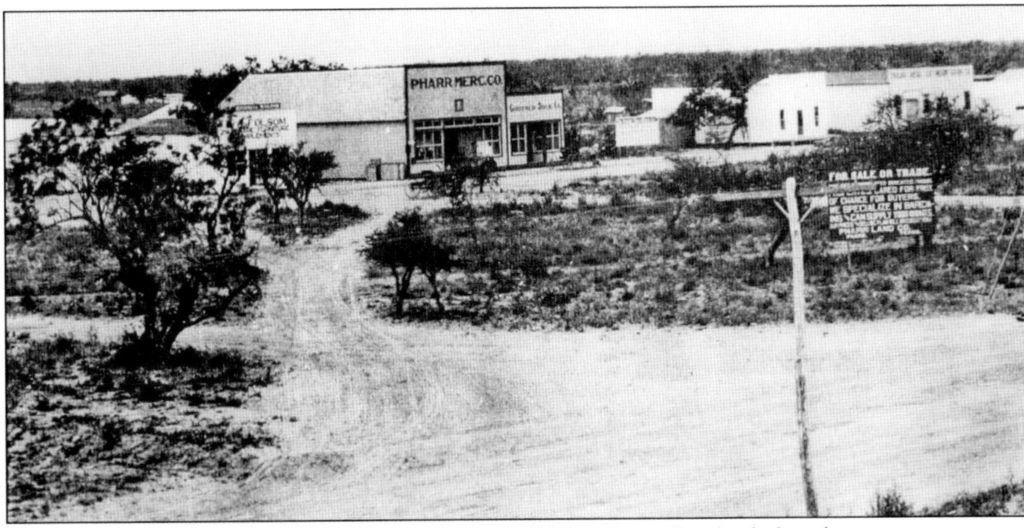

Pictured in this 1912 street scene are several small businesses that had already sprung up around Pharr after its founding in 1909. This photograph shows an excellent example of the steady growth the city experienced early on in the 20th century. However, at this point, there was still a whole lot of growing to do, as unstructured roads and plenty of brush and mesquite trees were still scattered all across town. (Courtesy of the Pharr Memorial Library Archives.)

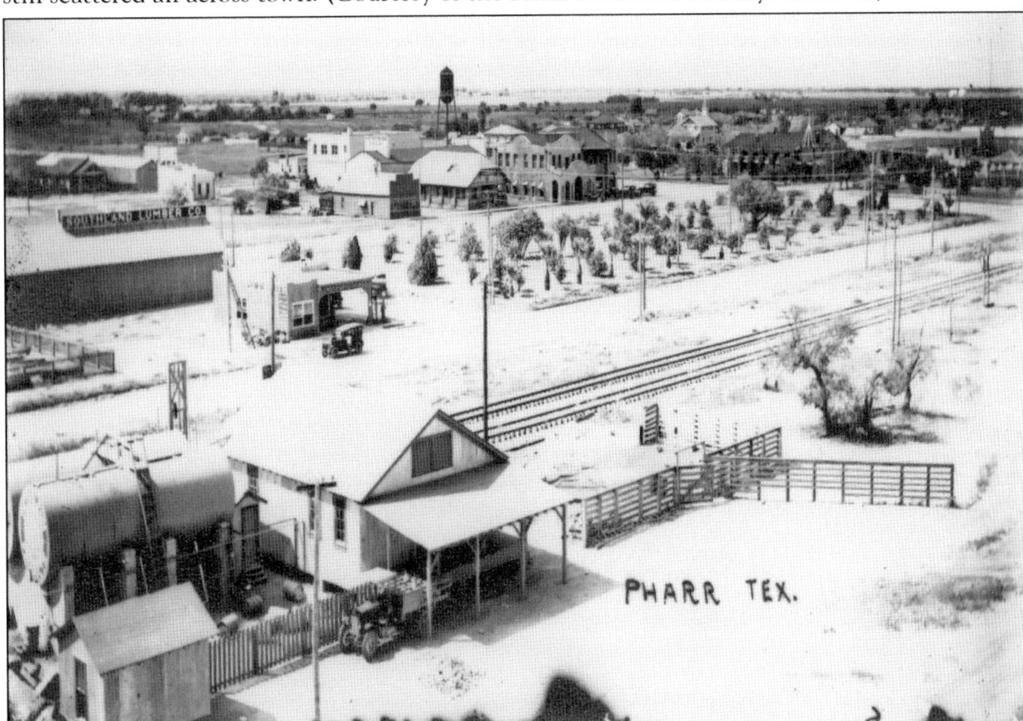

This 1920 aerial view of town was taken from the Pharr Equity elevator. The photograph was shot with the photographer facing south. In the distance, the First National Bank, city hall, and the Pharr Hotel are visible. The flatland Pharr sits on allows for a clear line of sight of the entire town. By this time, Pharr had undergone a serious transformation and expansion. (Courtesy of the University of Texas–Pan American Library and Special Collections Department.)

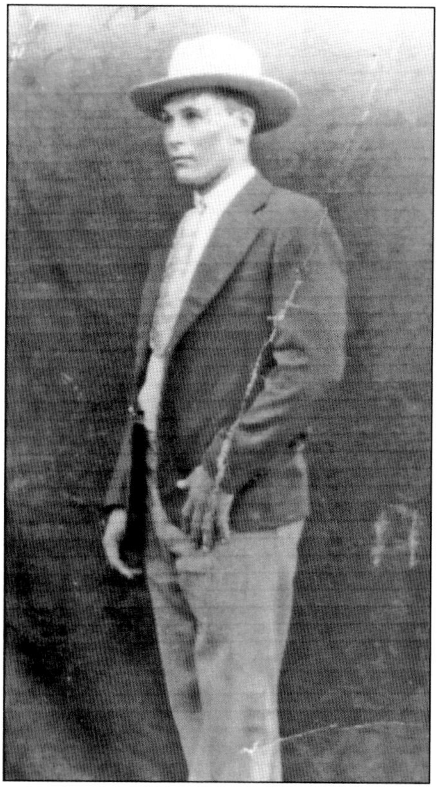

This man pictured is Julian Cantu. He held the title of Elmore and Stahl's iceman. As Pharr and the Rio Grande Valley were establishing themselves as agricultural hotbeds, the need to meet high demands for fruits and vegetables and to ship them out by way of refrigerator cars was constantly increasing. In order to preserve the fruits and vegetables better, a process known as "top icing" was implemented. Cantu would place a two-inch layer of crushed ice on top of the fruit and vegetables to preserve them. This process was later discontinued when it proved ineffective. (Courtesy of the Pharr Memorial Library Archives.)

This 1916 photograph is a street scene of the city, with the first Methodist church on the left-hand side. Note the road is unpaved and is very muddy. This mud accumulated from heavy rain that had been falling around town for quite some time. According to Capt. Herbert Wheaton Congdon, who arrived here in 1916 with his men to help protect the border, a local storyteller told him that a drought, lasting 18 to 29 months, had recently subsided. (Courtesy of the Museum of South Texas History.)

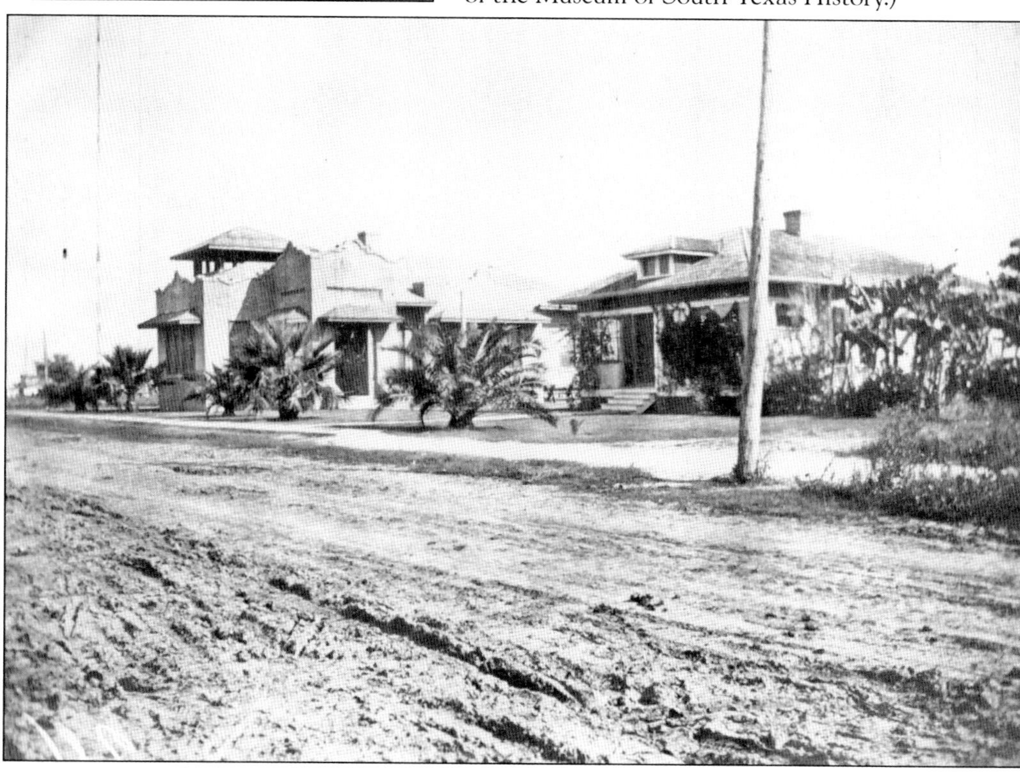

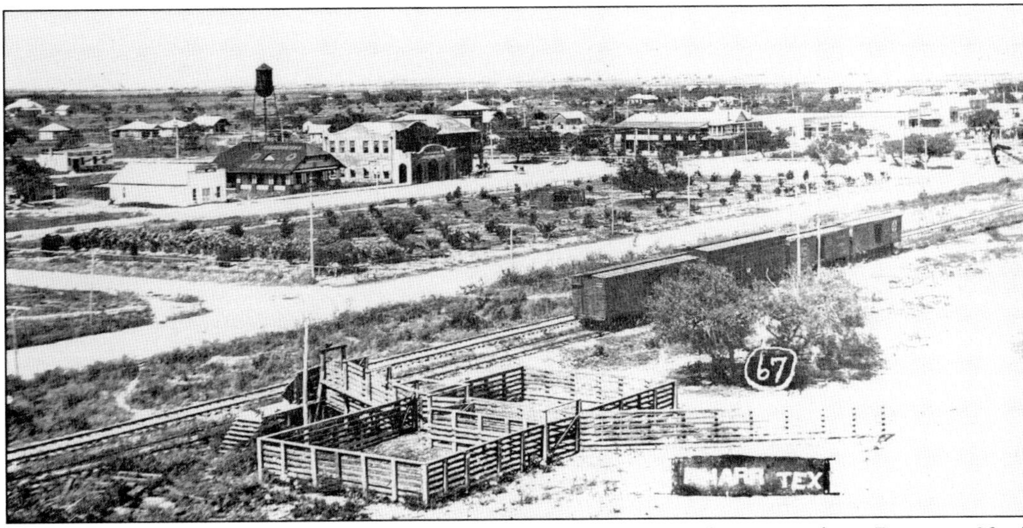

Pictured here in 1920 near Athol Street is the railway in town that runs along Business 83. A small wooden train platform can also be seen. In the distance, the downtown area of the city can be seen as well. The train was instrumental for the growth of Pharr. Traveling by rail became the main source of transportation for many people as trains allowed cargo, equipment, and loads to be moved from one place to another much quicker than any horse-, mule-, or ox-drawn wagon could. (Courtesy of the Pharr Memorial Library Archives.)

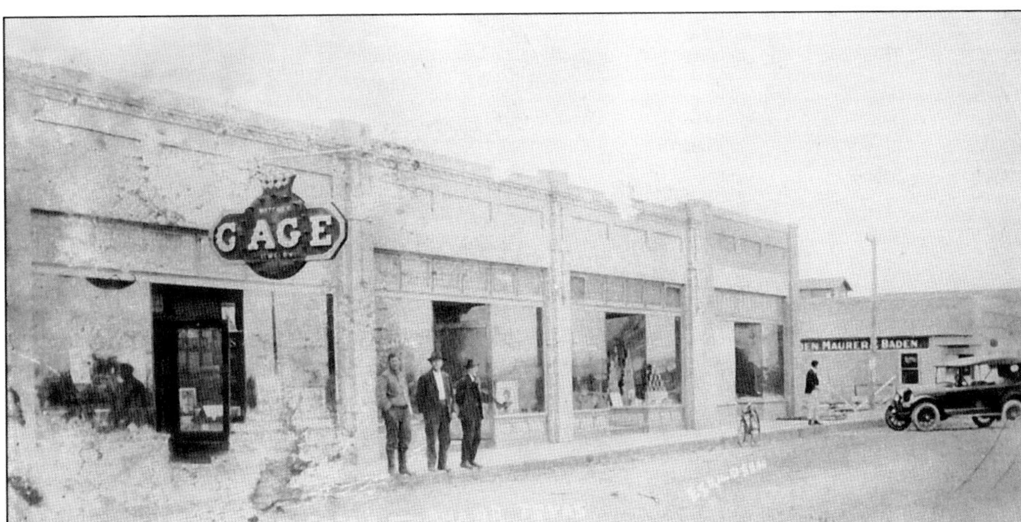

This 1922 view of South Cage Boulevard depicts the first buildings in the city. They were located just south of city hall. As Pharr prospered from the agriculturally rich land the Louisiana-Rio Grande Canal Company provided due to advancements in irrigation, Pharr's economy was boosted significantly, and more businesses downtown sprang up. The Cage Jewelry store, visible on the left, was owned and operated by the Gawthrop family. (Courtesy of the University of Texas–Pan American Library and Special Collections Department.)

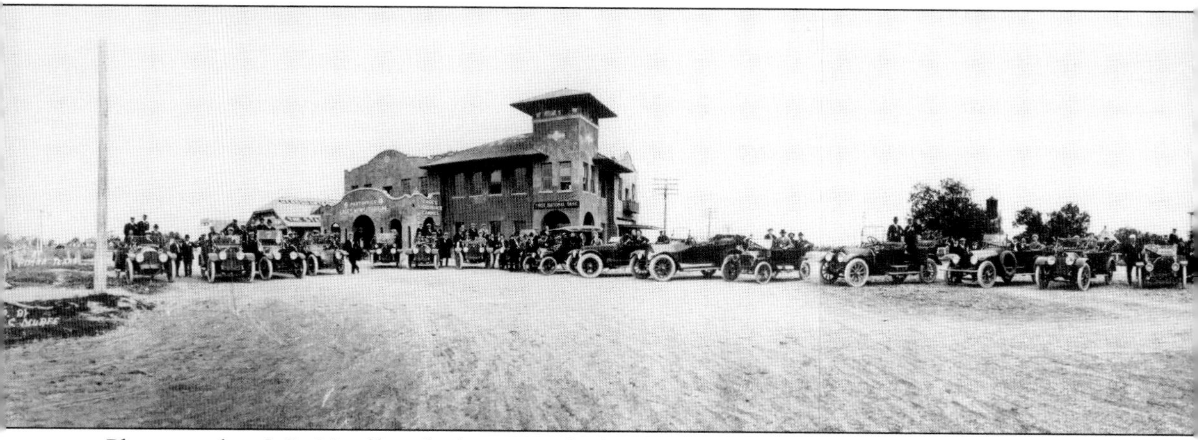

Photographer J.C. Murff took this one-of-a-kind panoramic photograph. The exact date is unknown, but it is believed to have been made around 1920. Seen from the intersection of Park Avenue and Cage Boulevard, this downtown area is the foundation of the city. Visible in the photograph are the city's first building on the left and the Pharr Hotel on the right. Standing and

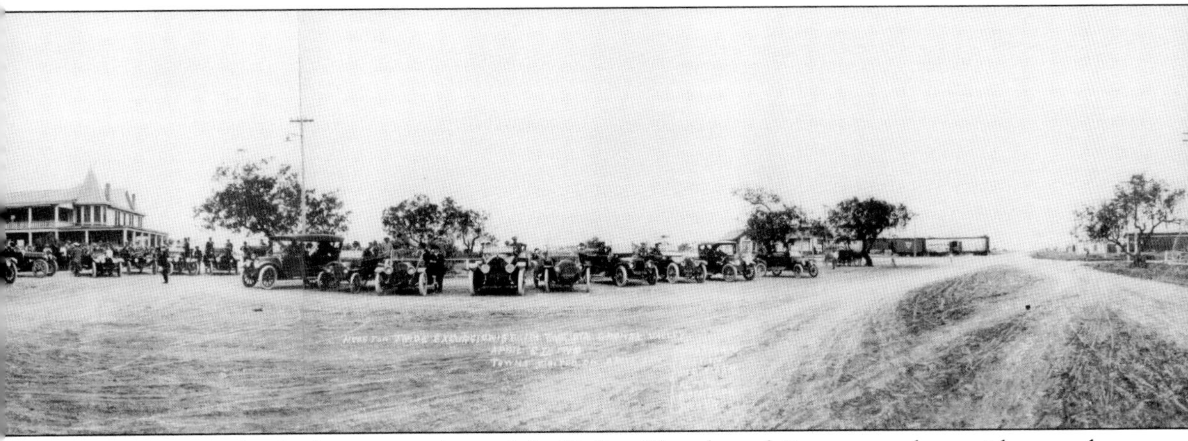

sitting in several vehicles are members of the Dallas Chamber of Commerce along with several other prospectors who came to visit Pharr, hoping to invest in land of their own. (Courtesy of the Museum of South Texas History.)

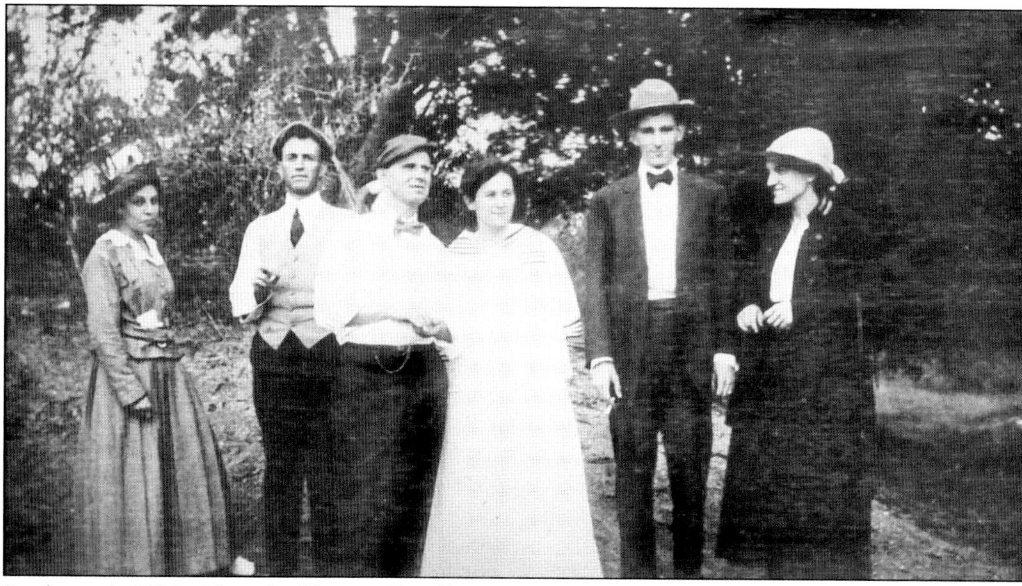

By the early 1920s, Pharr had been officially incorporated and was expanding significantly due to an agricultural boom, and so the need for a doctor in town was a must. Dr. Jill Devoti, the woman in the center wearing the white dress, is believed to be the city's first physician. Historically, women's inclusion in medicine had been restricted. (Courtesy of the University of Texas–Pan American Library and Special Collections Department.)

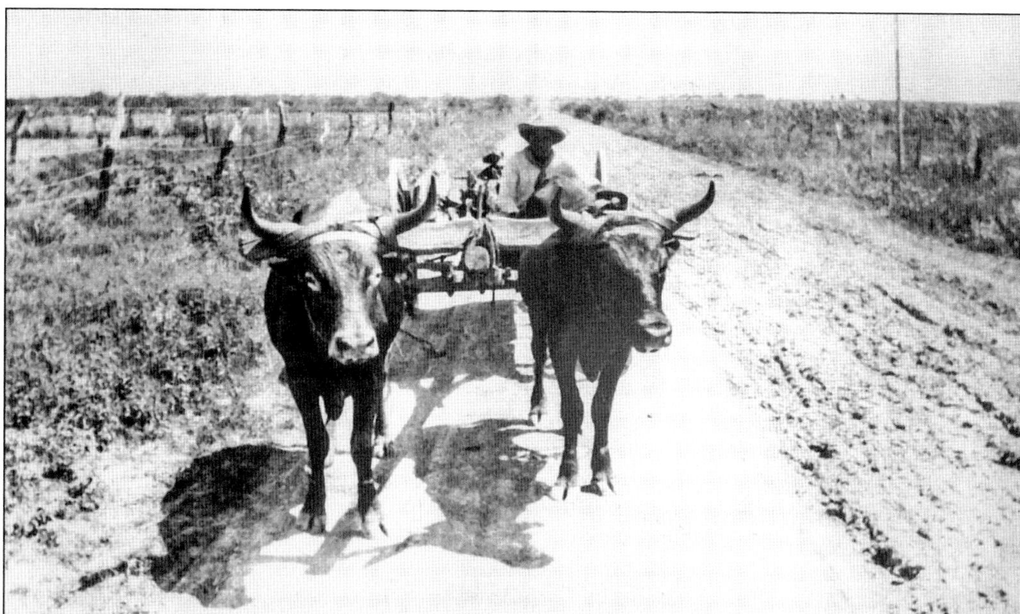

Although not as widespread as horse- or mule-drawn wagons, ox-drawn wagons were also used as a means of transportation for passengers and a way to transport loads from one place to another. Pictured in 1912 is an oxteam pulling a wagon and its passenger on Cage Boulevard. At this time, the city was in its early stages of establishment and incorporation. (Courtesy of the Pharr Memorial Library Archives.)

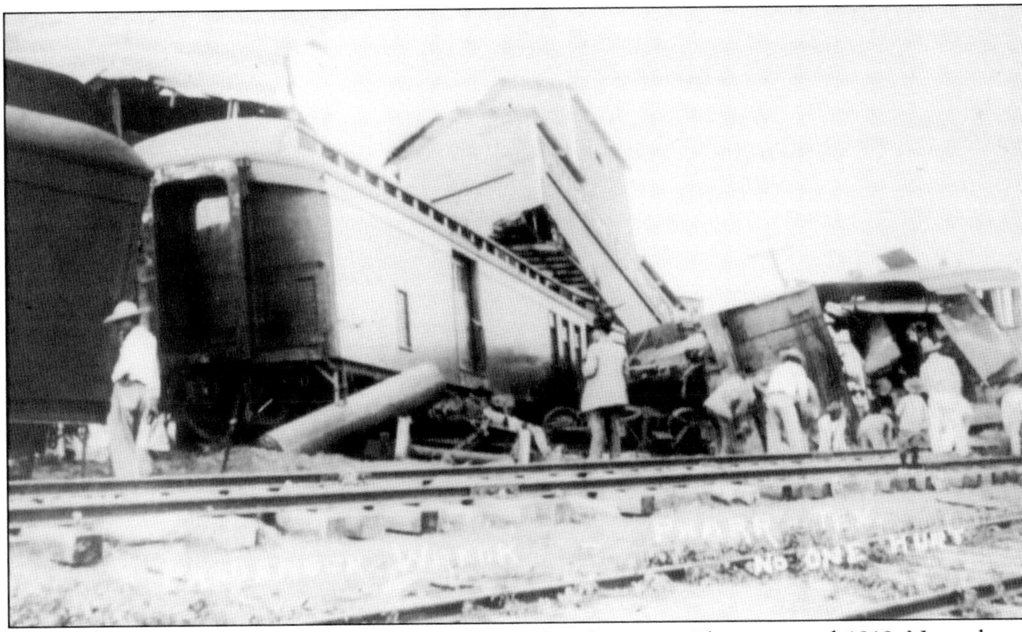

This is a unique photograph that shows a train derailment in Pharr around 1919. Not a lot of information about the wreck exists other than the fact that nobody on the train was hurt or killed. Train derailments did not occur often, but they certainly were not uncommon either. A significant number of train derailments occurred in Texas during the first half of the 20th century. (Courtesy of the University of Texas–Pan American Library and Special Collections Department.)

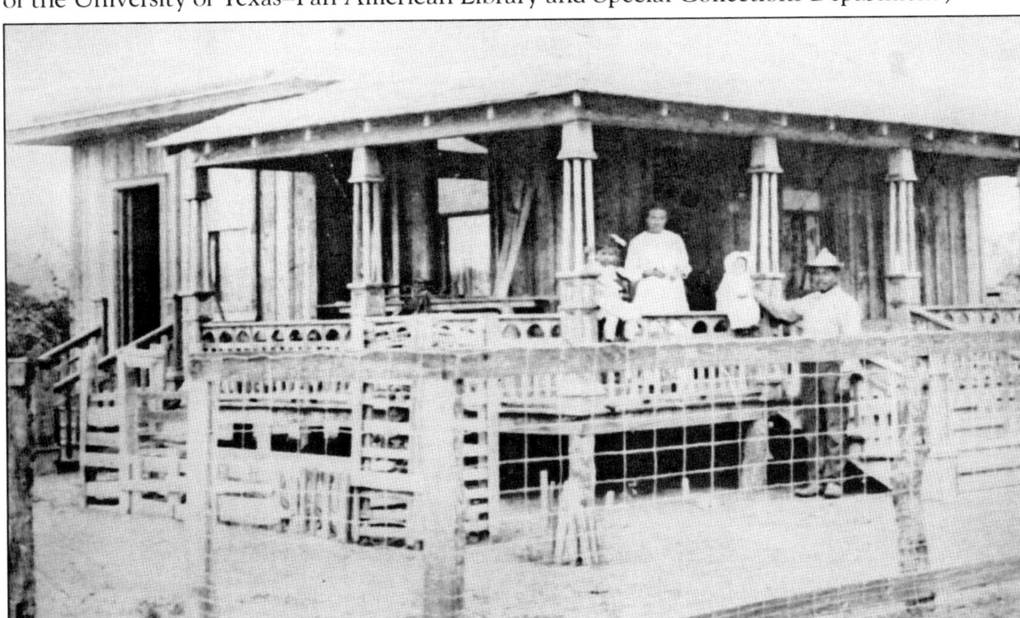

Pictured here on the porch of their home are members of the Contreras family. The house was built in 1911 by Dionicio Contreras and was located on the corner of Aster and Juarez Streets. The two young children are Rosa (left) and Elisa Contreras. This residence is an example of the typical wood-frame homes that were common around town during the early part of the 20th century. (Courtesy of the Pharr Memorial Library Archives.)

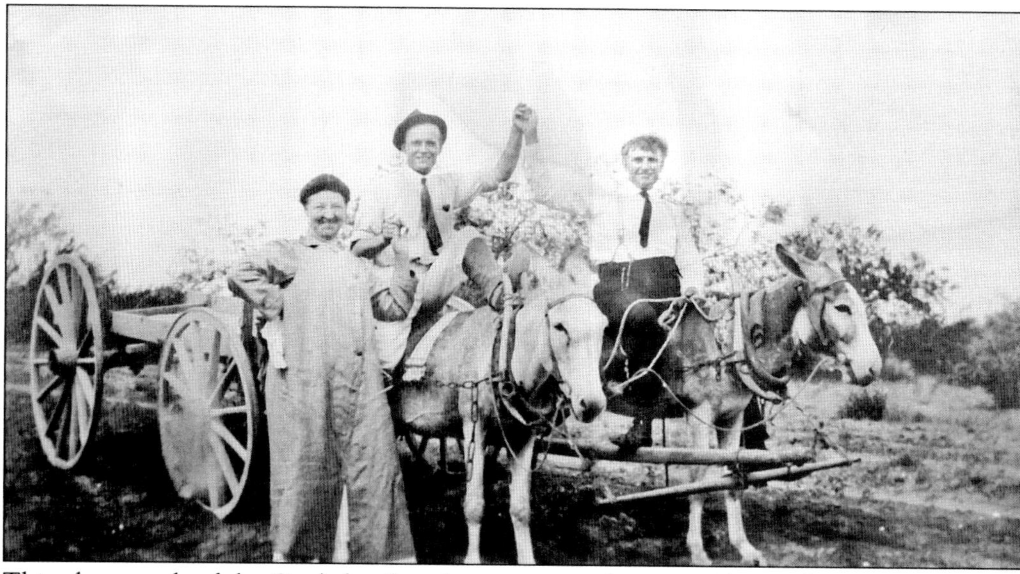

This photograph of the Cook family, taken sometime between 1911 and 1913, depicts them taking a break from work and smiling for the camera. The family's farmland was plentiful and filled with a variety of animals. Horse- and mule-drawn wagons, like the one pictured here, were a major source of transportation and help for the Cook family. The Cooks were here early on during the founding of Pharr, and they were one of the wealthiest families in town. (Courtesy of the University of Texas–Pan American Library and Special Collections Department.)

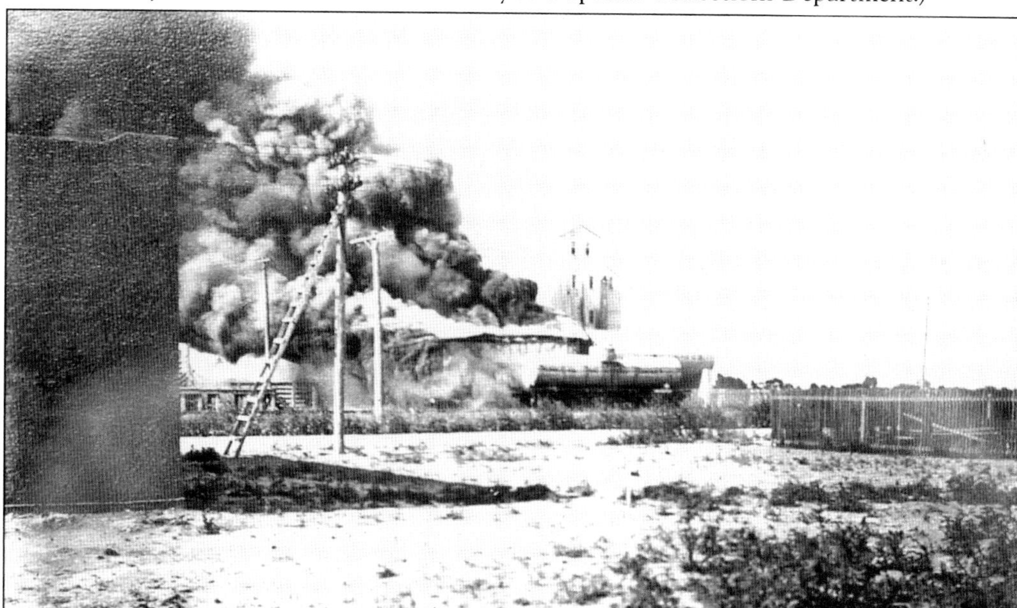

Seen here is as massive fire that occurred at Dixie Petroleum Products. The exact cause of the blaze is unknown, but disastrous fires in Pharr seemed commonplace at this time. In July 1916, a large fire decimated an entire square block. In this block were the Pharr Lumber Company, the Pharr Mercantile Company, Folsom Hardware Company, and the National Theater. With no firefighters or fire station established yet, these large fires caused significant damage. (Courtesy of the University of Texas–Pan American Library and Special Collections Department.)

This early-1920s photograph is of Loreto Brewster. An iceman for Elmore and Stah, he would deliver big blocks of ice to city residents. Local resident Emma Rosales remembers her family making *raspas*, which translates to "snow cones," out of the blocks of ice that were delivered to them. Other people simply placed the large block of ice in front of a steel fan so the air blown from the fan would be nice and cold. Loreto was said to have been a lawman before he became an iceman, hence the gun and holster. After being shot, Loreto retired from the law and found his calling at Elmore and Stahl. (Courtesy of Reyes and Anita Vela.)

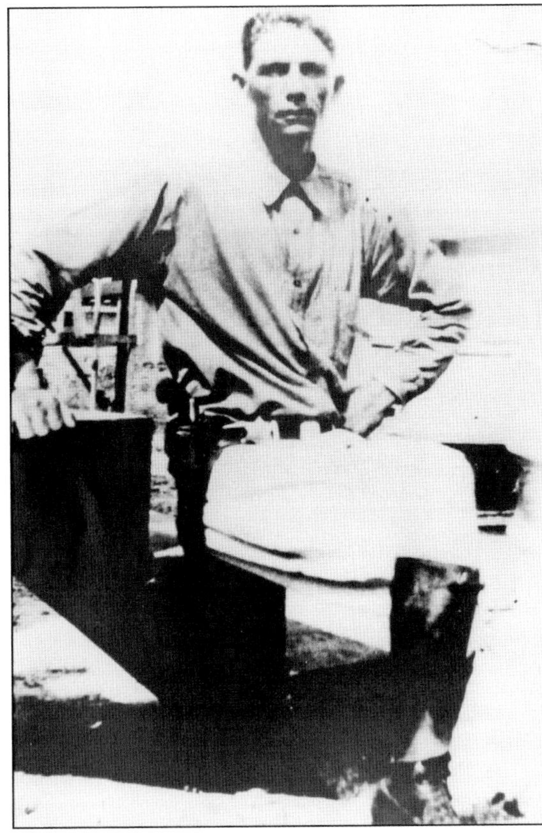

Pictured here around 1916 are two young children riding a horse through the downtown area of Pharr. Soldiers can be seen walking in the background in front of the Cage Jewelry store. Locals became accustomed to soldiers on the streets of Pharr when they were not out patrolling the border. (Courtesy of the University of Texas–Pan American Library and Special Collections Department.)

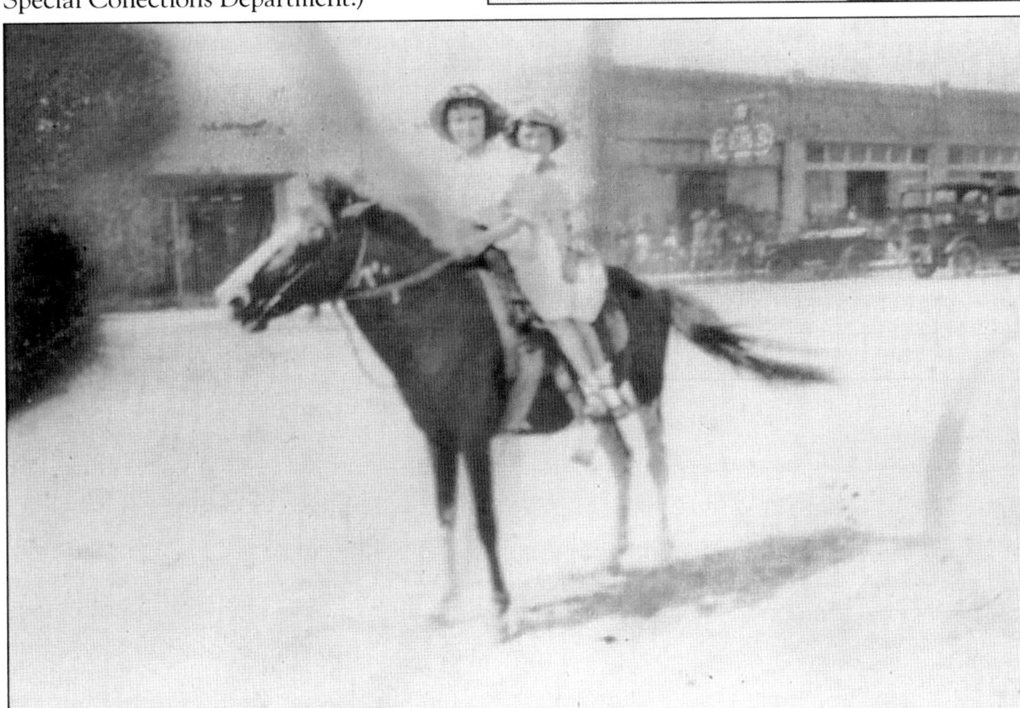

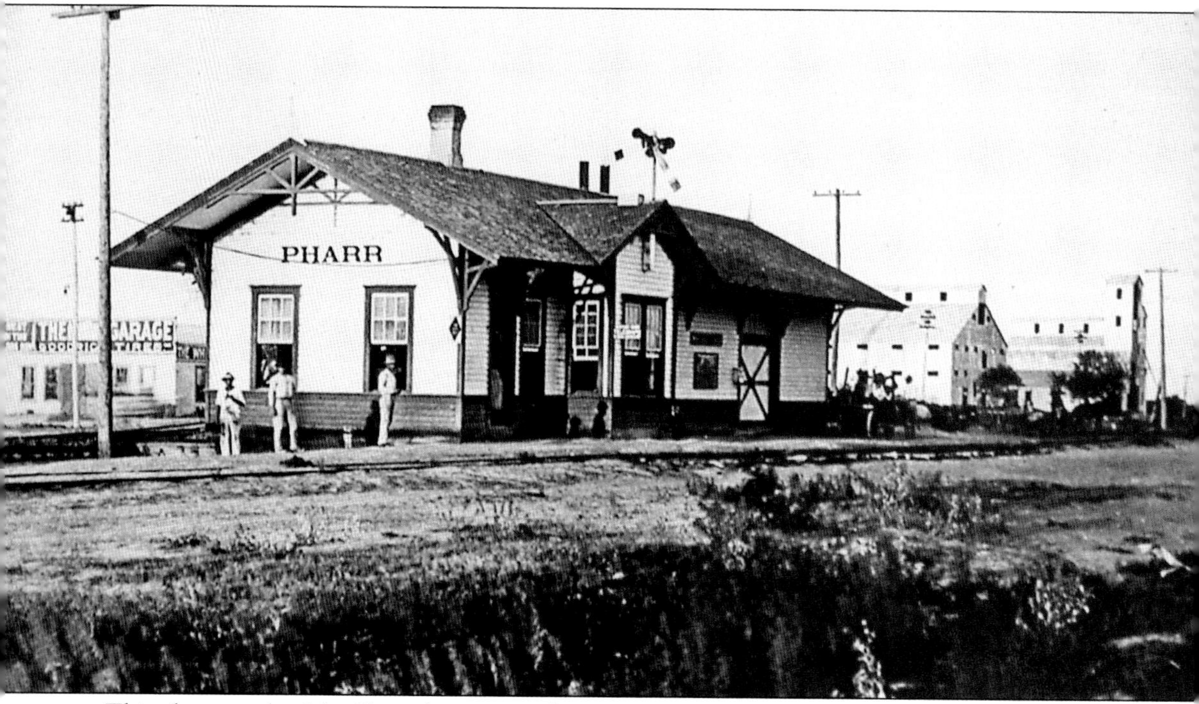

This photograph of the Pharr depot was taken around 1920 from Business 83. The depot uniquely overlooked the downtown area. Also visible in the right of the photograph are the grain elevator and alfalfa drier that belonged to the Pharr Mill and Elevator Company. The alfalfa drier burned down, entailing a huge financial loss. The company never fully recovered from it. (Courtesy of the University of Texas–Pan American Library and Special Collections Department.)

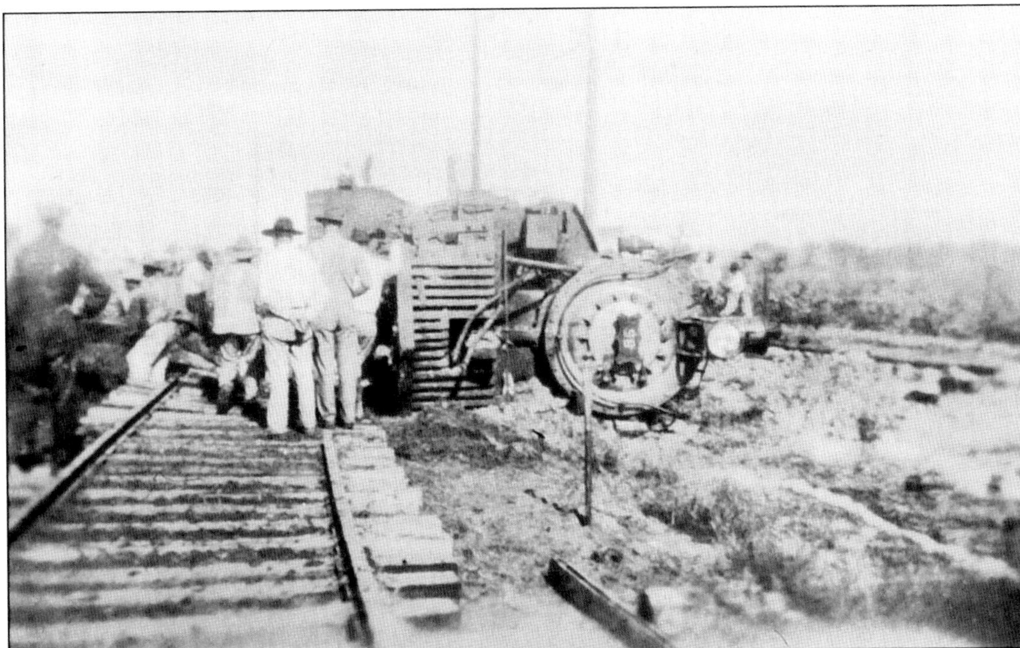

This is a frontal view of the train wreck that occurred in Pharr in 1919. The amazing thing about the wreck is that it occurred not long after leaving the Pharr depot. To date, there has never been a logical explanation as to why the train derailed. (Courtesy of the University of Texas–Pan American Library and Special Collections Department.)

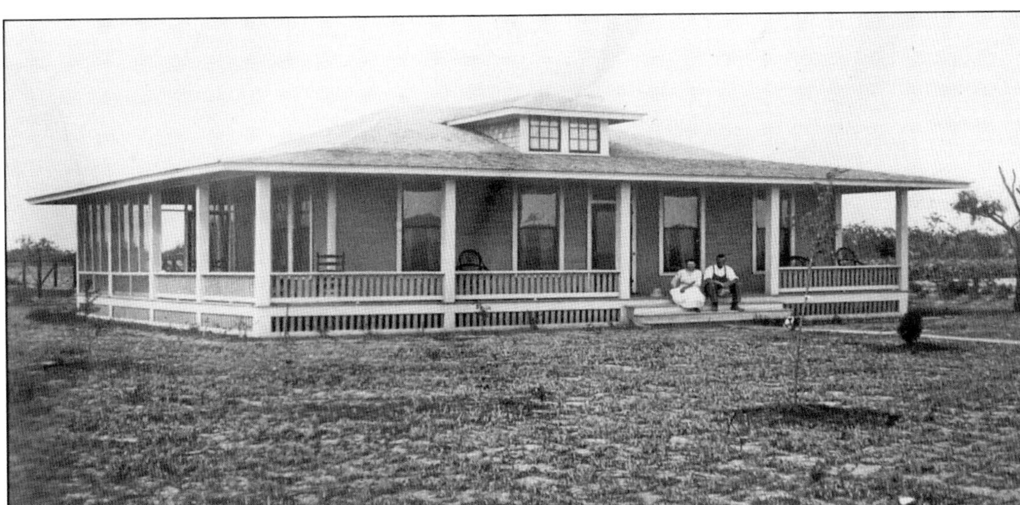

Sitting on the porch of their wood-frame home are Mr. and Mrs. John Cook. The Cook family owned a vast amount of land on the southeast side of town. Family members worked their land together and became very wealthy. Not everybody who invested in land in Pharr at this time was as fortunate as the Cooks. Many families came down to South Texas to take a chance at becoming wealthy off the large tracts of land available, but their dreams did not always pan out. (Courtesy of the University of Texas–Pan American Library and Special Collections Department.)

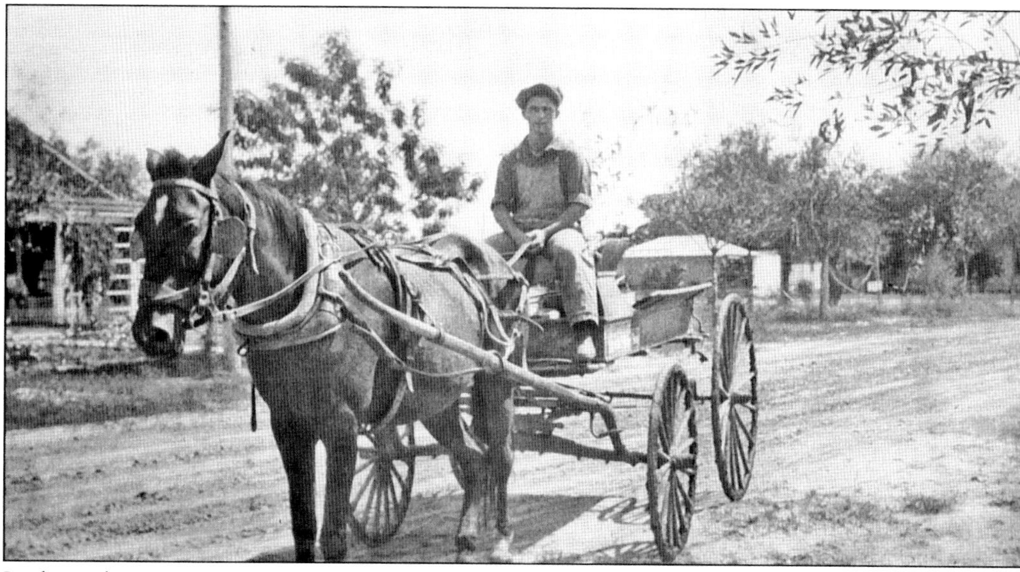

In the early 1920s, transportation in Pharr was still primitive. In 1927, however, the Missouri Pacific Railroad, linking Brownsville to Pharr and other towns, became the chief means for transporting local produce to numerous markets. It became less common to see farmers transporting goods in horse-drawn wagons. Eventually, the railroad partnered with the Valley Electric & Ice Company (later Central Power and Light Company) to introduce refrigerated cars and icing stations at freight depots to transport up to 60 carloads of citrus and vegetables in a short period of time. By the end of the decade, the Central Power and Light Company provided electricity, water, and ice to a large number of homes in Pharr. (Courtesy of the University of Texas–Pan American Library and Special Collections Department.)

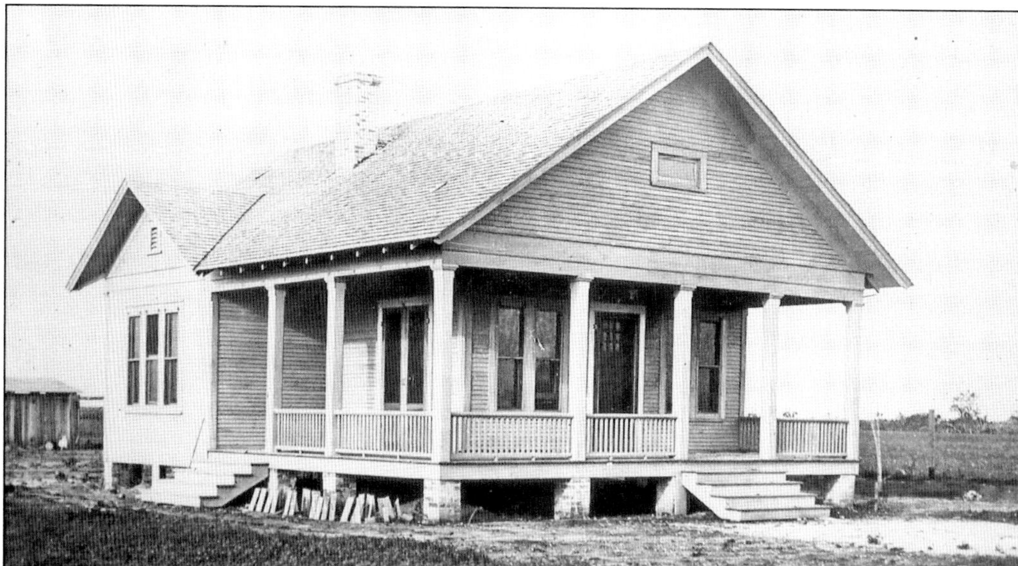

This 1911 frame home is a typical style that was visible around town during this period, as Pharr was slowly but steadily expanding in the early 20th century. Due to its relatively hot weather, Pharr is known for wooden homes; they were ideal because they had many windows to allow for a fresh breeze. (Courtesy of the University of Texas–Pan American Library and Special Collections Department.)

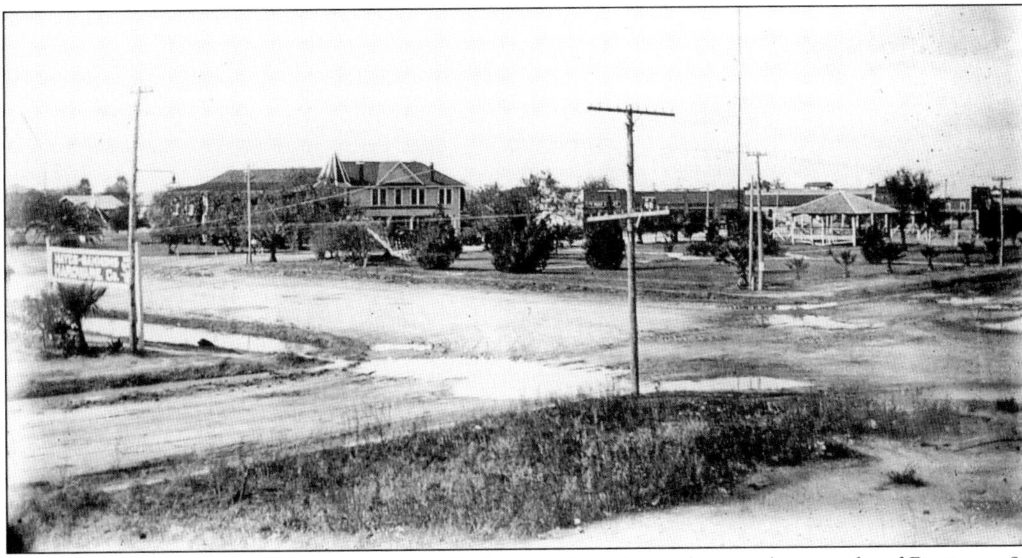

This view of the Pharr Hotel and Pharr Park was taken from the northeast side of Business 83 and Cage Boulevard after a downpour passed through town. Heavy rains are what Pharr and the Rio Grande Valley crave, as the region is a hotbed of agriculture. Pharr is known to suffer from serious droughts. (Courtesy of the University of Texas–Pan American Library and Special Collections Department.)

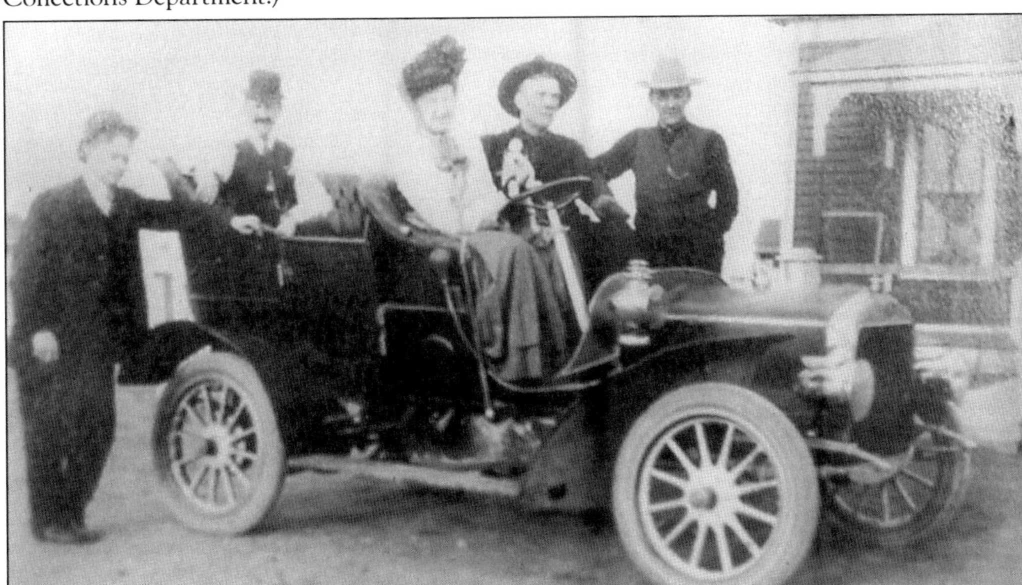

There were very few families around town who could afford the luxury of owning an automobile. Most people would simply just walk or ride horses to get around, but the Cook family was fortunate enough to have amassed enough money to own a car. Mrs. Cook is sitting on the passenger side while Mr. Cook sits on the driver's side. The steering wheel is actually located in the middle. Early on in automobile production, there was no standardized steering wheel location. The car the Cooks are driving is more than likely a 1911 Stutz Bearcat, produced by the Stutz Motor Company, which operated from 1911 to 1935. This was considered a luxury vehicle at the time. (Courtesy of the University of Texas–Pan American Library and Special Collections Department.)

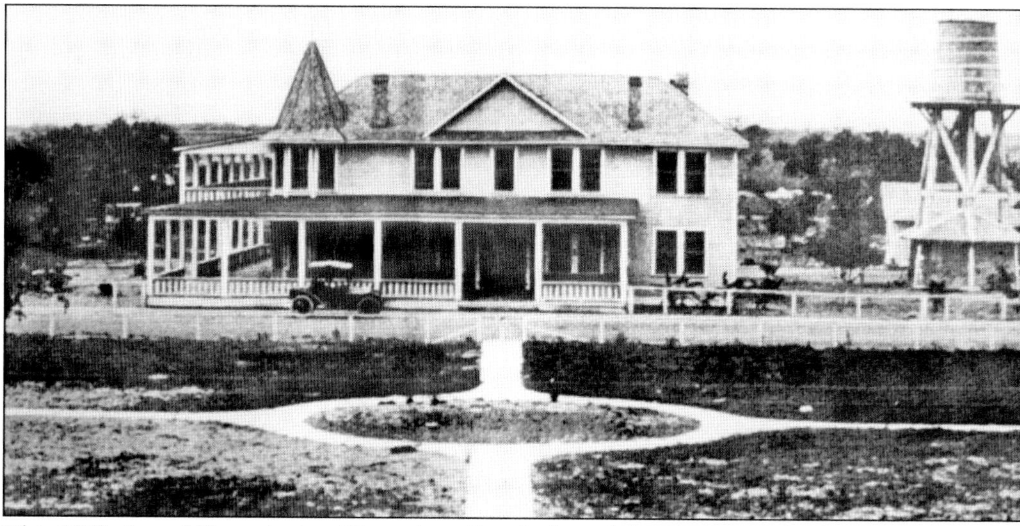

This 1910 view of Pharr depicts Showplace City Park and the Pharr Hotel. The park played host to several band concerts. When visitors arrived in town via train, this beautiful area was one of the first things they saw. This was probably such a delight for them to see. Showplace Park was situated along Business 83. (Courtesy of the Pharr Memorial Library Archives.)

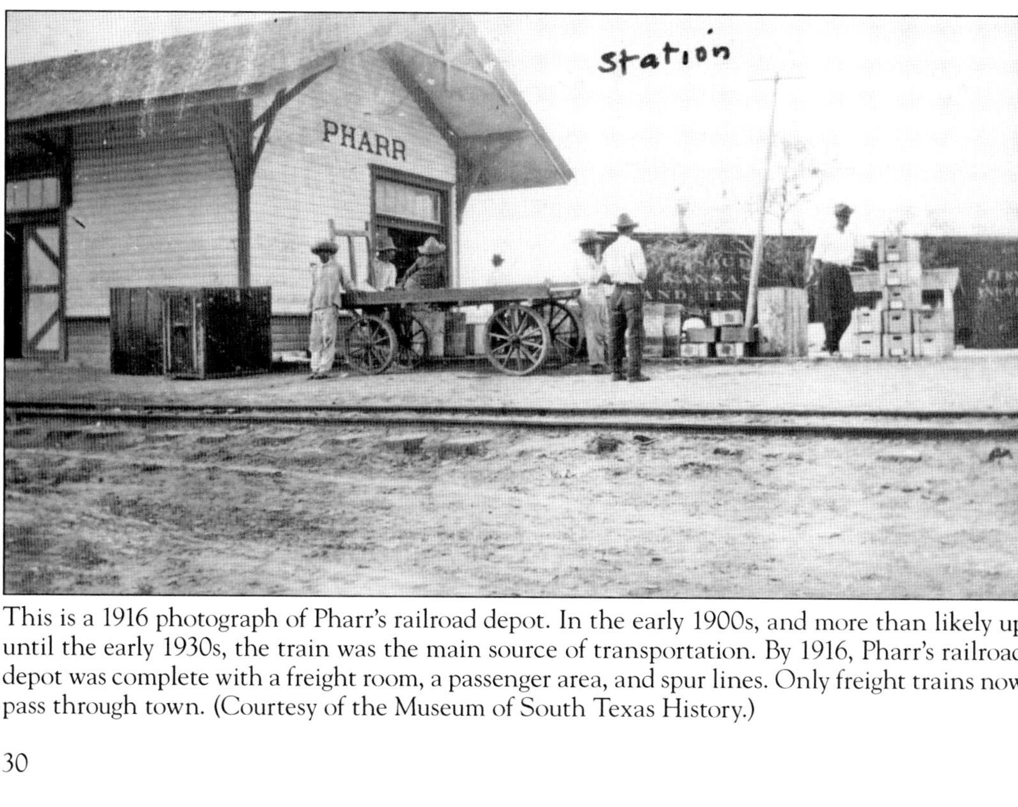

This is a 1916 photograph of Pharr's railroad depot. In the early 1900s, and more than likely up until the early 1930s, the train was the main source of transportation. By 1916, Pharr's railroad depot was complete with a freight room, a passenger area, and spur lines. Only freight trains now pass through town. (Courtesy of the Museum of South Texas History.)

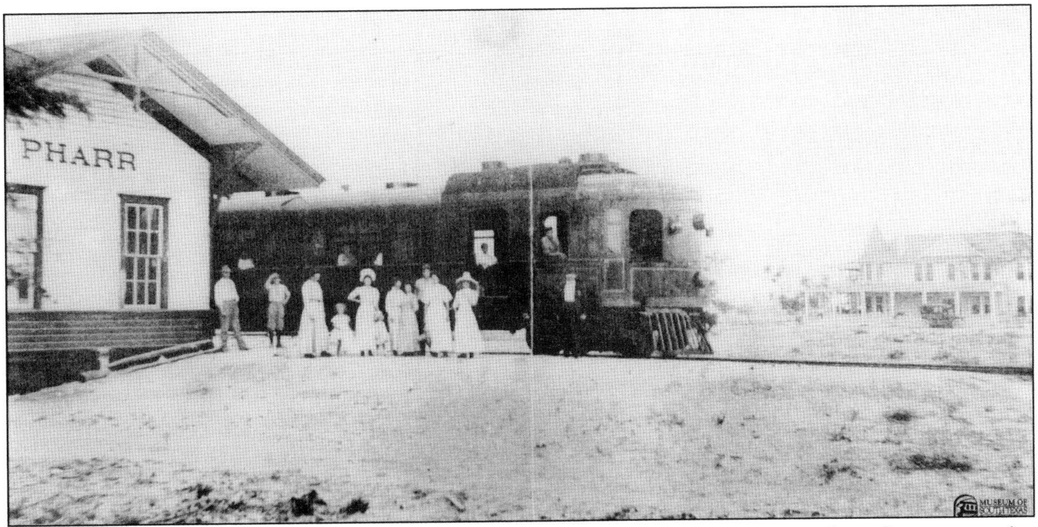

Pictured here are several individuals, mostly women and children, waiting to board a train at the Pharr depot. Sticking his head out of a window at the front of the train is the railroad engineer. On the right-hand side in the distance is the Pharr Hotel. It was quite a spectacle for hotel guests to see trains passing by, loading and unloading cargo, and transporting and dropping off passengers. (Courtesy of the Museum of South Texas History.)

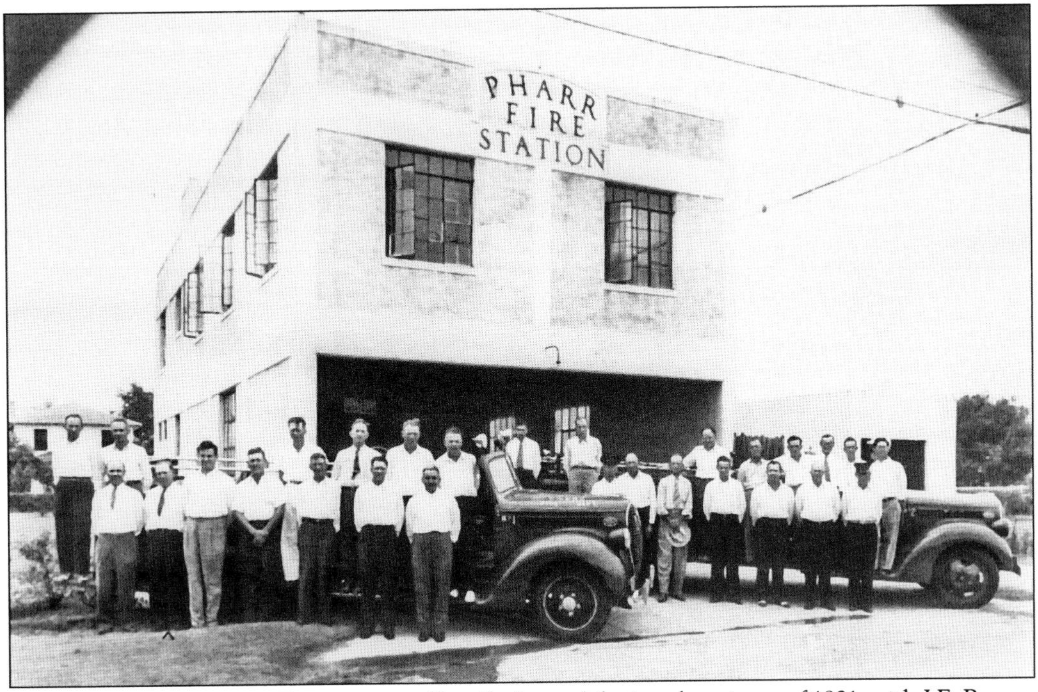

The volunteer Pharr Fire Department officially formed during the winter of 1921, with J.E. Rogers as chief. Prior to 1921, these volunteers used hose reels left behind by National Guard troops, who left the city due to the outbreak of World War I, as the city's first firefighting capability. This fire station was erected in 1928 when the city commissioned assistant fire chief O.C. Brown to build it. The former station now has a Texas Historical Marker. (Courtesy of the Pharr Memorial Library Archives.)

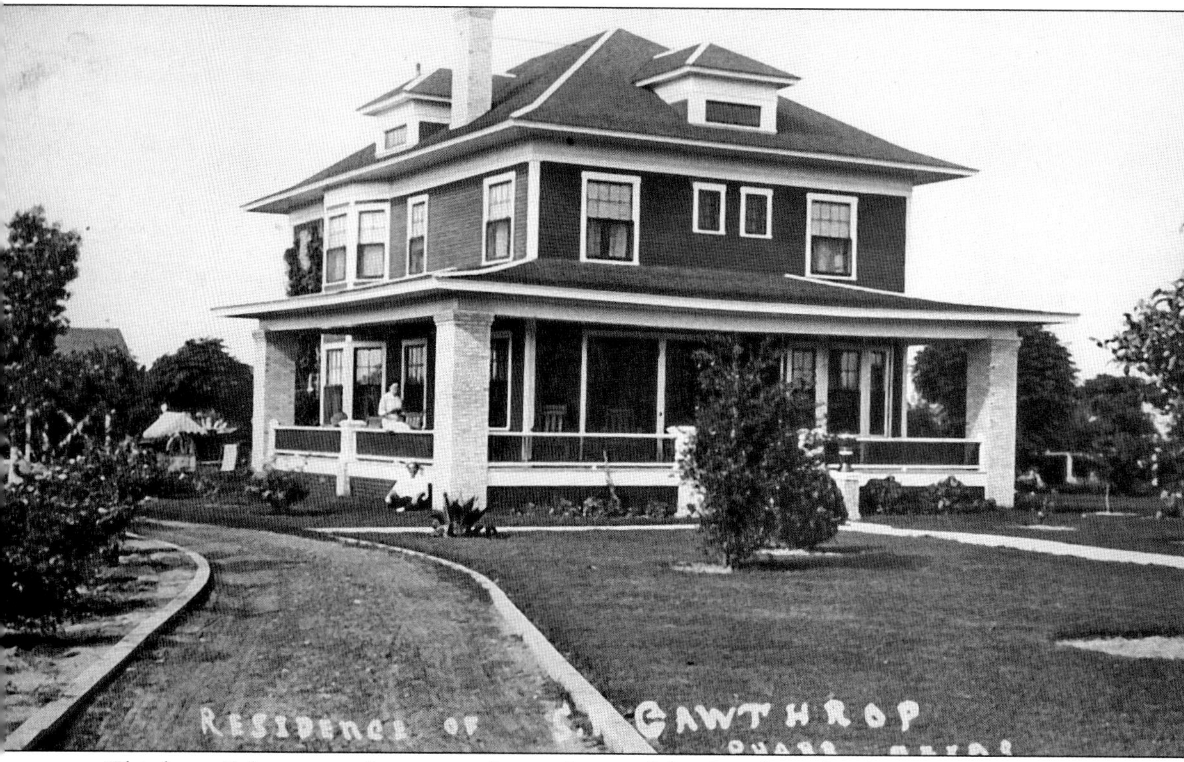

This beautiful two-story home was the residence of the Gawthrop family. Mr. Gawthrop owned the first jewelry store in the city. The house was located on the corner of Bluebonnet and Caffrey Streets. After the Gawthrop family, Virginia Polk then resided in the home. She was the postmaster for the city for approximately 30 years. The post office today is located just one block north of this house. (Courtesy of the University of Texas–Pan American Library and Special Collections Department.)

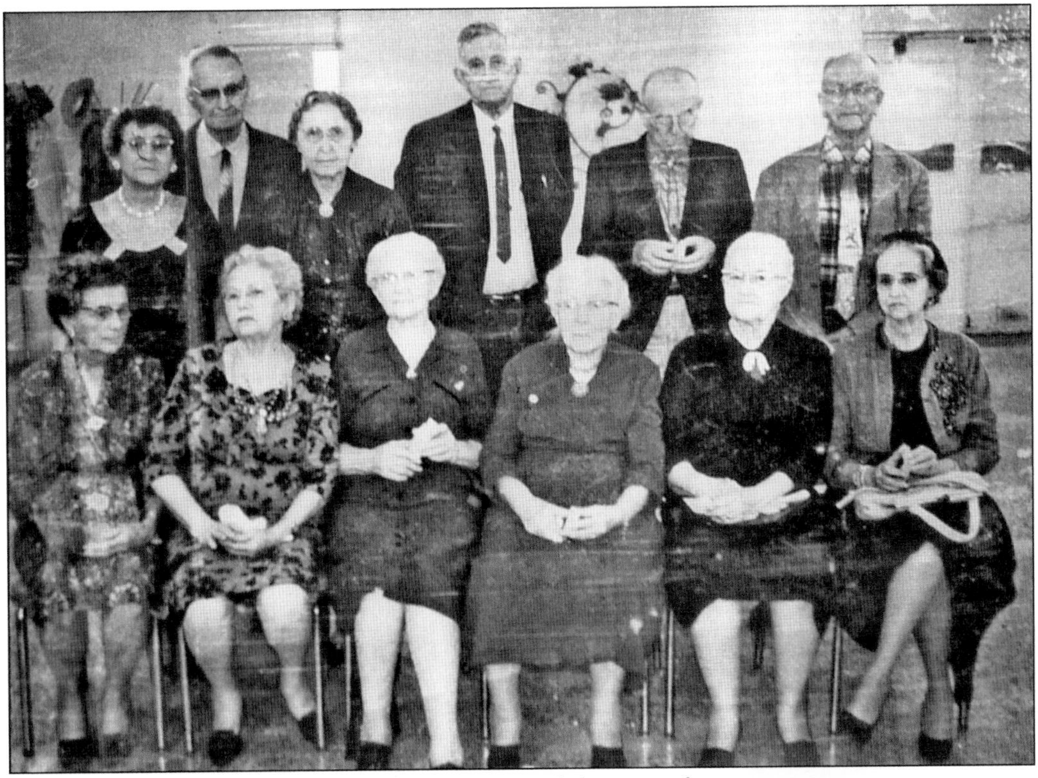

Pictured here at the Texan Hotel are pioneers of the city of Pharr who came before 1920. The most notable and notorious person pictured here is Tom Mayfield, the tallest man in the center. He was a former Texas Ranger and a towering man known to instill fear in the eyes of many of the Mexicans and Mexican Americans who resided in town. Mayfield definitely killed an unknown number of Mexicans. He spoke with a raspy voice; some say that was because he had throat cancer, but others say it was because he was nearly hanged to death before being cut down, thus ripping his vocal cords and forever altering his voice. Mayfield died in 1966 in the neighboring town of San Juan, Texas. (Courtesy of the University of Texas–Pan American Library and Special Collections Department.)

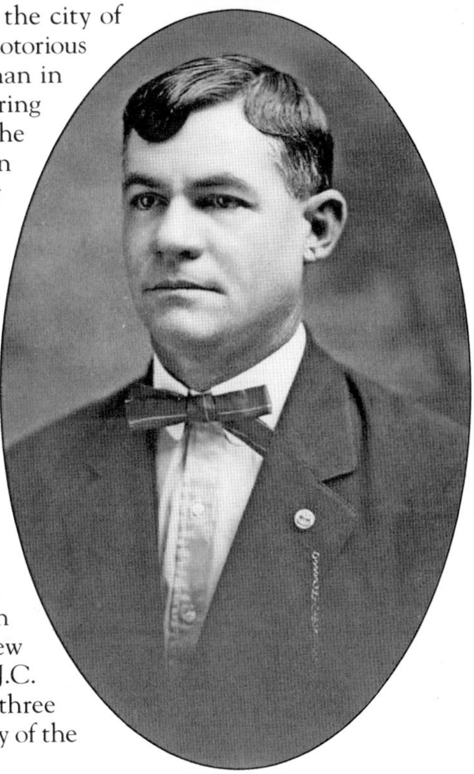

Pictured here sometime between 1909 and 1920 is a Mr. Muñoz. The exact identity of this man is unknown, but he appears to be a wealthy Mexican American gentleman. To be a rich Mexican American during this time was quite a feat. Most men in town with money were white. However, there were a few wealthy men who were not, and those men were J.C. Martinez, Antonio Saeta, and Manuel Othal. All three were all known to be worth a lot of money. (Courtesy of the Library of Congress.)

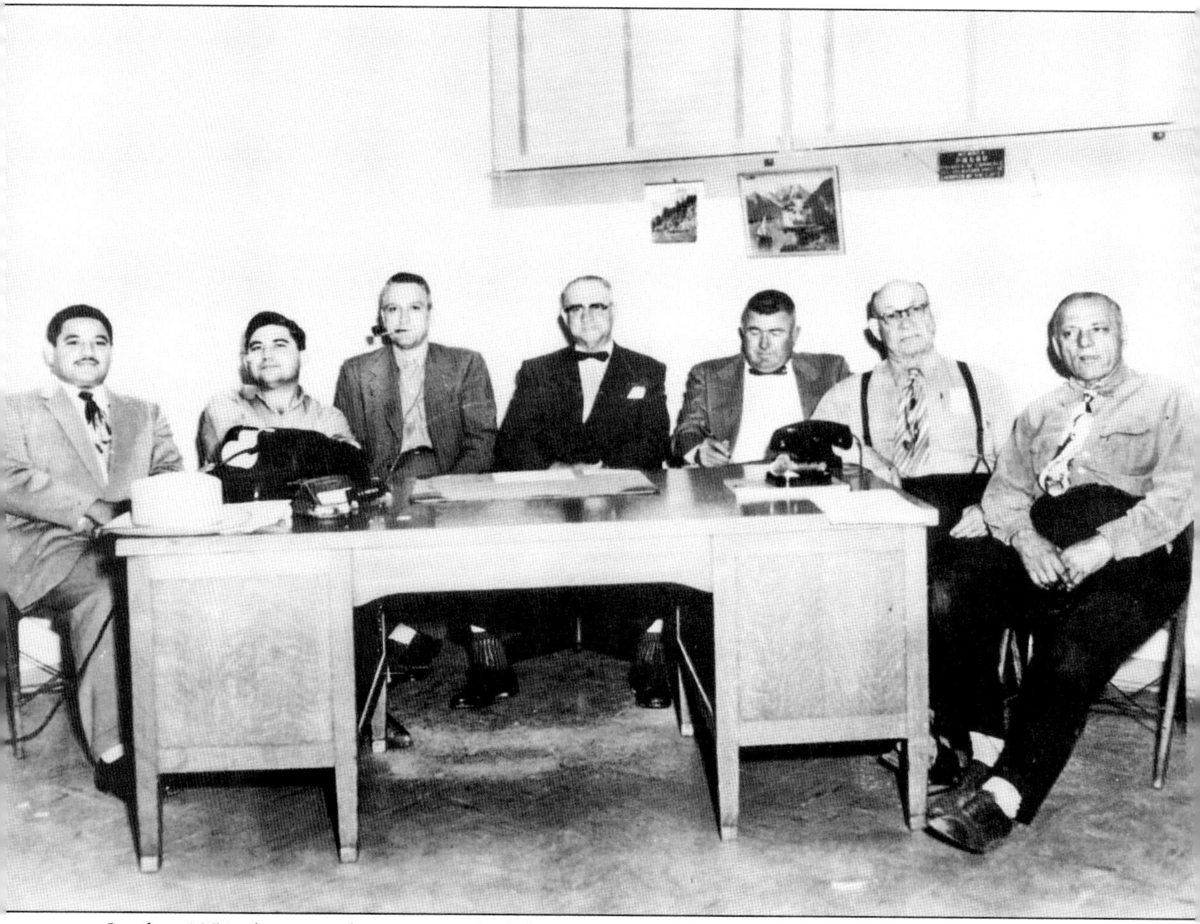

In this 1954 photograph are several of the men who made up Pharr's city hall. Six of these men can be identified. They are, from left to right, Roy Cortez, Tony Villegas, Bob Lattimore, Mayor James H. Witten (the man with the black suit and bow tie), a Mr. Shoemaker, and Pat Schroder, who was the city commissioner. These men, and others before them, laid the foundation for the individuals who run the city today. (Courtesy of Tony Villegas.)

Two

The New York and Tennessee National Guardsmen

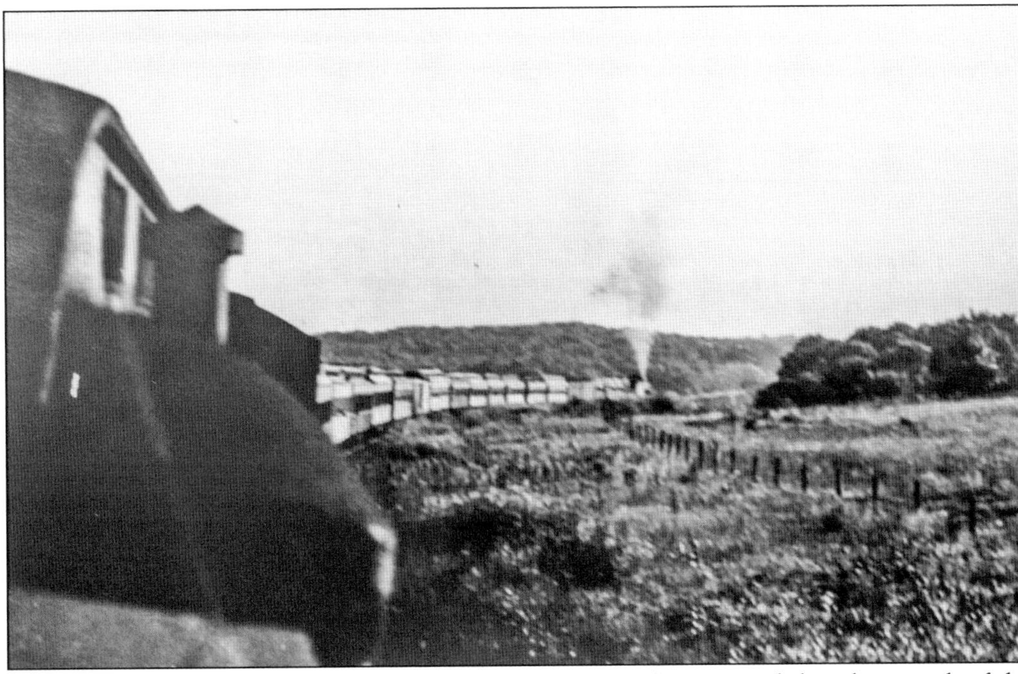

On his trip to South Texas, Capt. Herbert Wheaton Congdon snapped this photograph of the New York 23rd Infantry's train heading southbound. According to Congdon, once he and his men arrived in Pharr on July 11, 1916, the first thing they noticed about it was the heat. Unfortunately, they would find out from locals that they had arrived at a relatively "cool" time with plenty of rain. These men were sent to South Texas by the US government to patrol the Rio Grande and keep a lookout for the notorious Pancho Villa and his men. (Courtesy of the New York State Military Museum.)

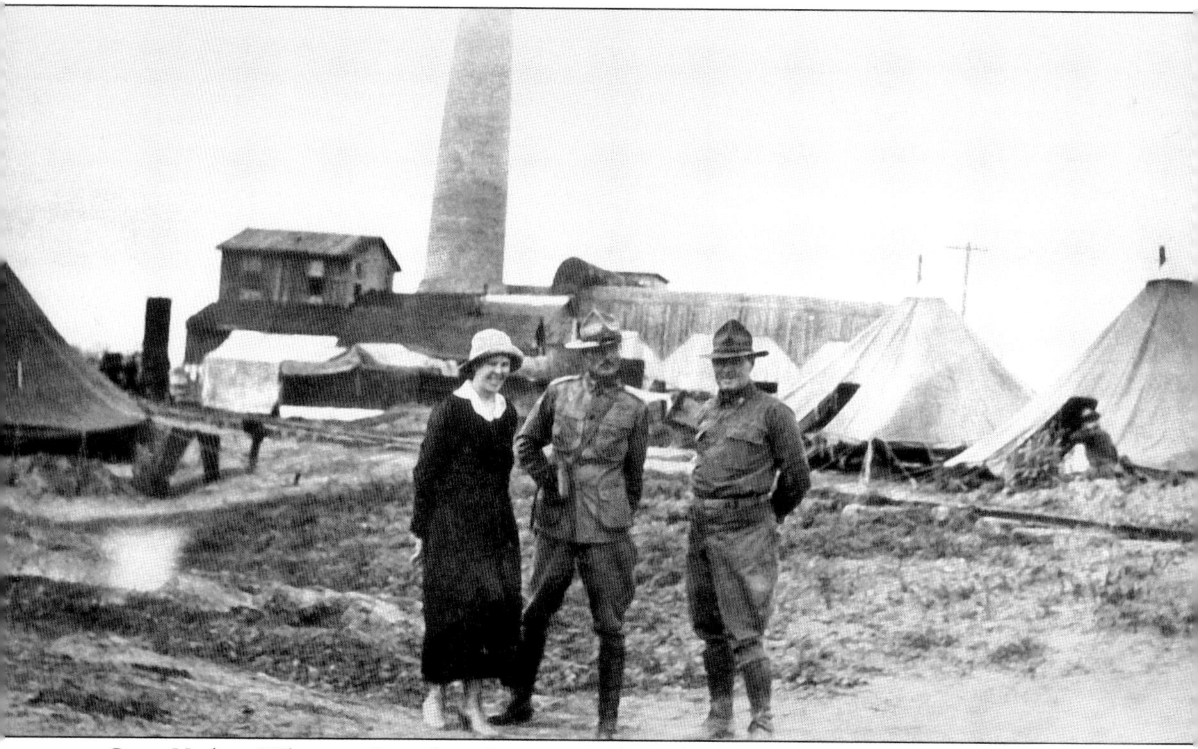

Capt. Herbert Wheaton Congdon, the man on the right wearing his captain pin on his collar, is standing here with an unidentified man and woman in front of "tent city." The New York National Guard was mobilized along the Mexican border to act as reserves for the punitive expedition, and as border patrols, hoping to catch the Mexican bandit Pancho Villa. (Courtesy of the University of Texas–Pan American Library and Special Collections Department.)

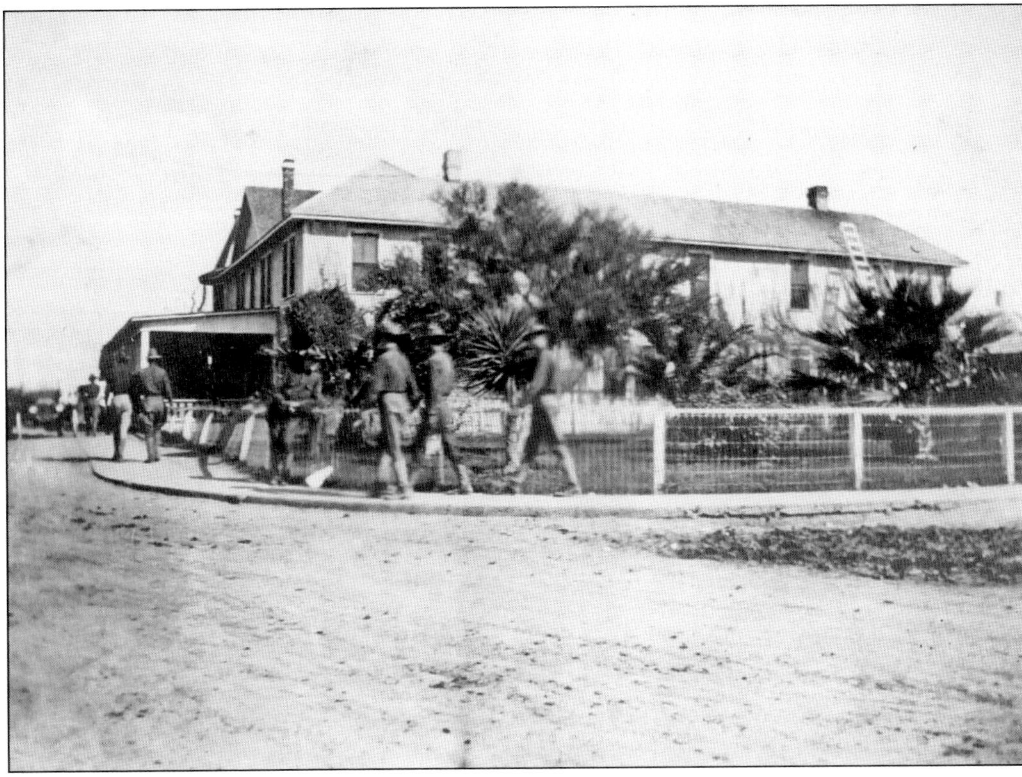

Pictured here are several National Guardsmen rounding a street corner on the west side of the Pharr Hotel. Seeing these soldiers walking around town during this time was not out of the ordinary. These National Guardsmen from Tennessee and New York called Pharr their home for nearly a year until they were called back due to the United States' participation in World War I after 1917. (Courtesy of the Museum of South Texas History.)

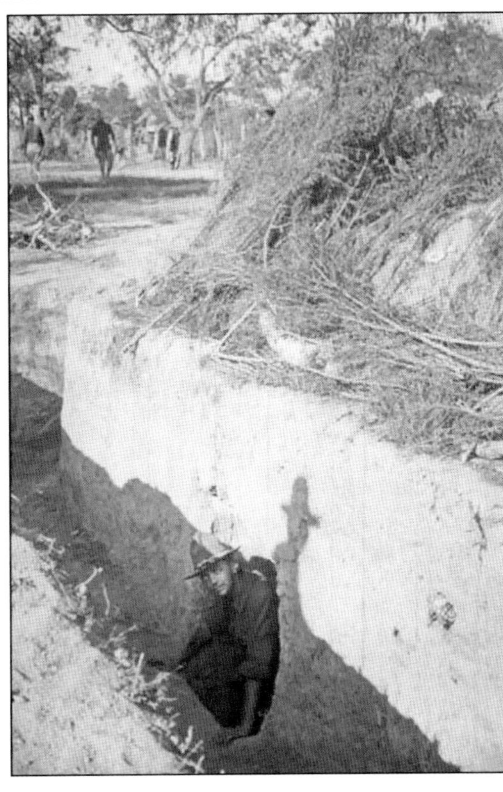

Being accustomed to much cooler weather in New York, the soldiers of the 23rd Infantry were very uncomfortable in the blistering Texas heat. The men would do anything they could to stay out of the hot weather. Pictured here is a solider sitting in a man-made trench attempting to get cool. In addition to the heat, the men had to become accustomed to dangerous wildlife consisting of scorpions, centipedes, tarantulas, and snakes. (Courtesy of the New York State Military Museum.)

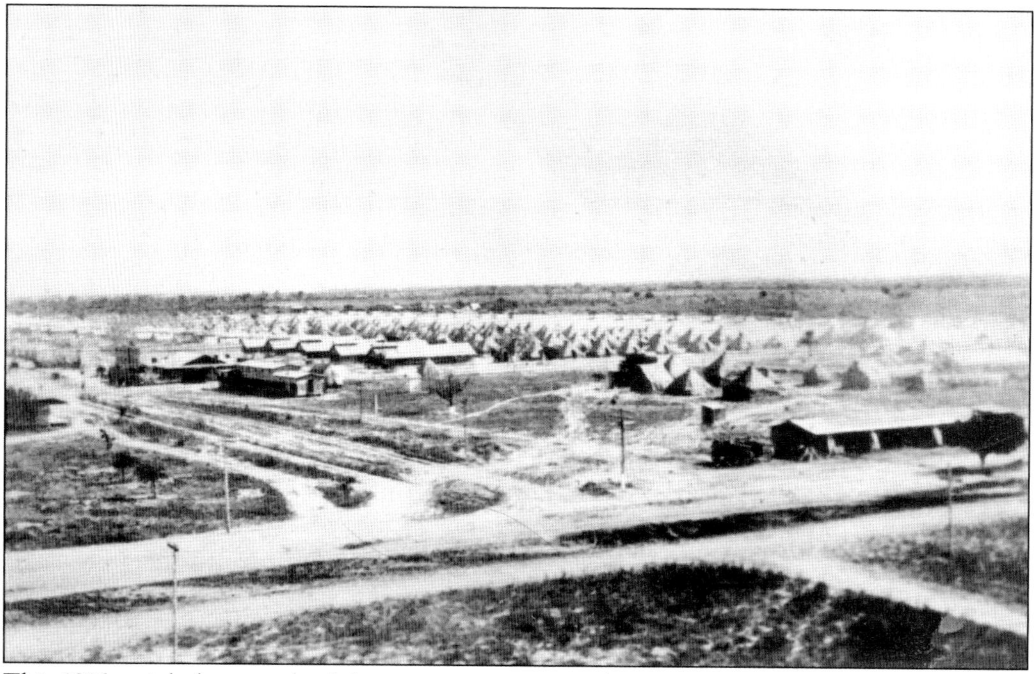

This 1916 aerial photograph of the main encampment for troops was taken by a photographer facing south. Visible are the many barracks and tents that housed the troops for the duration of their time in Pharr. The 23rd Infantry arrived in Pharr on July 11, 1916, and departed on January 2, 1917. The 74th Infantry arrived on July 10, 1916, and departed February 14, 1917. (Courtesy of the University of Texas–Pan American Library and Special Collections Department.)

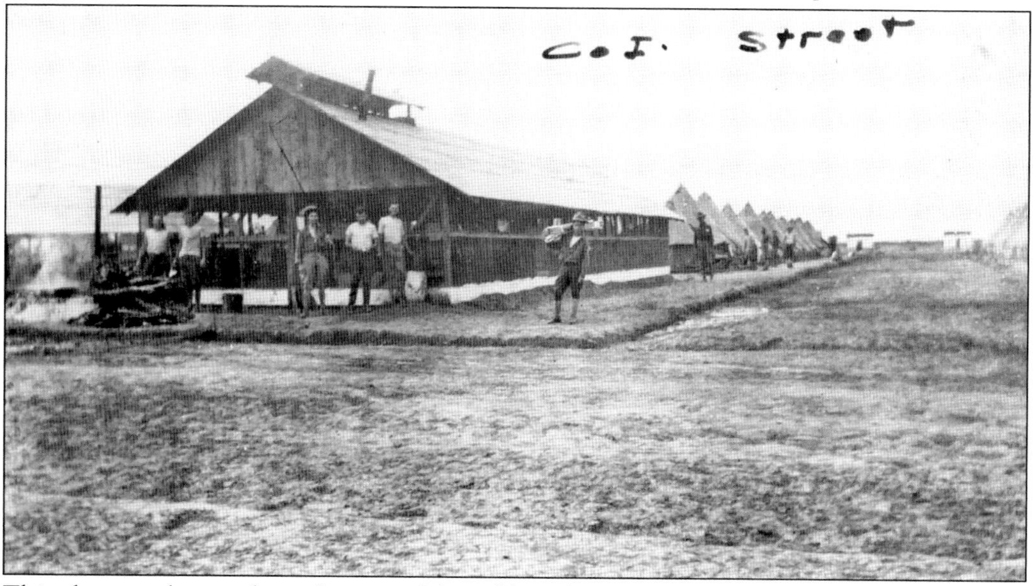

This photograph provides a close-up of the soldiers' barracks and tents. As the soldiers arrived during a time when rain fell heavily in Pharr, the living conditions at first were very uncomfortable. The mud that resulted from the heavy rain shocked the soldiers because of its texture, which was extremely thick, slippery, and sticky. Living conditions improved once the rain stopped and the mud dried. (Courtesy of the Museum of South Texas History.)

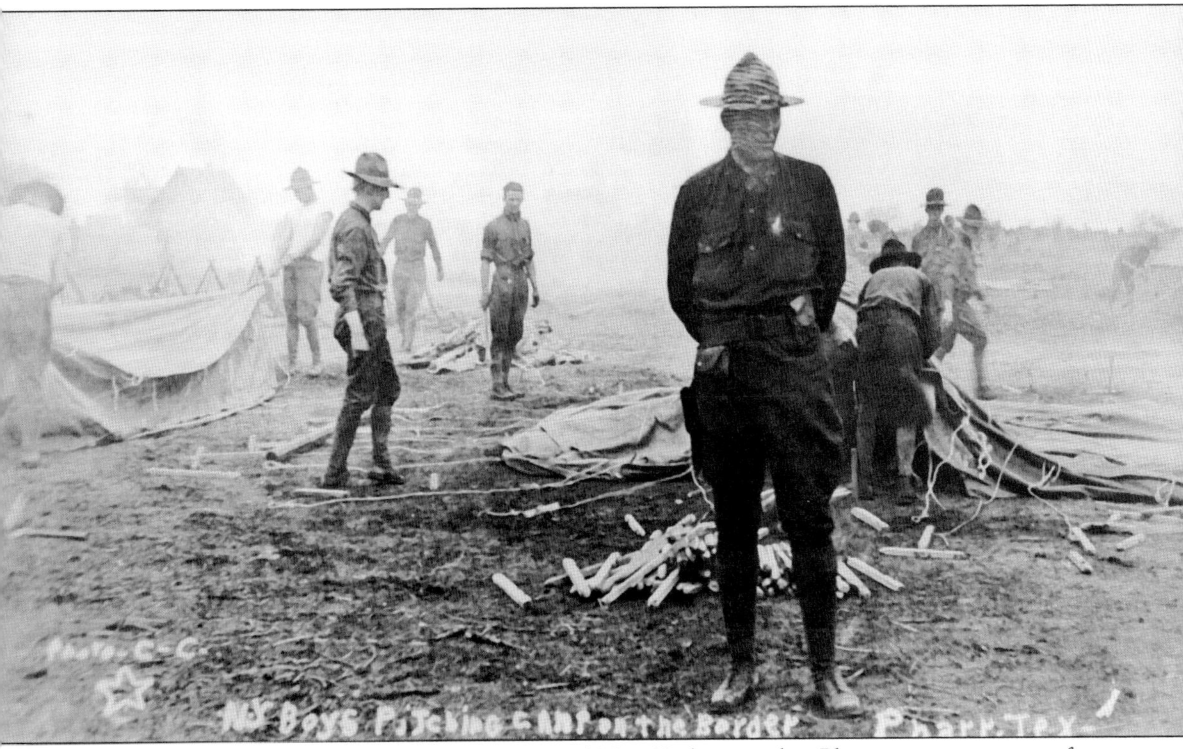

As the National Guardsmen from Tennessee and New York arrived in Pharr, it was necessary for them to set up their campgrounds in their new home. Here are several New York soldiers pitching their tents. Local resident Sindulfo Villarreal, who has now passed on, used to tell stories about the soldiers from New York not being able to withstand the incredible heat. He said the best soldiers for withstanding the heat were the ones from Tennessee. He claimed to have witnessed several New York men passed out on the floor from heat exhaustion. (Courtesy of the University of Texas–Pan American Library and Special Collections Department.)

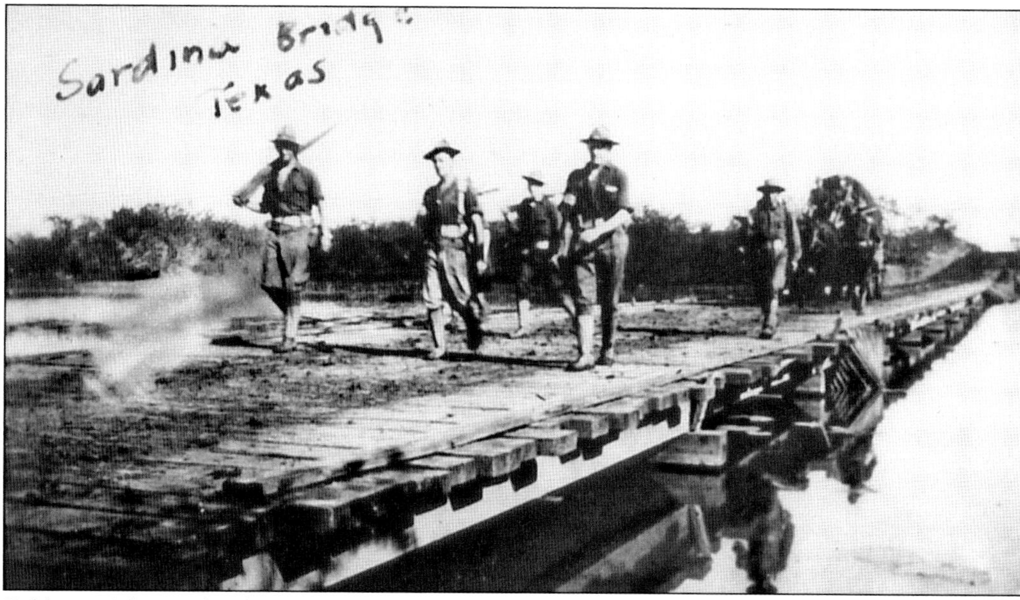

Soldiers of the 23rd Infantry from Brooklyn, New York, can be seen crossing the Sardina Bridge in this picture. Infantrymen and cavalry would cross this bridge daily to train where the city's levees are located. The journey from camp to the training grounds was quite a hike on foot. The Sardina Bridge and Sardina Lake no longer exist, but the soldiers' training grounds can still be seen today on South Jackson Road. (Courtesy of the University of Texas–Pan American Library and Special Collections Department.)

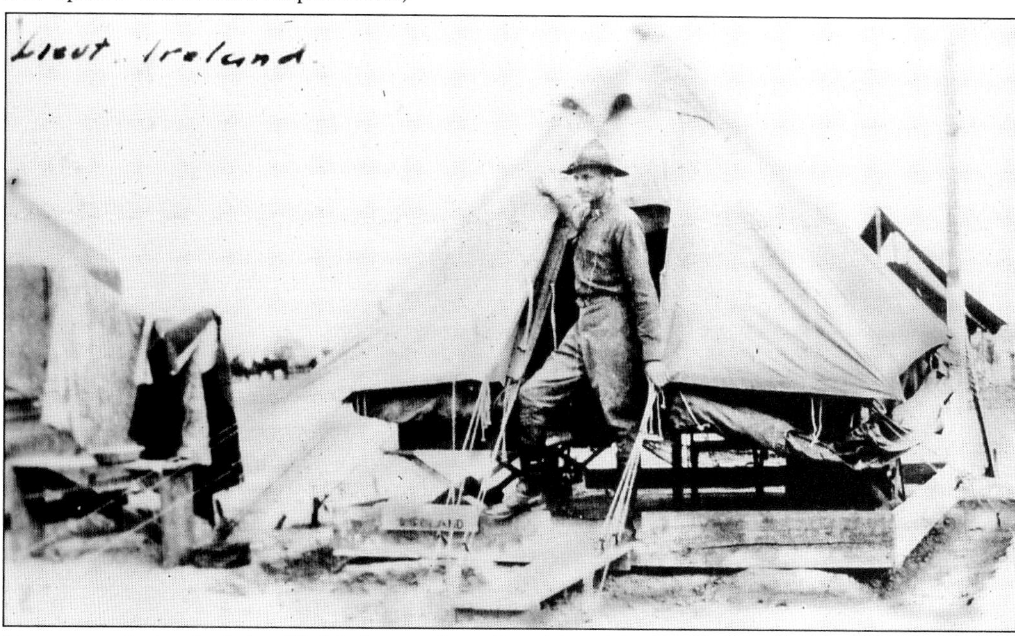

Lieutenant Ireland of the 23rd Infantry from Brooklyn, New York, is pictured here getting out of his tent. The soldiers' main campgrounds were established in a large vacant lot, located just southwest of Pharr's downtown area. The campgrounds were littered with soldiers' tents and came to be known as "tent city" to locals and to the soldiers themselves. (Courtesy of the University of Texas–Pan American Library and Special Collections Department.)

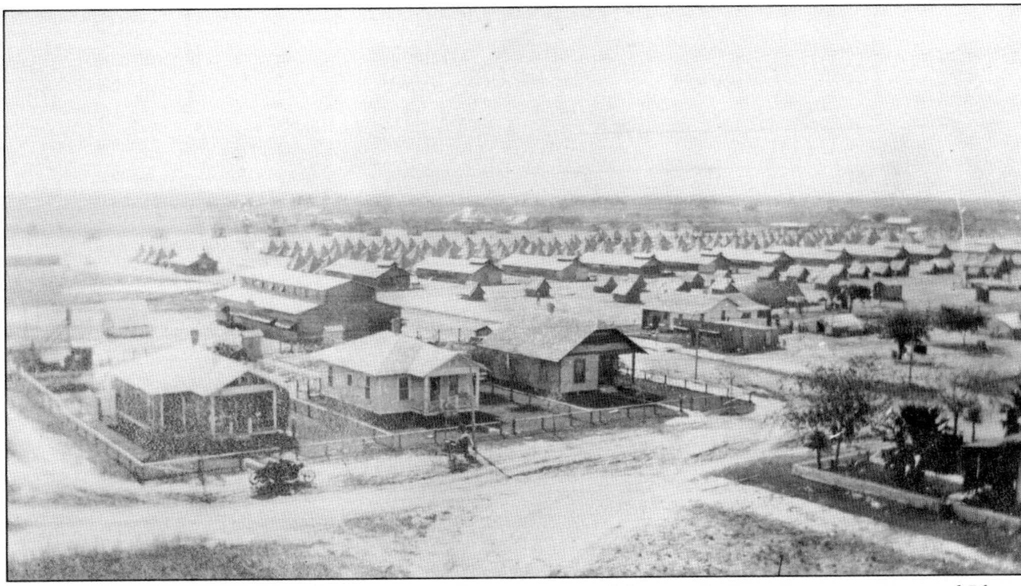

Located next to the soldiers' campgrounds were several homes belonging to natives of Pharr. Visible on the lower left-hand corner of this photograph are several of those houses. Local residents got to know many of the soldiers very well and considered them friends. It was not uncommon for locals to invite soldiers into their homes for lunch or dinner. (Courtesy of the University of Texas–Pan American Library and Special Collections Department.)

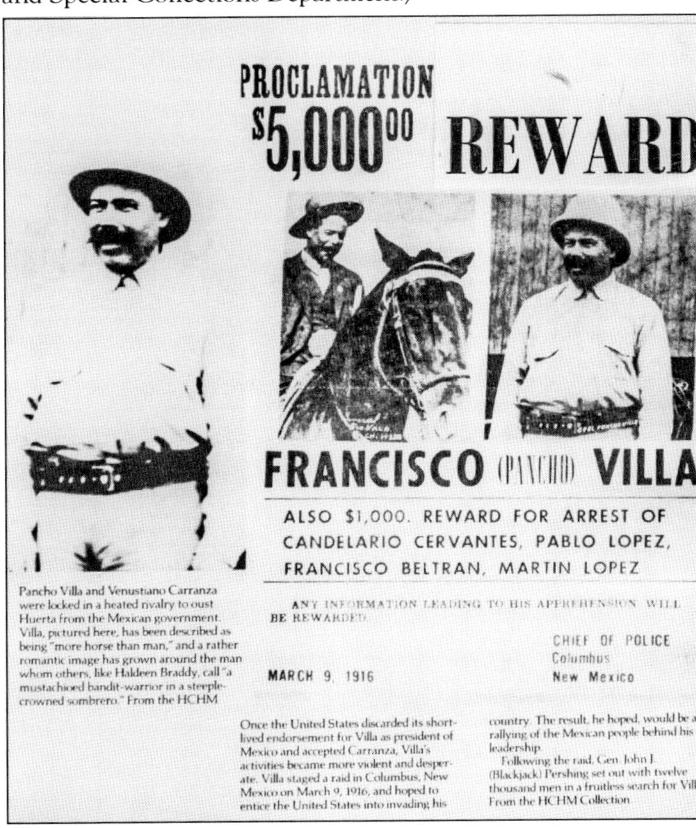

PROCLAMATION

$5,000.00 REWARD

FRANCISCO (PANCHO) VILLA

ALSO $1,000. REWARD FOR ARREST OF CANDELARIO CERVANTES, PABLO LOPEZ, FRANCISCO BELTRAN, MARTIN LOPEZ

ANY INFORMATION LEADING TO HIS APPREHENSION WILL BE REWARDED.

MARCH 9, 1916

CHIEF OF POLICE
Columbus
New Mexico

Pancho Villa and Venustiano Carranza were locked in a heated rivalry to oust Huerta from the Mexican government. Villa, pictured here, has been described as being "more horse than man," and a rather romantic image has grown around the man whom others, like Haldeen Braddy, call "a mustachioed bandit-warrior in a steeple-crowned sombrero." From the HCHM

Once the United States discarded its short-lived endorsement for Villa as president of Mexico and accepted Carranza, Villa's activities became more violent and desperate. Villa staged a raid in Columbus, New Mexico on March 9, 1916, and hoped to entice the United States into invading his country. The result, he hoped, would be a rallying of the Mexican people behind his leadership.

Following the raid, Gen. John J. (Blackjack) Pershing set out with twelve thousand men in a fruitless search for Villa. From the HCHM Collection.

This March 9, 1916, newspaper clipping depicts the infamous Pancho Villa. This reward for his capture was put out in New Mexico the day Pancho Villa and his bandits crossed the United States–Mexico border with a force estimated between 500 and 1,000 men and attacked the town of Columbus, New Mexico. Seven American soldiers were killed. Villa's raids frightened American citizens along the border from New Mexico to the Rio Grande Valley. These raids are the reason the New York and Tennessee National Guards were posted along the border in Pharr, Mission, and McAllen. (Courtesy of the Pharr Memorial Library Archives.)

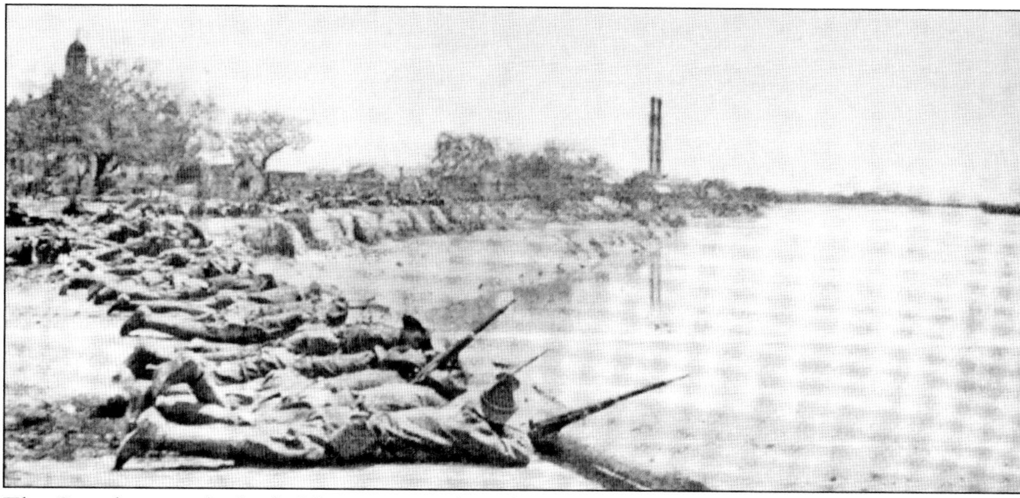

The Guardsmen, who hailed from New York and Tennessee, were put through constant intensive training. These soldiers were always waiting for possible orders for an invasion of Mexico—an order that never came. Pictured here along the border are soldiers conducting maneuver and tactical exercises in case an invasion actually occurs. For Capt. Herbert Wheaton Congdon, the most exciting part of duty was the outpost work along the Rio Grande. Along the river were a series of outposts and outguards that the 23rd Infantry would man. It was Congdon's job to inspect these fortifications periodically. On several occasions, the men would come into face-to-face contact with coyotes and wildcats during reconnaissance missions. One particular night, the No. 3 outguard reported hearing, on the opposite bank of the Rio, a woman screaming followed by the sound of a gunshot and finally a deep silence. (Courtesy of the New York State Military Museum.)

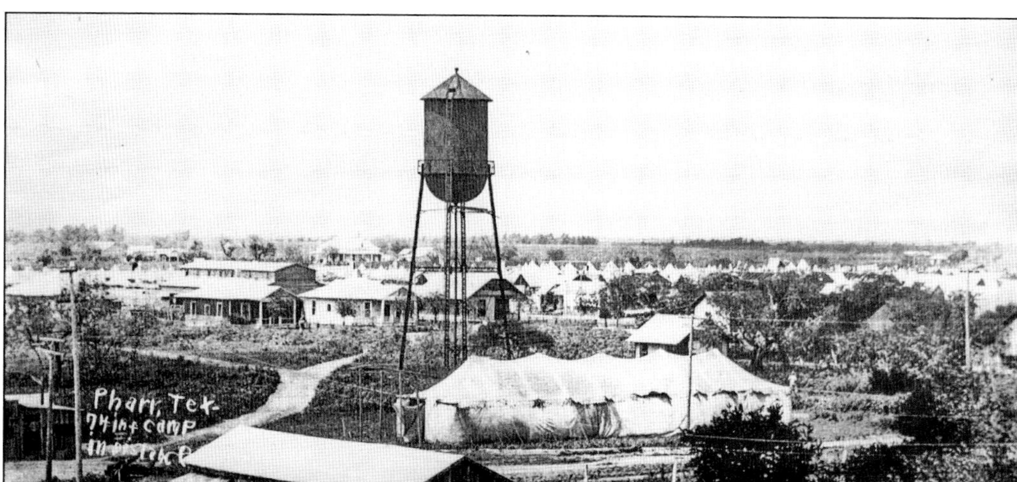

This medium-sized campground was home to New York's 74th Infantry National Guardsmen. The 74th Infantry hailed from the same area as the 23rd Infantry. The 74th's campground was not as large and was situated on the southeast side of town, opposite that of the 23rd. (Courtesy of the University of Texas–Pan American Library and Special Collections Department.)

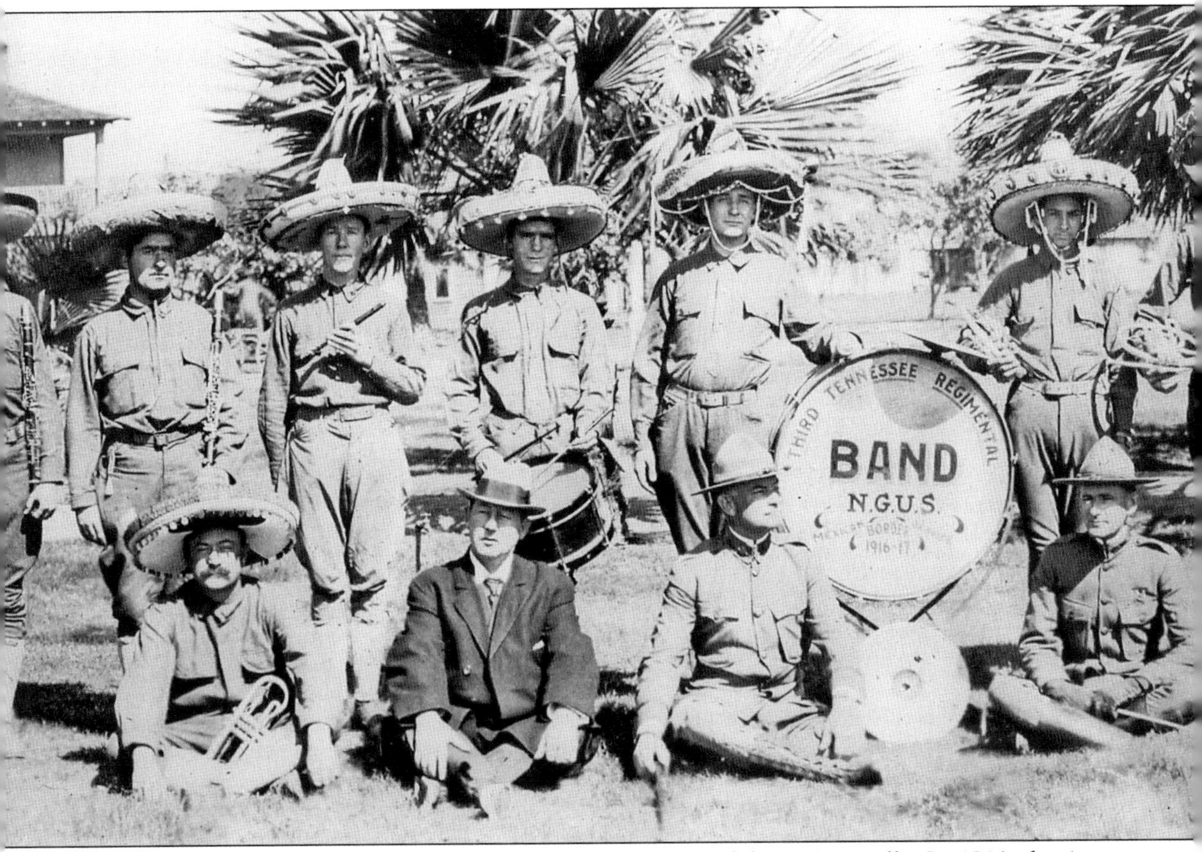

Pictured here in 1916 is the 3rd Tennessee Regimental Band from Knoxville. In 1916, the 1st Tennessee Infantry was called into service along the Mexican border to defend against incursions by bandits under Pancho Villa. The regiment mobilized June 26 and was mustered into federal service in July, training for Mexican border duty at Eagle Pass, Texas. After training, the men were relocated to Pharr until their departure on March 20, 1917. (Courtesy of the University of Texas–Pan American Library and Special Collections Department.)

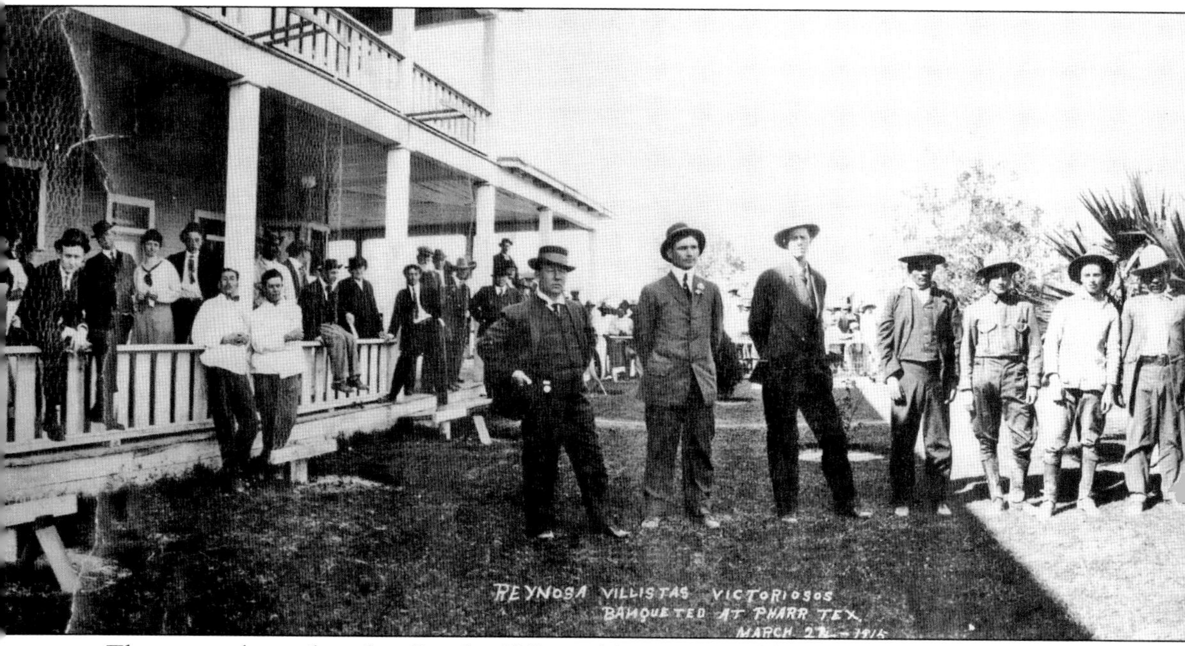

There was always fear that Pancho Villa and his men would invade the Rio Grande Valley. Chances are he was never here, but he had plenty of supporters. Pictured here are Villa supporters, better known as Villistas. In March 1915, the Villistas took control of Reynosa, Tamaulipas, in Mexico. A banquet to honor these men and their victory in Reynosa was held at the Pharr Hotel.

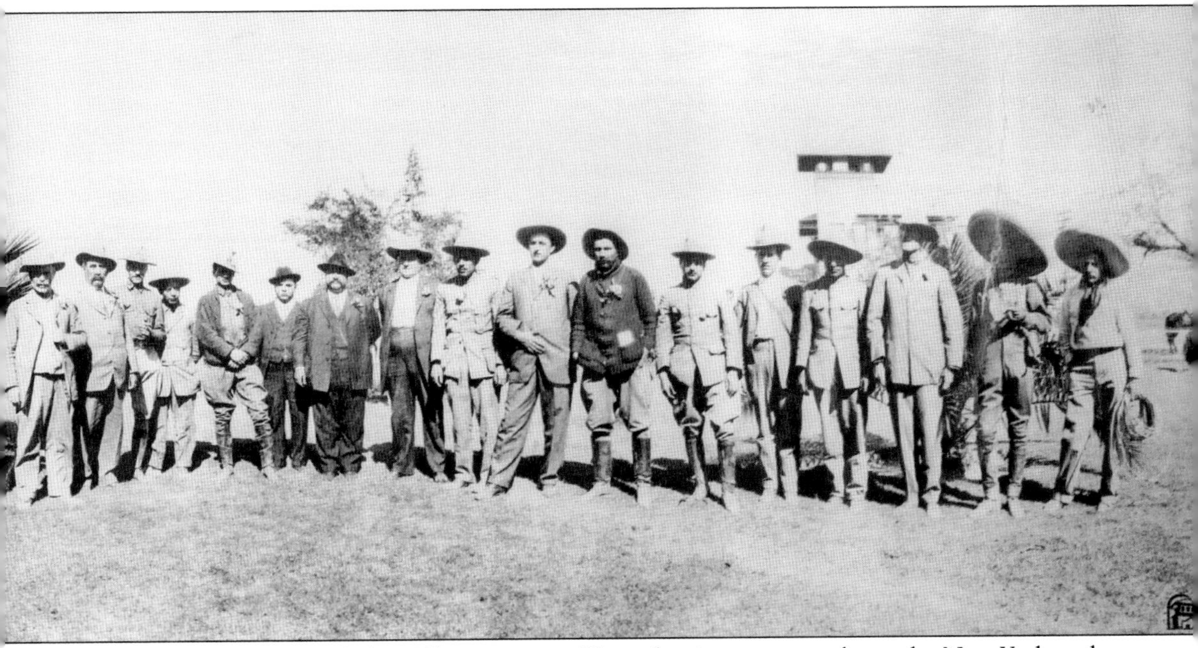

It is unclear how accepted the Villistas were in Pharr, but just one year later, the New York and Tennessee National Guardsmen were mobilized to the border. This is another panoramic image taken by photographer J.C. Murff. (Courtesy of the Museum of South Texas History.)

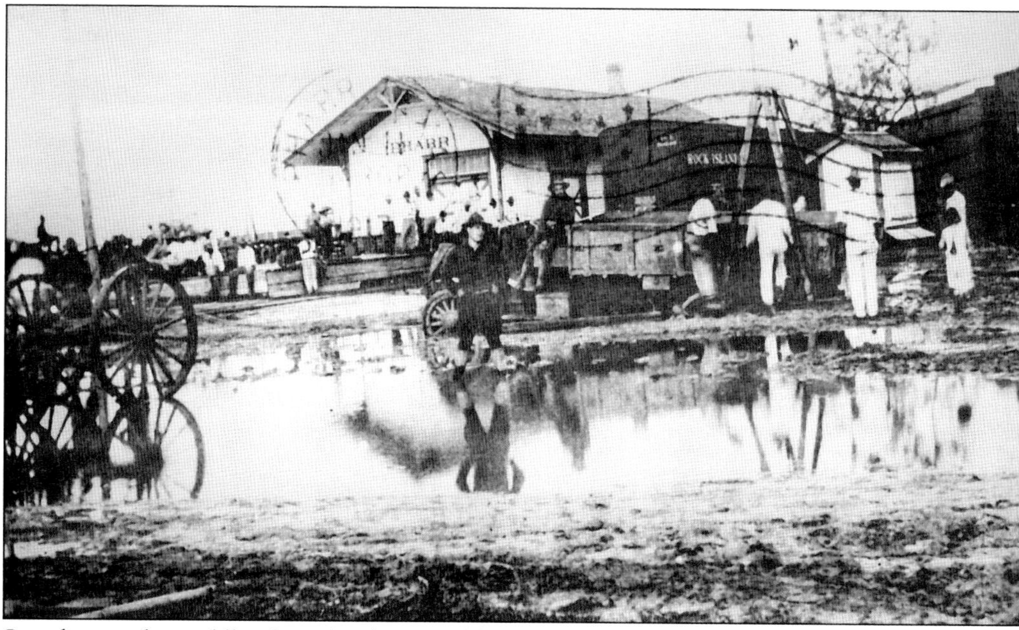

Standing in the middle of a rather large puddle in front of Pharr's railroad depot is a soldier from either the Tennessee or New York National Guard. Because the roads around town had not been paved at the time of this picture in 1917, large muddy puddles were very common after a heavy downpour. These puddles could make life and travel very difficult. (Courtesy of the Pharr Memorial Library Archives.)

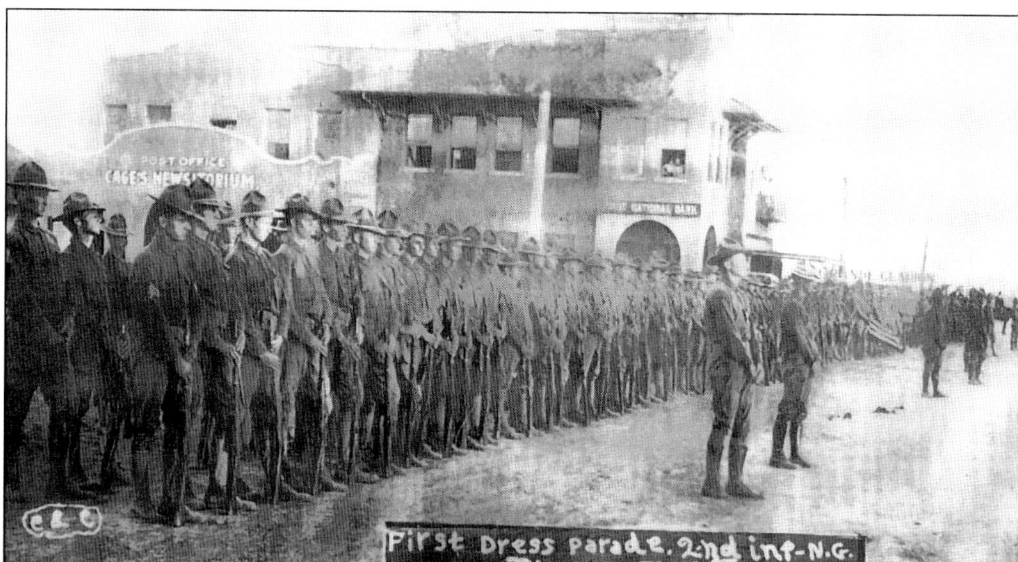

Pictured here in 1916 in front of the city's first building are soldiers from New York and Tennessee; they are participating in their traditional dress parade, a formal ceremony in which troops are formed, assessed, and read important orders. The earliest account of a dress parade is documented in the *Regulations of the Confederate States Army* published in 1861. Maj. Gen. Frederick Funston was in charge of every single man who reported for Mexican border service. (Courtesy of the Pharr Memorial Library Archives.)

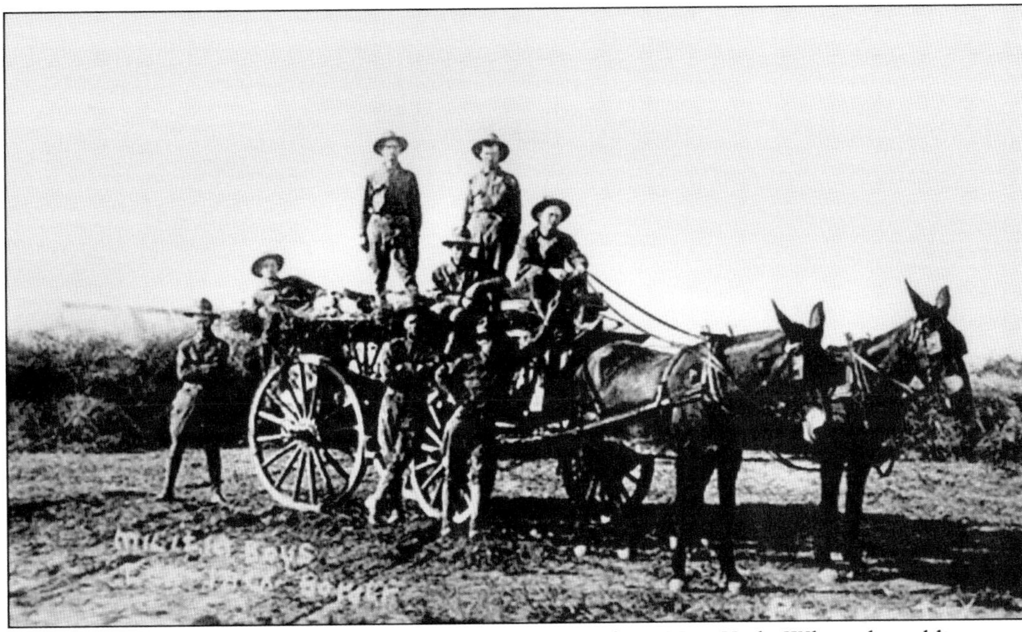

Pictured here in 1916 are members of the 74th Infantry from New York. When the soldiers were not out being drilled by their commanding officers, there was not a whole lot to do to pass the time in the blistering heat. For most of the men, the most exciting part of duty was the outpost work along the Rio Grande. (Courtesy of the Pharr Memorial Library Archives.)

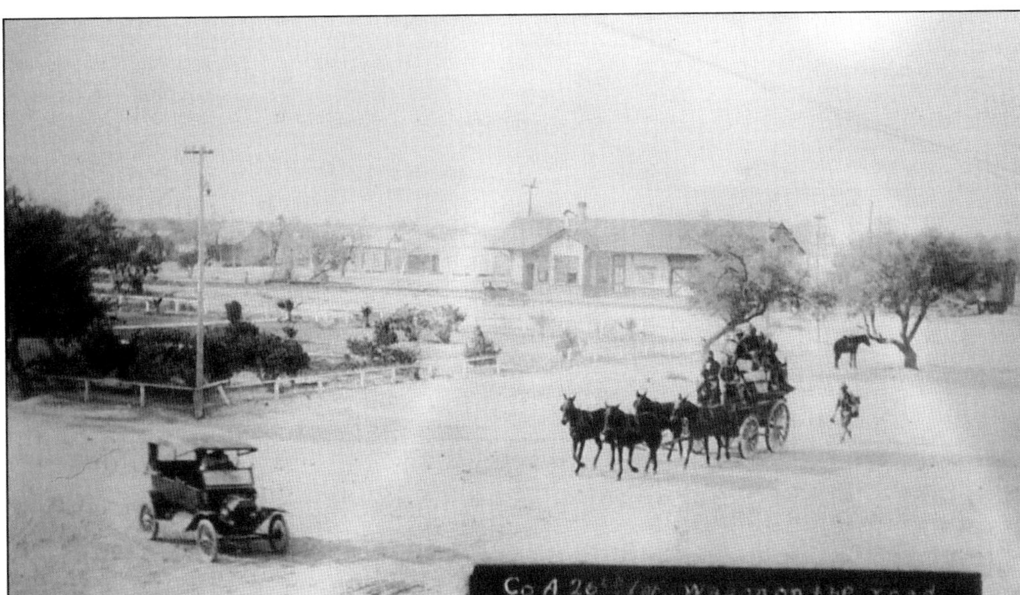

This photograph was taken in 1915 and shows the Pharr railroad depot in the background. Also pictured are soldiers from New York's 23rd Infantry riding with some cargo on a mule-drawn wagon while one soldier carrying a bag follows. The soldiers were traveling south on Cage Boulevard and were more than likely heading to their campgrounds. (Courtesy of the University of Texas–Pan American Library and Special Collections Department.)

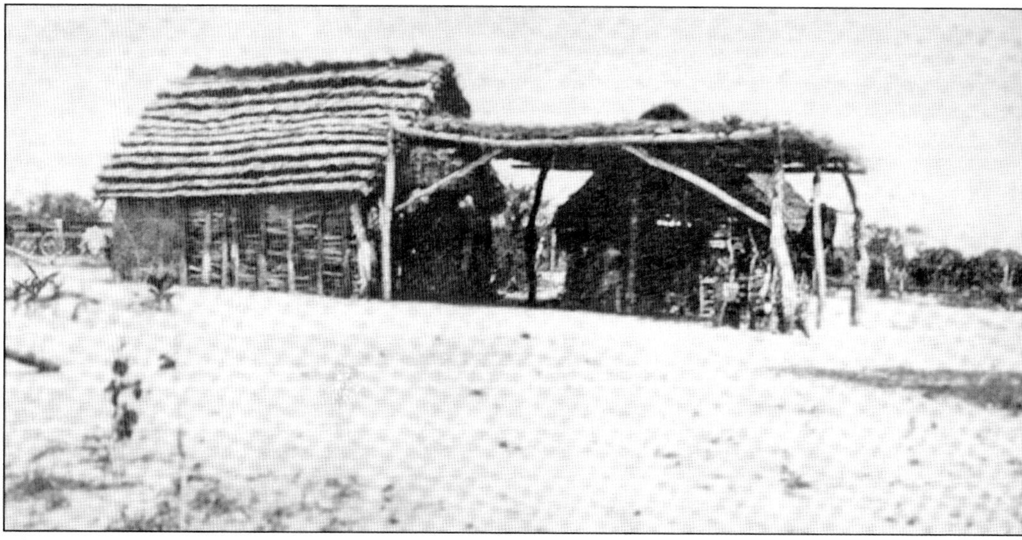

This 1916 hut is the type of native dwelling that was typically seen along the Rio Grande at the time. It was not uncommon for soldiers to visit the huts and camps of Mexicans who lived mostly in the brush. The Mexicans were said to be very hospitable once their suspicions of the American soldiers subsided. (Courtesy of the New York State Military Museum.)

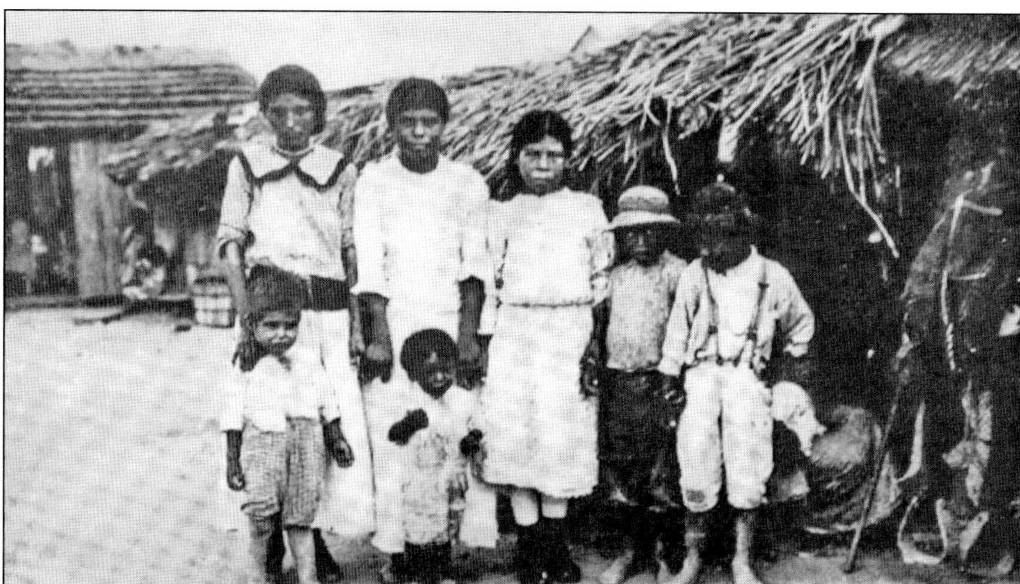

Pictured here sometime in 1916 is a small Mexican family. They resided at the time in the outskirts south of Pharr along the Rio Grande. According to an account by soldier John O'Ryan, these Mexicans resembled a number of Indian tribes. O'Ryan also claimed that the majority of these Mexicans spoke a version of Spanish known as "Mex." The soldiers referred to these people as "peons." (Courtesy of the New York State Military Museum.)

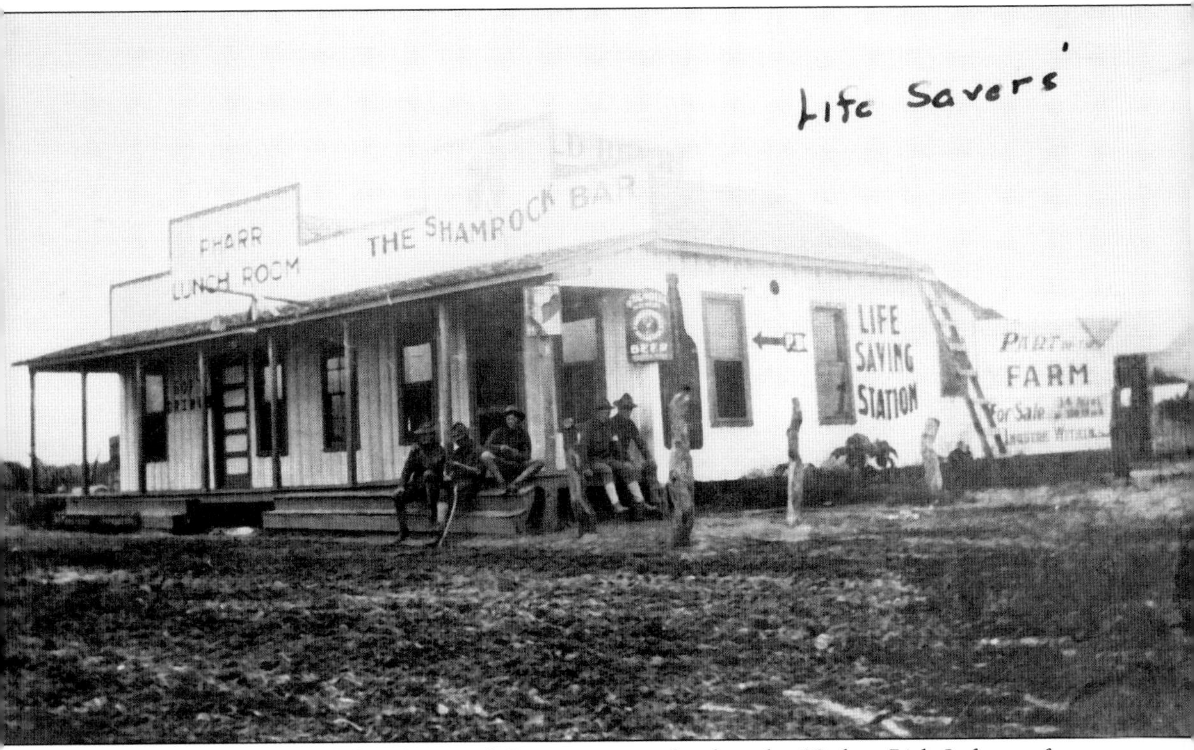

Pictured here in front of the Shamrock Bar are men of either the 23rd or 74th Infantry from New York. The order known as G.0.7. was issued prohibiting officers and men of the New York Division from consuming intoxicating liquors in any form. However, Major General Funston, the man in charge of all the troops on the border, was quoted saying, "There is no danger of G.0.7. being applied to Fort Sam Houston," which was at that time his headquarters. (Courtesy of the Museum of South Texas History.)

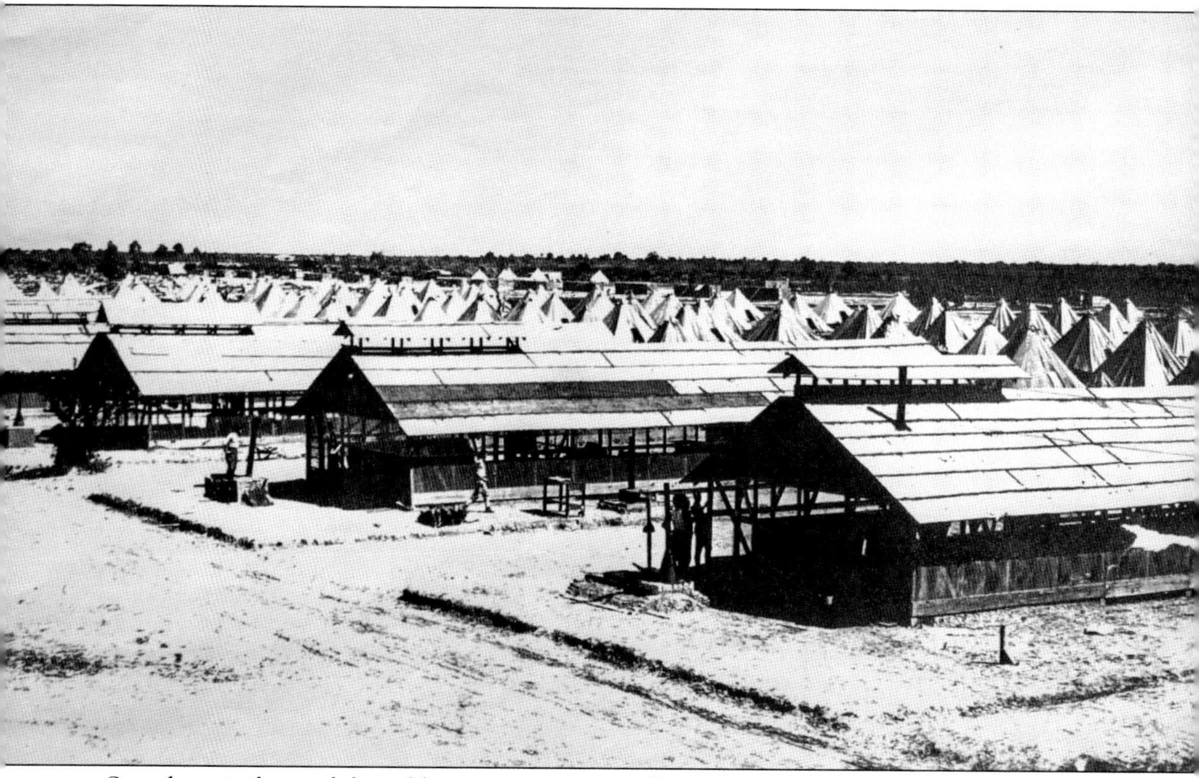

Seen here in front of the soldiers' tents are the military mess halls, also known as chow halls. Soldiers would eat their three square meals per day here. If soldiers still found themselves hungry, it was not uncommon for them to make their way to the Shamrock Bar or to a local's house to eat some food. (Courtesy of the Museum of South Texas History.)

Three

The Agricultural Boom

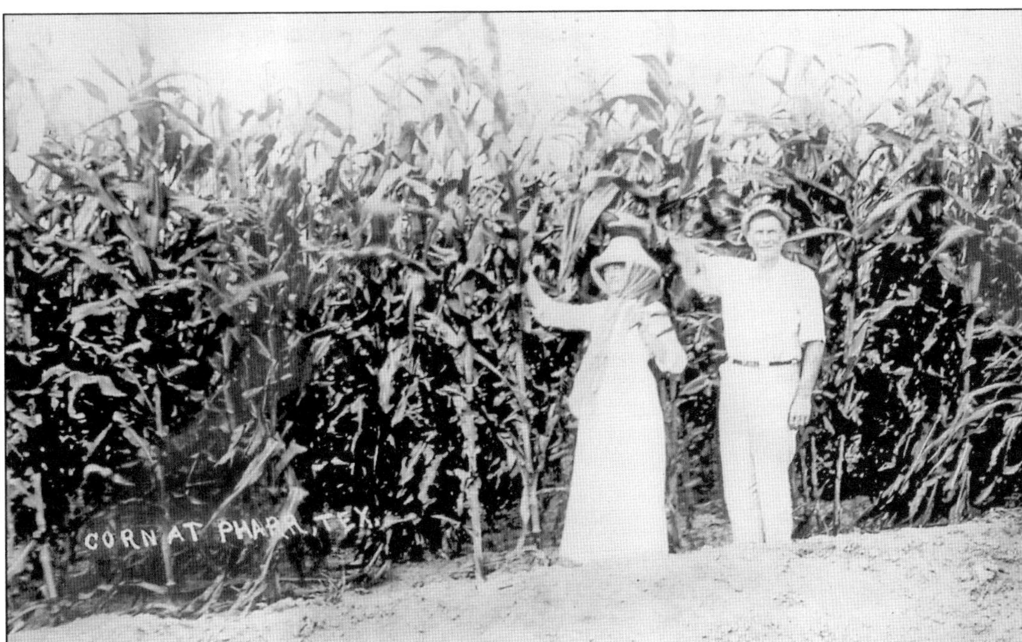

This early-1900s photograph depicts an unidentified man and woman standing in front of a cornfield. Crops like corn, cotton, sorghum, carrots, and many other types of fruits and vegetables ran rampant. Pharr's location in the South Texas Plains vegetation area allowed it to be an agriculturally rich town. (Courtesy of the University of Texas–Pan American Library and Special Collections Department.)

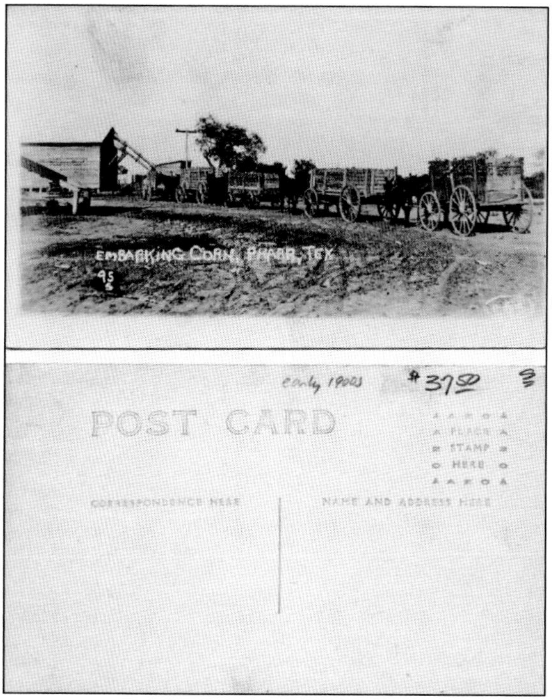

This early-1900s Pharr, Texas, postcard depicts several horse-drawn wagons transporting corn. Corn is typically planted from February to April and is harvested from July to October. In 1913, Texas planted some seven million acres in corn and harvested an average of 21 bushels per acre. Pharr was instrumental in this amount of corn planted and harvested. (Courtesy of Southern Methodist University, Central University Libraries, DeGolyer Library.)

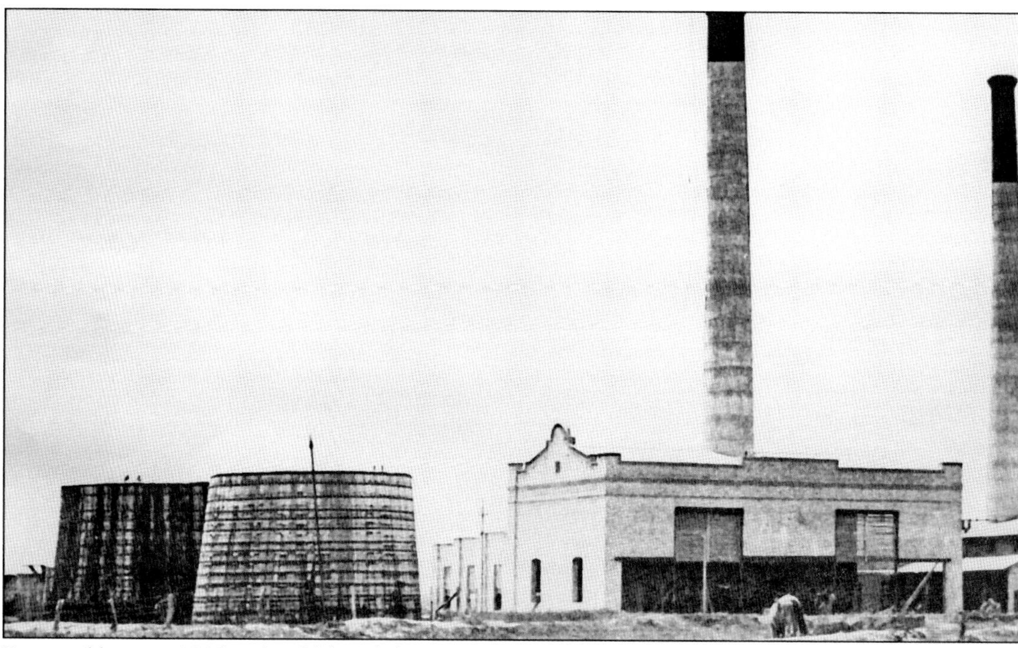

Pictured here in 1915 is the Old Hidalgo Pump House. The pump house currently sits in Hidalgo, Texas, but its origins began in Pharr when Henry Newton Pharr and his partner John C. Kelly commissioned a Mr. Gore, a civil engineer, to construct an irrigation system with a main canal that could supply water for at least 16,000 acres. Gore's completed pump house pumped water directly from the Rio Grande, to the main canal, and then to local farms; making the land very fertile. The pump house has since been decommissioned, but the City of Hidalgo maintains the pump house as a great local museum. (Courtesy of the Museum of South Texas History.)

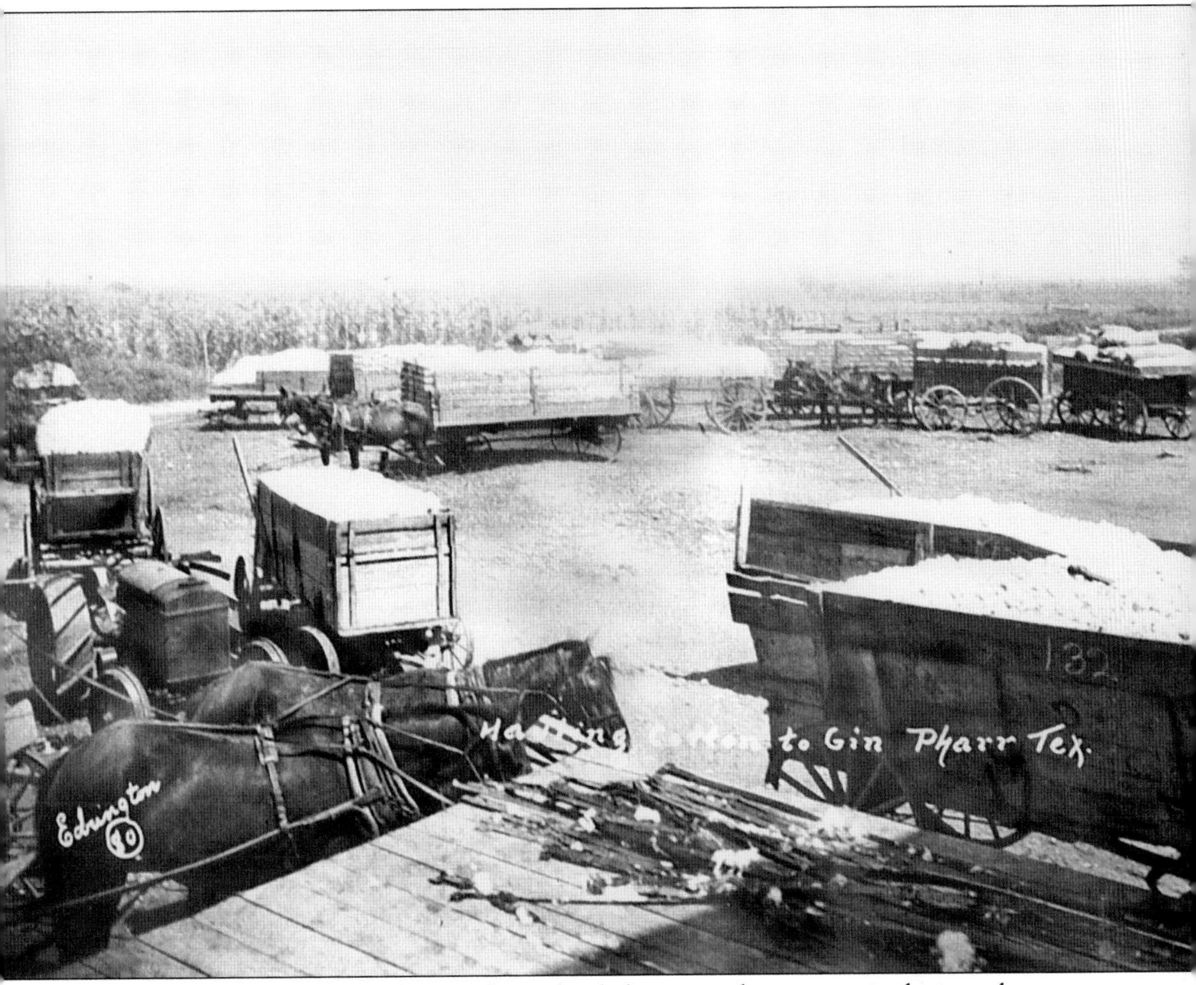

This late-1920s photograph of cotton being hauled to a nearby cotton gin depicts what soon became an old way of life for farmers in Pharr. Cotton was dominant in East and Central Texas until a sudden shift to the Rio Grande Valley occurred in the 1920s. However, the Texas Cotton Acreage Control Act of 1931 drastically halted cotton production in Pharr and across Texas, and so the cotton boom declined. (Courtesy of the University of Texas–Pan American Library and Special Collections Department.)

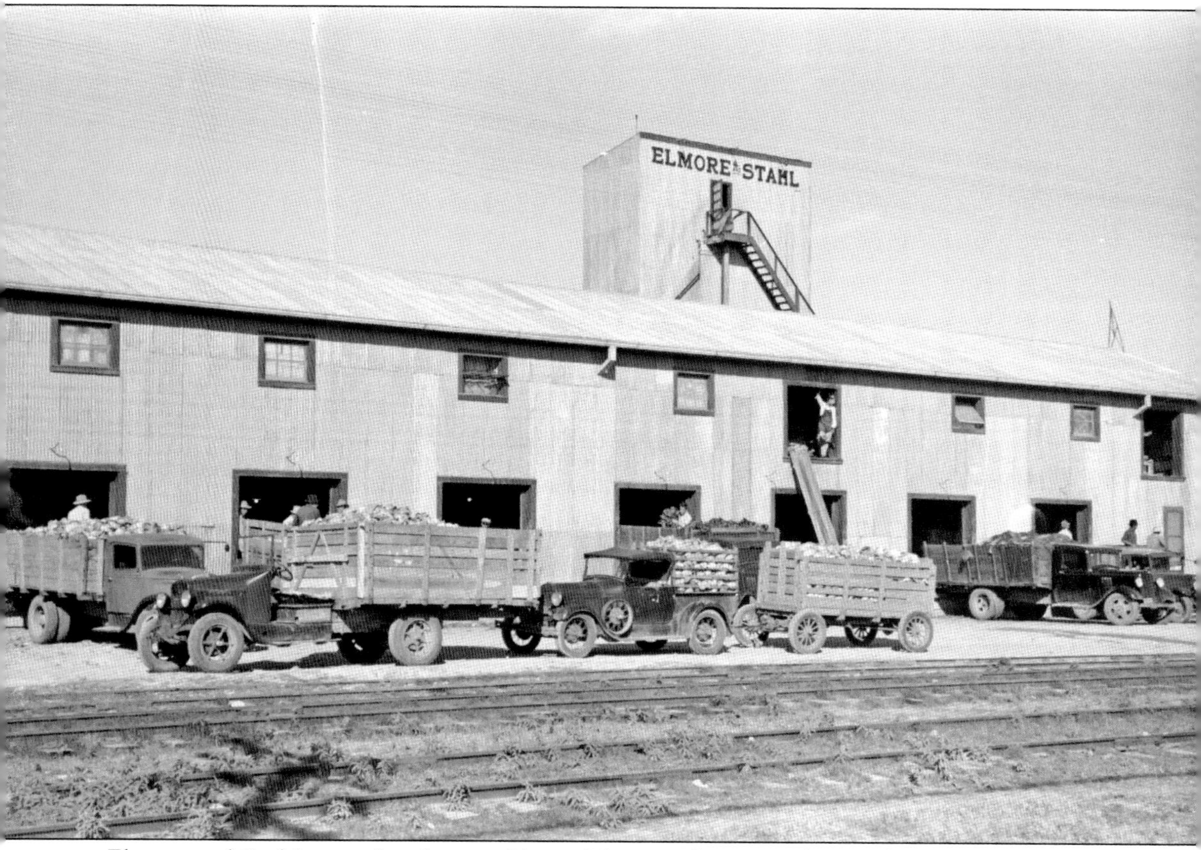

Elmore and Stahl was a local vegetable and fruit packing warehouse that served the city for quite some time, especially during the fruit and vegetable boom that spread across South Texas during the late 1930s and early 1940s. This 1939 picture shows truckloads of produce being hauled away. Local resident Ruben "Sepi" Rosales, born in 1928, remembers working on the warehouse's second floor, assembling the boxes that would store the fruits and vegetables. (Courtesy of the Library of Congress.)

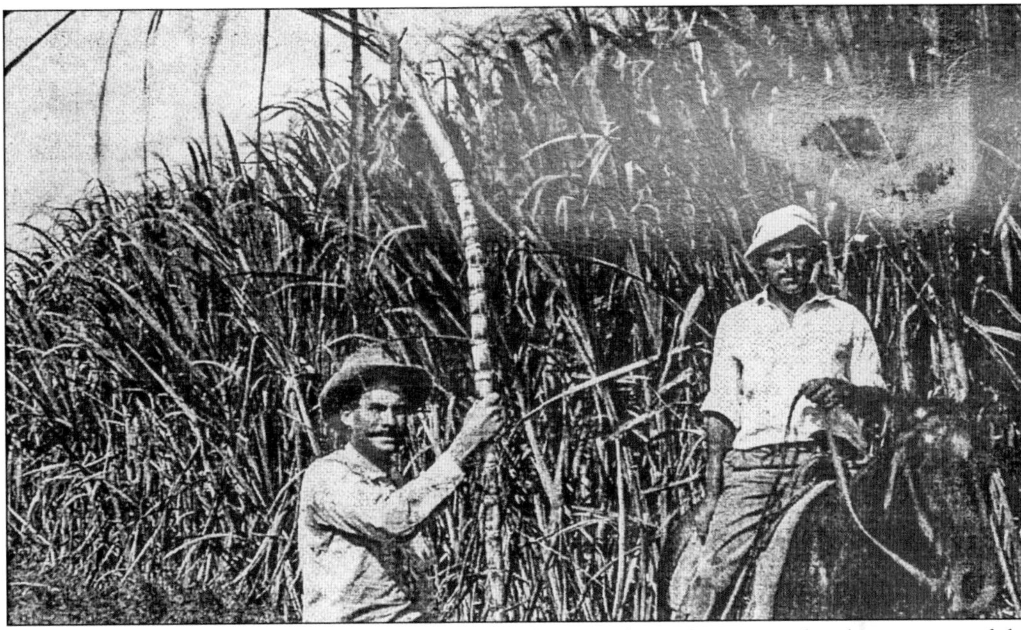

Pictured here are two unidentified sugarcane workers in Pharr. Sugarcane has been a part of the Rio Grande Valley agricultural landscape for more than 200 years. It was introduced here in the early 1800s, and five major sugar mills were in operation by 1913. However, the United States' involvement in World War I brought on economic and political hardships that caused these sugar mills to close. Fortunately, the sugarcane industry in the valley was reborn in the 1960s. (Courtesy of the University of Texas–Pan American Library and Special Collections Department.)

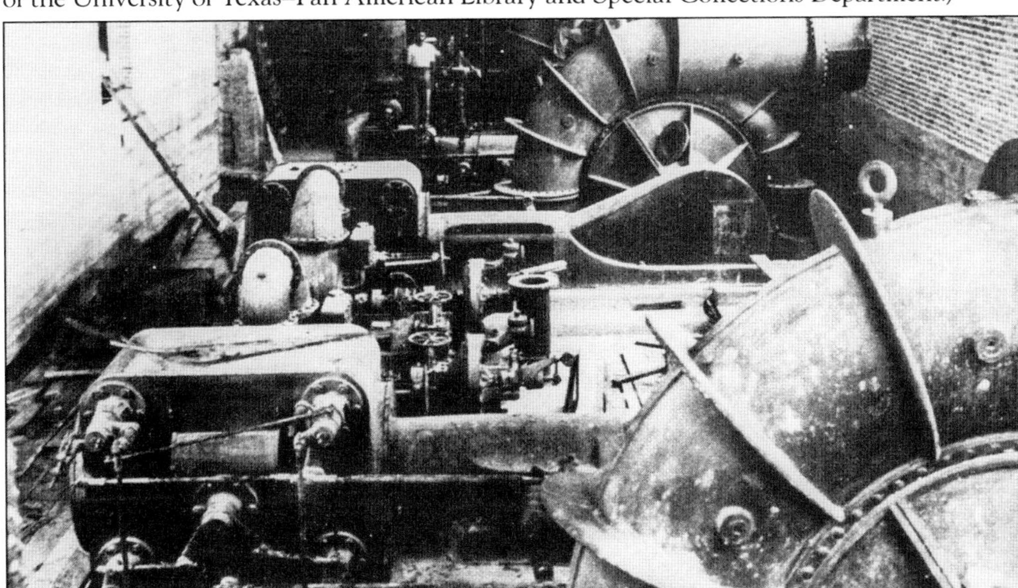

This undated picture shows several of the intake pipes that are located inside the Old Hidalgo Pump House. The pump house once sat on the Rio Grande, but a flood in 1933 changed the course of the river. The river was then flowing half a mile away from the pump house. A channel was then dug from the pump house to the river to bring river water into these huge intake pipes. (Courtesy of the Pharr Memorial Library Archives.)

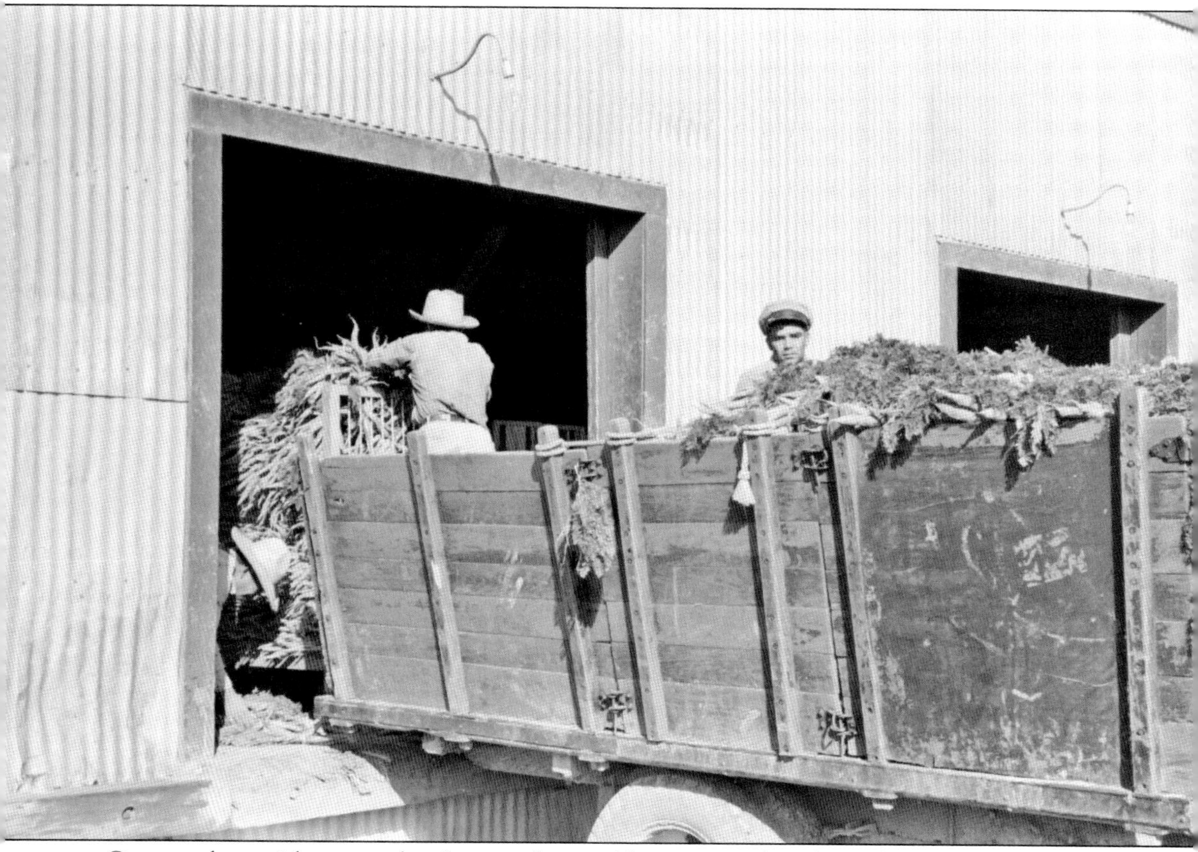

Carrots, along with many other fruits and vegetables, grew in abundance due to the agriculturally rich soil that was made possible by the city's irrigation system. Unloading a truckload of carrots, these three unidentified men are pictured in 1939 at Elmore and Stahl. Production was steadily increasing moving into the 1940s. (Courtesy of the Library of Congress.)

Ella Beth Melton was an entrant in the annual "birthday party" fashion show in Weslaco, Texas. The event was organized by the chamber of commerce to highlight the fruit and vegetables grown in the Rio Grande Valley, and area citizens created and modeled clothing made from local fruit, vegetables, and flowers. Ella was representing the Kiwanis Club of Pharr and won the first-prize vegetable division. The dress is made of grapefruit peels with a train of sliced onions wrapped individually in cellophane; she is holding a bouquet of turnips and carrots with fern. (Courtesy of the University of North Texas Libraries.)

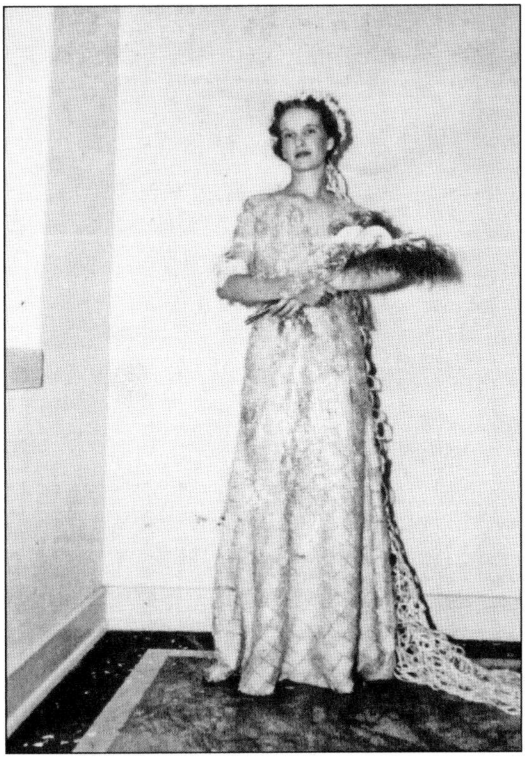

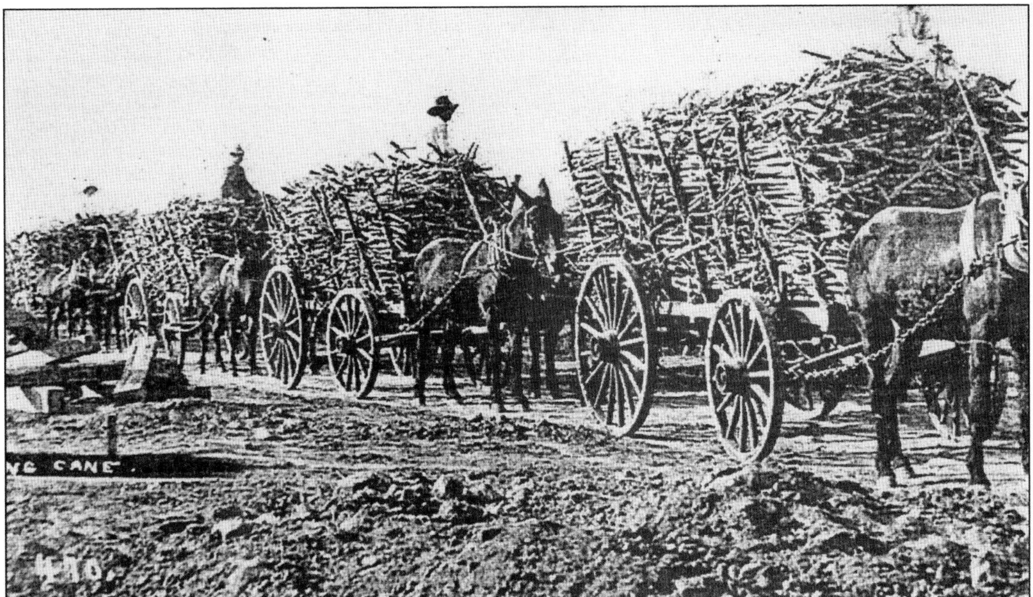

Since sugarcane grows rampant in South Texas, it is no surprise that cities like Pharr have allowed Hidalgo County to become the largest producer of sugarcane in the entire state of Texas. Pictured here around 1915 are several horse-drawn wagons hauling large amounts of cane stalks to be used for milling. (Courtesy of the University of Texas–Pan American Library and Special Collections Department.)

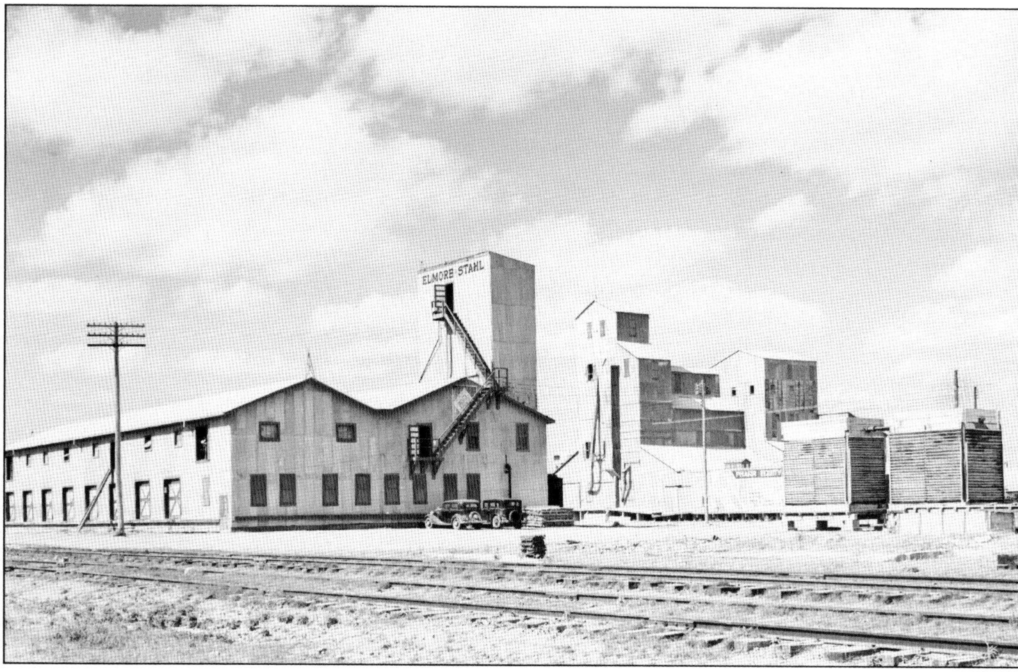

This 1939 photograph of Elmore and Stahl was taken from the south side of the railroad tracks on Business 83. Located right behind Elmore and Stahl is the Pharr Equity. Standing in this exact location today, one will notice that the area looks much the same, though Pharr Equity is no longer there. (Courtesy of the Library of Congress.)

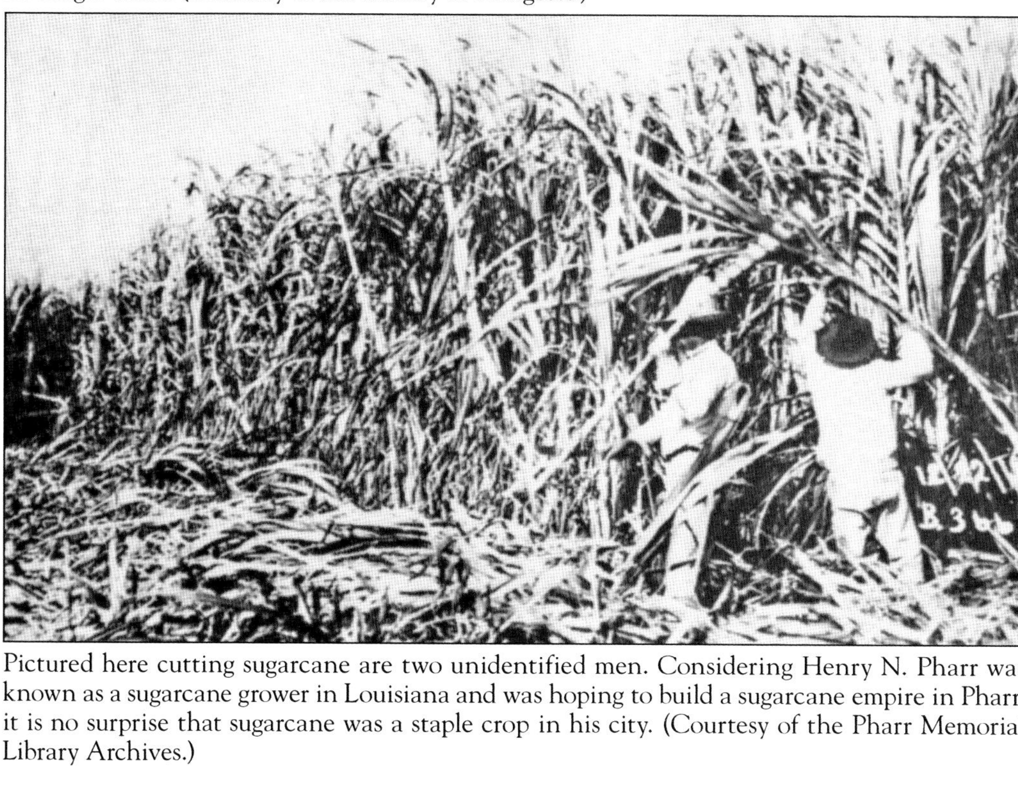

Pictured here cutting sugarcane are two unidentified men. Considering Henry N. Pharr was known as a sugarcane grower in Louisiana and was hoping to build a sugarcane empire in Pharr, it is no surprise that sugarcane was a staple crop in his city. (Courtesy of the Pharr Memorial Library Archives.)

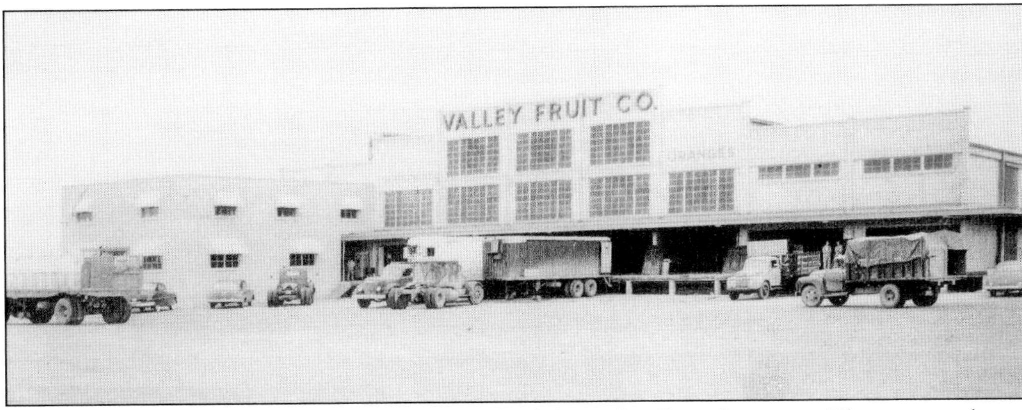

J.H. Williams and his stepson Roy Weir established the Valley Fruit Company. Their careers began out of a small garage, but when business boomed over the next 10 years, Williams purchased a 14-acre lot, located on North Cage Boulevard, in 1939 to accommodate their growing business. The Valley Fruit Company building was officially built in 1947, establishing it as a major packer and shipper of grapefruit in the global market. (Courtesy of the University of Texas–Pan American Library and Special Collections Department.)

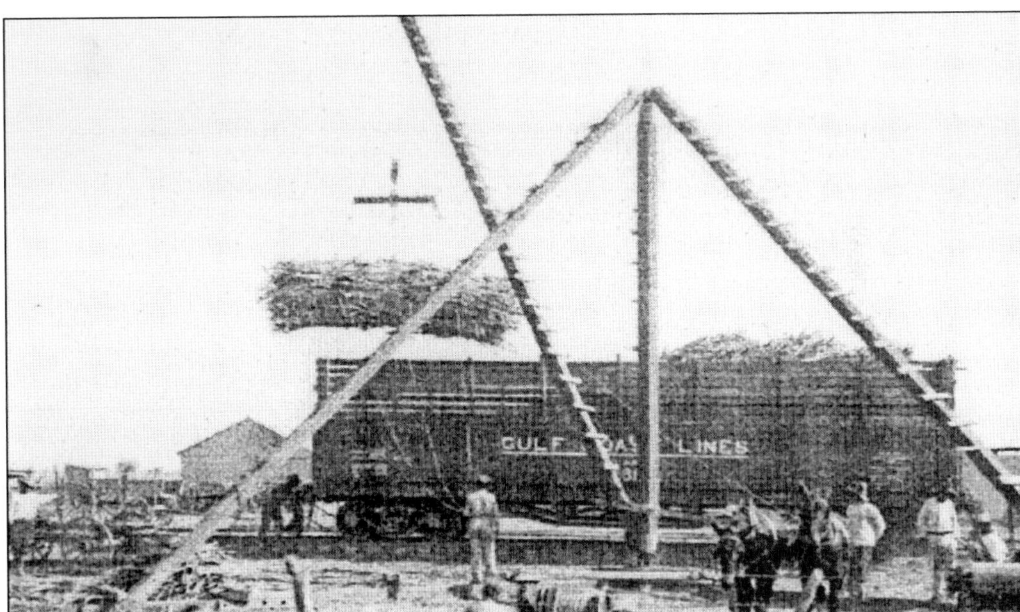

The world demand for sugar is the primary reason for sugarcane agriculture. A total of 80 percent of the world's sugar is produced from sugarcane while the other 20 percent is produced from sugar beets. These men here are loading a large amount of sugarcane stalks onto this railcar to be shipped out. The Rio Grande Valley established itself as the largest sugarcane producer in the region and the state. (Courtesy of the University of Texas–Pan American Library and Special Collections Department.)

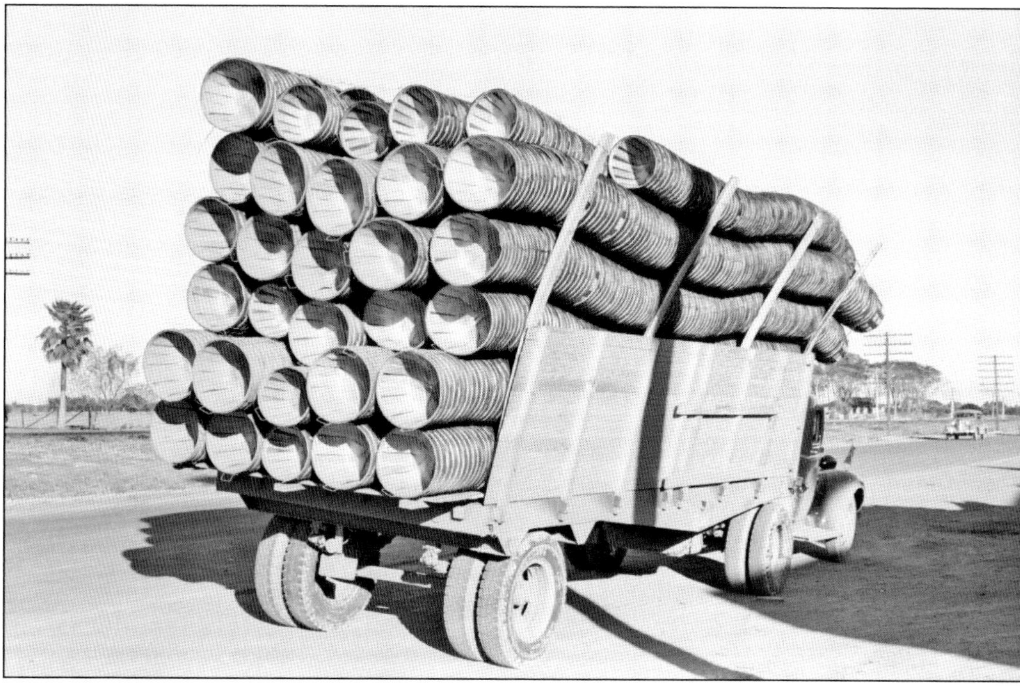

Due to an agricultural expansion in South Texas during the 1920s, plenty of laborers were needed to work the fields to pick fruits and vegetables. Typically, these workers were Mexicans and Mexican Americans. Due to the Great Depression and repatriation efforts, work and production slowed down, but things picked up again during the 1940s. This 1939 picture shows a truckload of baskets getting ready to be sent into the fields. (Courtesy of the Library of Congress.)

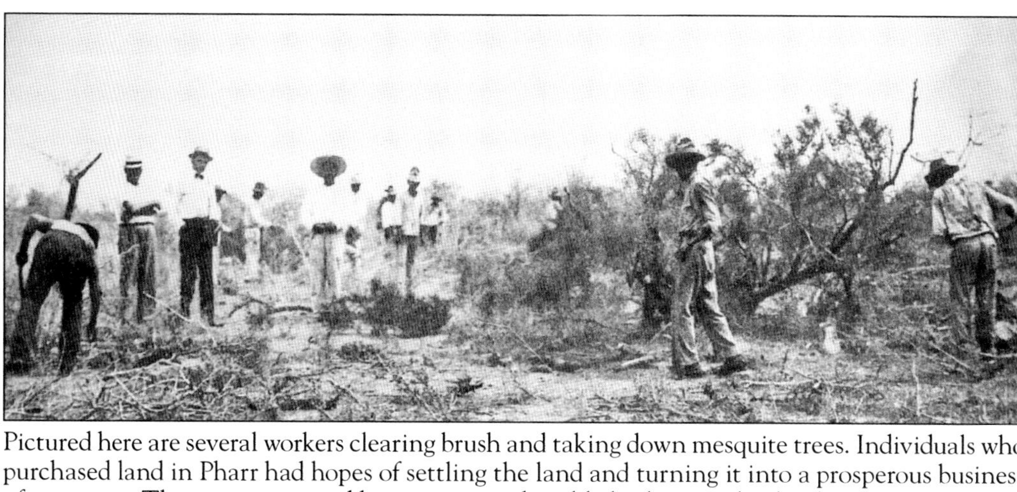

Pictured here are several workers clearing brush and taking down mesquite trees. Individuals who purchased land in Pharr had hopes of settling the land and turning it into a prosperous business of some sort. These men pictured here are more than likely clearing this land so that the owners of the property could prosper from it. (Courtesy of the Pharr Memorial Library Archives.)

Four

Street Scenes and Businesses

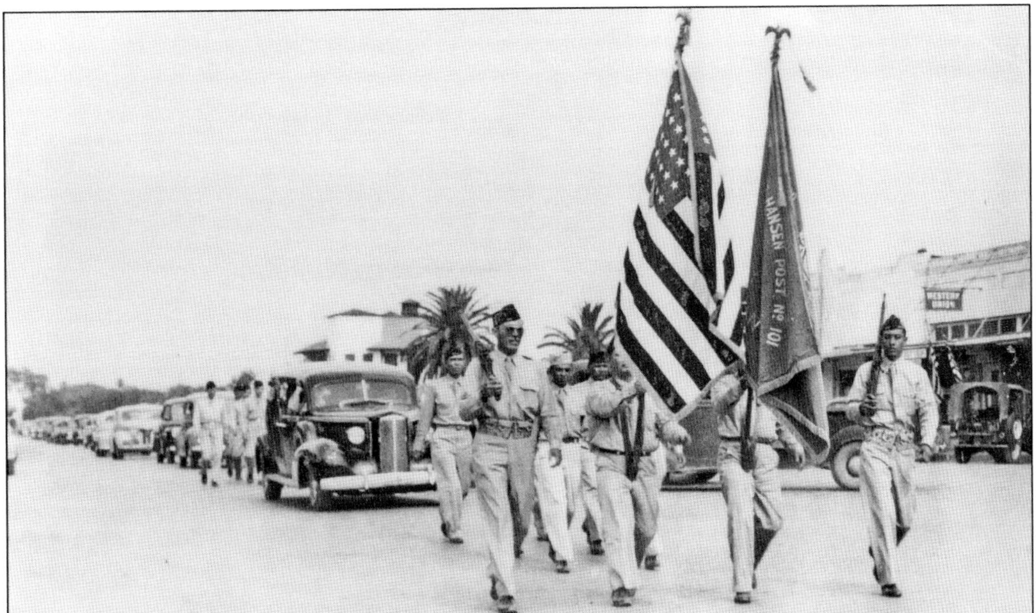

Pictured here in the early 1940s are several US military men who are proudly serving their country during World War II. It is unclear exactly what is occurring, but it is assumed that a funeral is taking place for a fallen soldier. They are marching west on Park Avenue through the downtown area of the city. Similar to Bedford, Virginia, the American town with the highest per capita casualties on D-day, Pharr had plenty of its young men serve and fight overseas during World War II. One of Pharr's sons even stormed Omaha Beach, in Normandy, France, during Operation Overlord, also known as D-day. Several others fought in Europe and the Philippines. (Courtesy of Tony Villegas.)

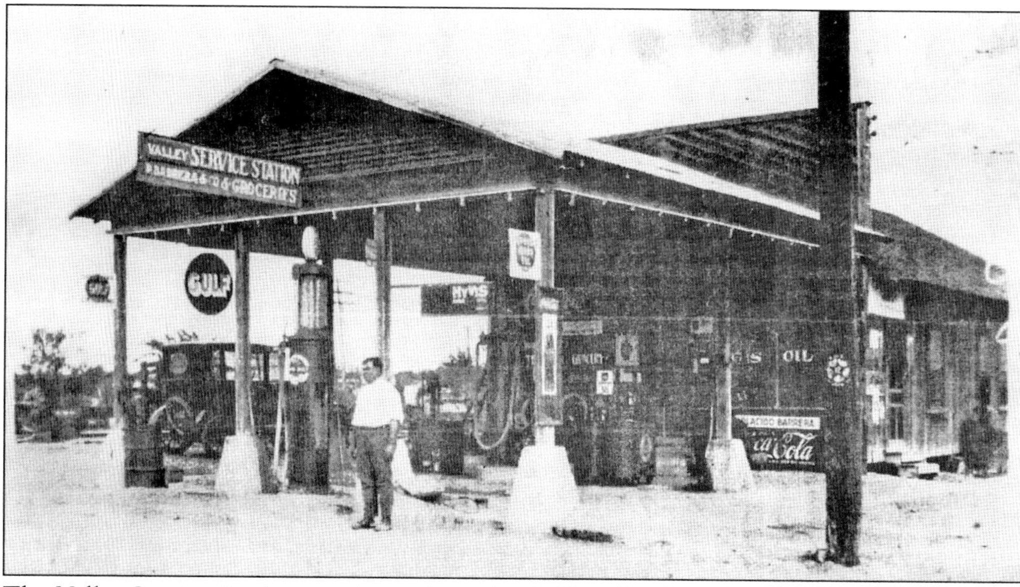

The Valley Service Station was located on North Cage Boulevard and East Clark Avenue. It was owned and operated by Placido Barrera (pictured). The station's gas pumps were operated manually. The exact date of this photograph is unknown, but it was more than likely taken in the 1920s. (Courtesy of the Pharr Memorial Library Archives.)

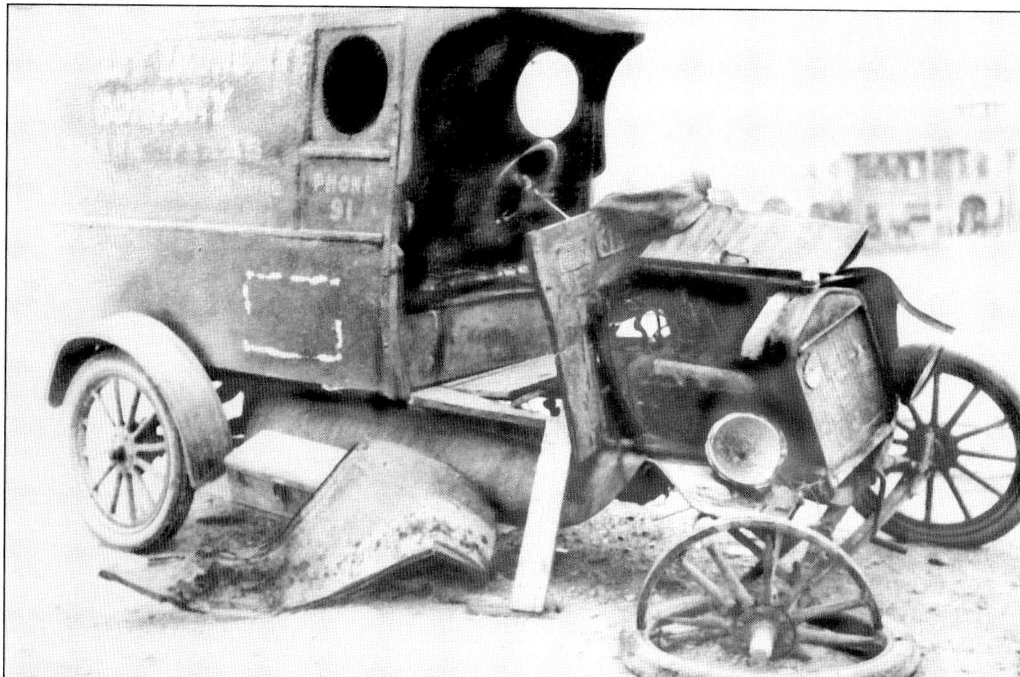

This 1920 photograph shows a totaled vehicle belonging to the Valley Laundry Company, located in Pharr. The reasons for this wreck are unknown; no other vehicle was involved in the accident. Halted in the center of town on Cage Boulevard and Business 83, the car was clearly struck by something large. Thankfully, nobody was hurt. (Courtesy of the University of Texas–Pan American Library and Special Collections Department.)

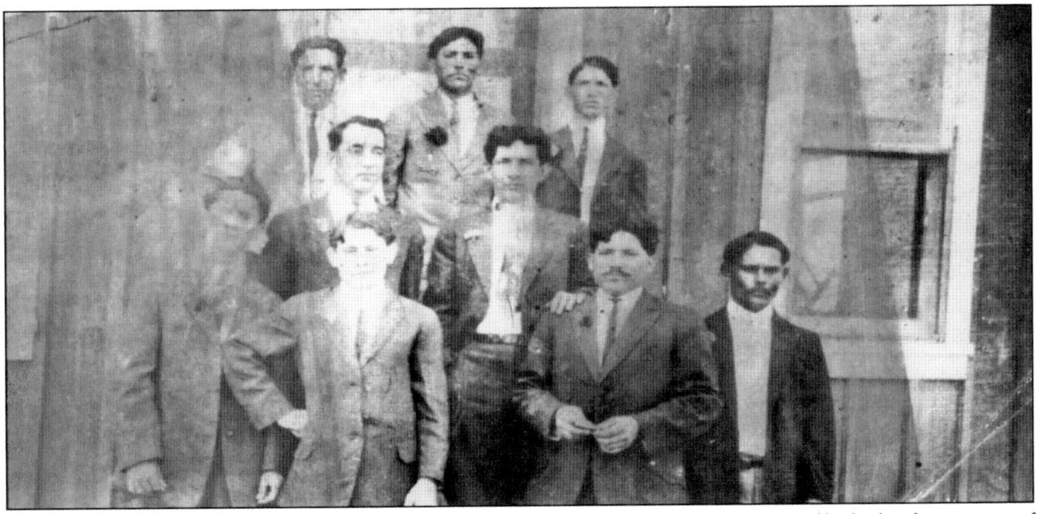

This damaged photograph was taken sometime in 1913. These men are all clerks for many of the Pharr business establishments. They are all bilingual and hold important positions. In the third row are Alonzo Benavidez (left) and Salvador Villegas (center); in the second row is Juan "Cheno" Rodriguez (right). He was murdered by a man named Lupi Edwards in the company of Texas Rangers at 205 West Park Avenue inside the Pharr Mercantile. In the first row are Lazaro Gonzalez (left) and Antonio Villegas (right), who witnessed the murder of Rodriguez. (Courtesy of Tony Villegas.)

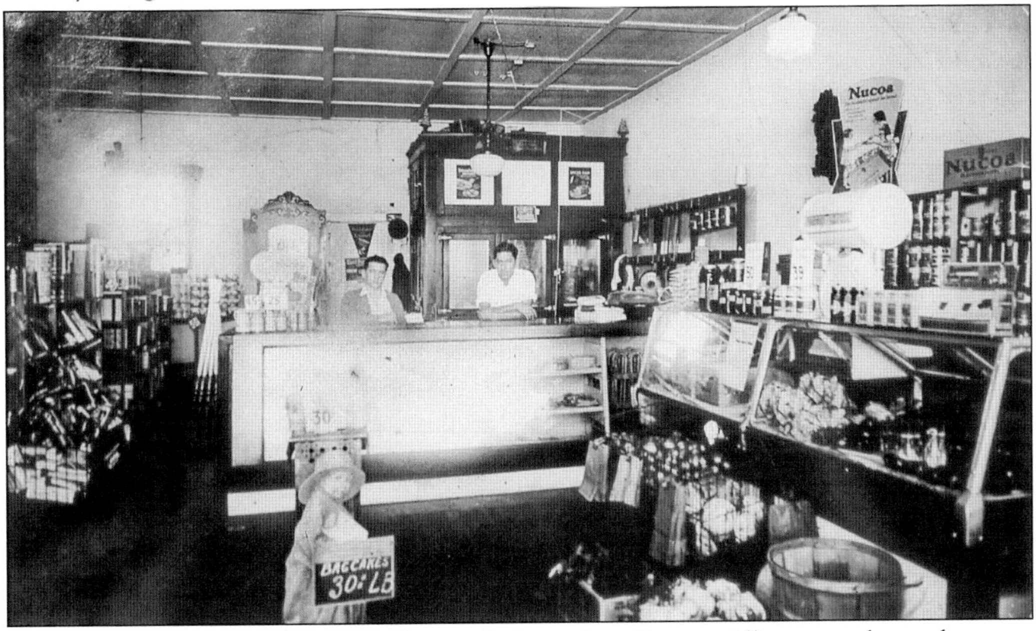

Pictured in 1928 are Frank and Joe Guioco. Independent Grocers Alliance market and grocery was located on West Park Avenue in the downtown area of the city. The store was located on the south side of the railroad tracks meaning that Mexicans were not allowed. The north side of the tracks was designated for minorities. Eventually, the store met stiff competition and went out of business when Piggly Wiggly came to town, followed by H-E-B grocery store, which still operates in Pharr today. (Courtesy of the University of Texas–Pan American Library and Special Collections Department.)

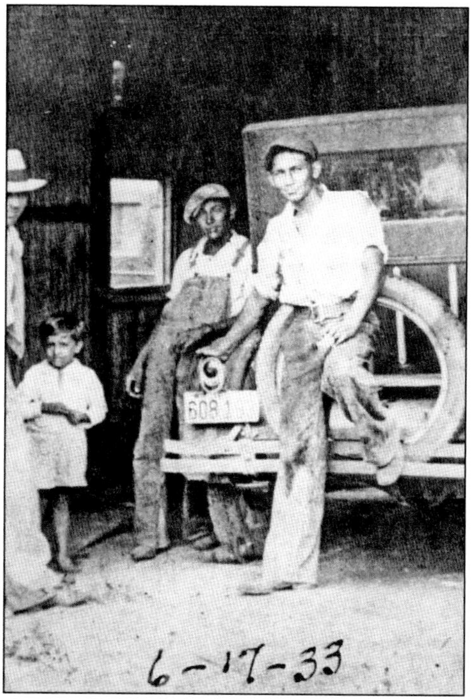

The best mechanic in town was said to be Prajedis Rios; he is believed to be the man on the far right leaning against the car. If there was a problem with a car, he could fix it. He was known for taking a large screwdriver and placing it on the engine of a car. He would then put his ear to the screwdriver and listen. From that alone, he could tell what was wrong with the engine. He truly was a one-of-a-kind mechanic. The little boy in the photograph is Leo Gonzalez, who is still alive today. (Courtesy of the University of Texas–Pan American Library and Special Collections Department.)

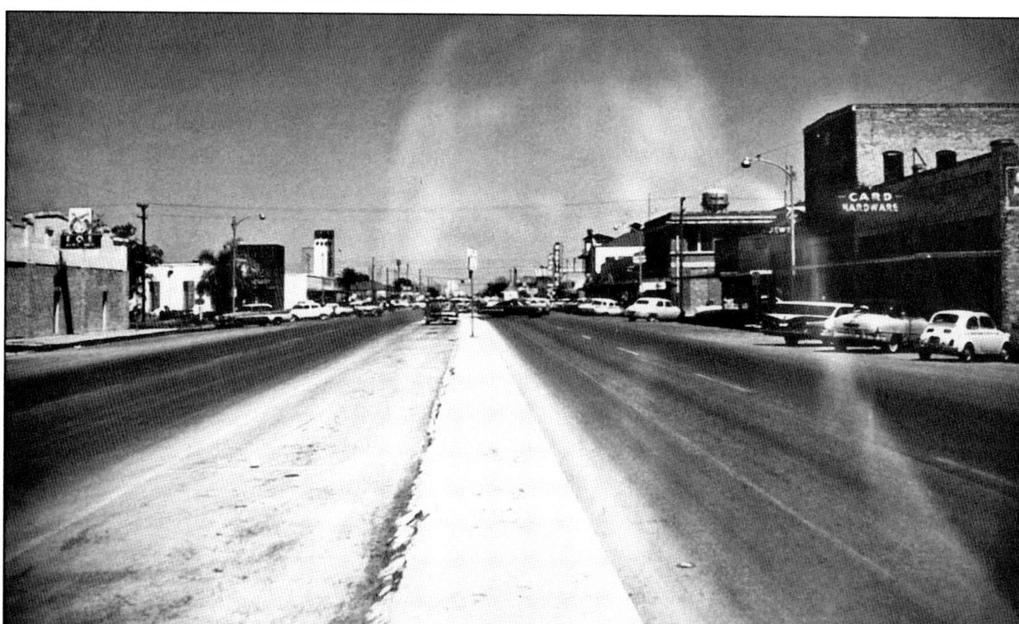

This 1950s street view facing north was photographed from the center of Cage Boulevard. On the left-hand side, the Fraternal Order of Eagles building can be seen. It burned to the ground, and the group's new home was eventually situated across the street, where it still stands today. In the distance is Martin's Café. It was originally Junction Café but was renamed for a short period when the Martin family owned it. The name was changed back to Junction Café once the Martins sold the business. The current owners of the Junction Café are Raul and Criselda Fong. (Courtesy of the University of Texas–Pan American Library and Special Collections Department.)

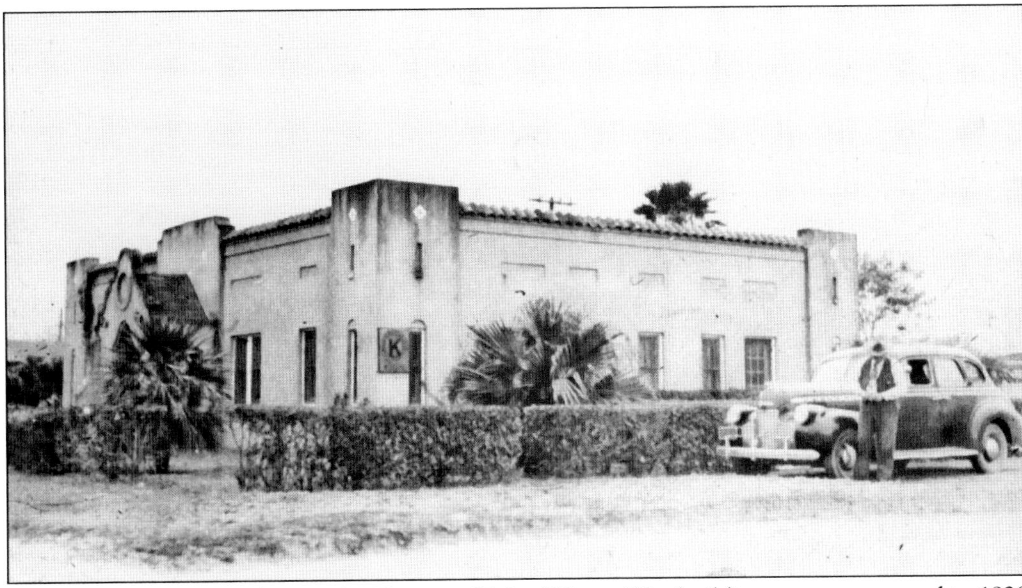

This 1940 photograph depicts the Kiwanis Club of Pharr. The building was constructed in 1928, 13 years after the formation of the first Kiwanis club in Detroit, Michigan, and one year after the Pharr club was chartered. Designed to serve as a community center, it has been used for a variety of different functions and meetings and housed offices of the city chamber of commerce. It became a Texas Historic Landmark in 1981. (Courtesy of the University of Texas–Pan American Library and Special Collections Department.)

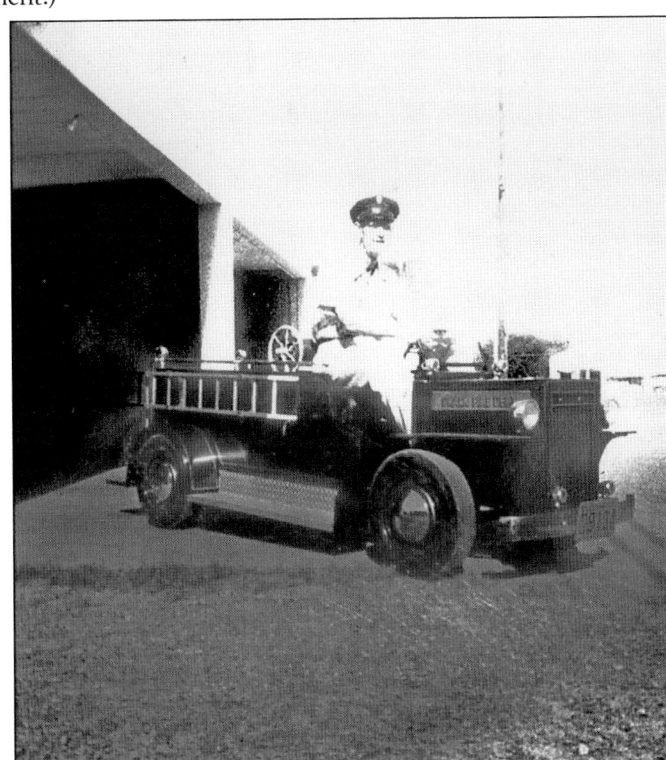

Frank Guioco, manager and proprietor of Independent Grocers Alliance market and grocery store located on Park Avenue, is pictured here sitting on top of a model fire truck in the 1940s. By this time, the Pharr Fire Department had been established, resulting in a significant firefighting presence in the city. (Courtesy of the University of Texas–Pan American Library and Special Collections Department.)

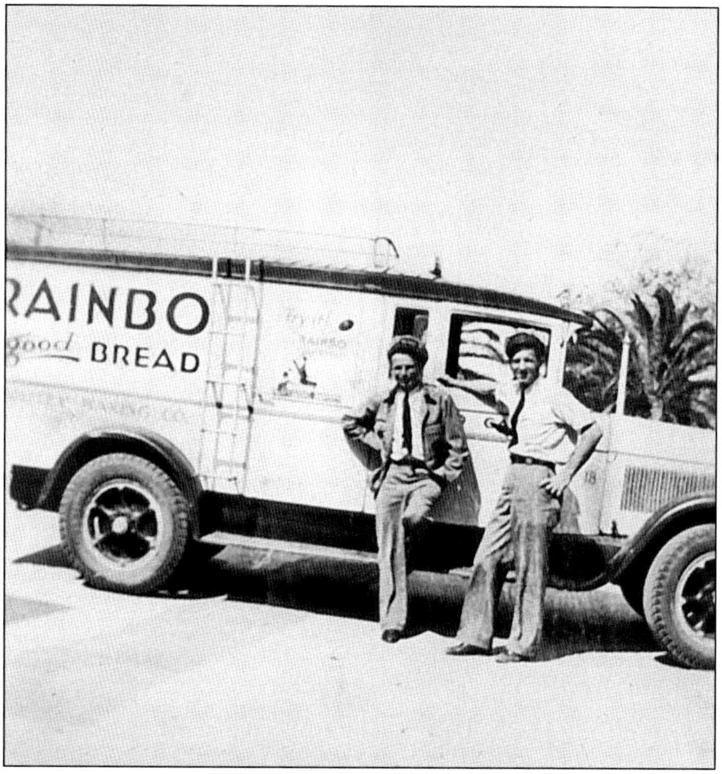

This picture, taken sometime during the 1930s, shows two deliverymen standing by their Rainbo Bread truck. Rainbo Bread was delivered to the white people living on the south side of the tracks. However, if a person had money, white or not, he or she could purchase Rainbo, considered the "expensive" bread. Mexicans typically bought sweet bread from Don Jose, who delivered bread from La Estrella Bakery in McAllen, Texas, or they stuck to eating the tortillas made at home. (Courtesy of the University of Texas–Pan American Library and Special Collections Department.)

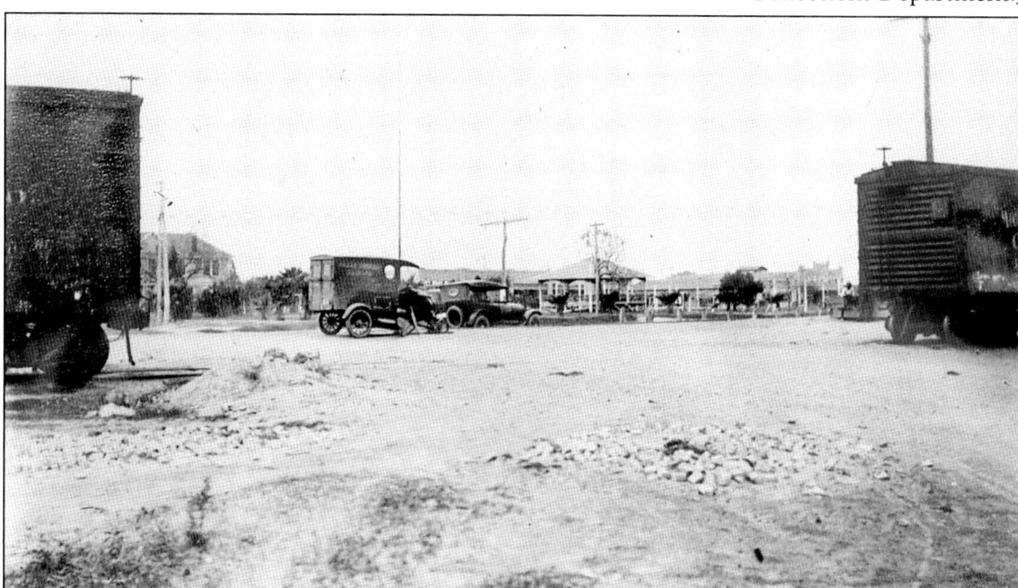

This photograph depicts another angle of the wrecked laundry vehicle that sat in the middle of the street for quite some time. There was a break in the train running along Business 83 that allowed for this photograph to be taken. Facing southwest, the Pharr Hotel is visible on the left-hand side, and the Pharr Park, with its beautiful gazebo located on Park Avenue, is visible right in the center of the photograph in the distance. (Courtesy of the University of Texas–Pan American Library and Special Collections Department.)

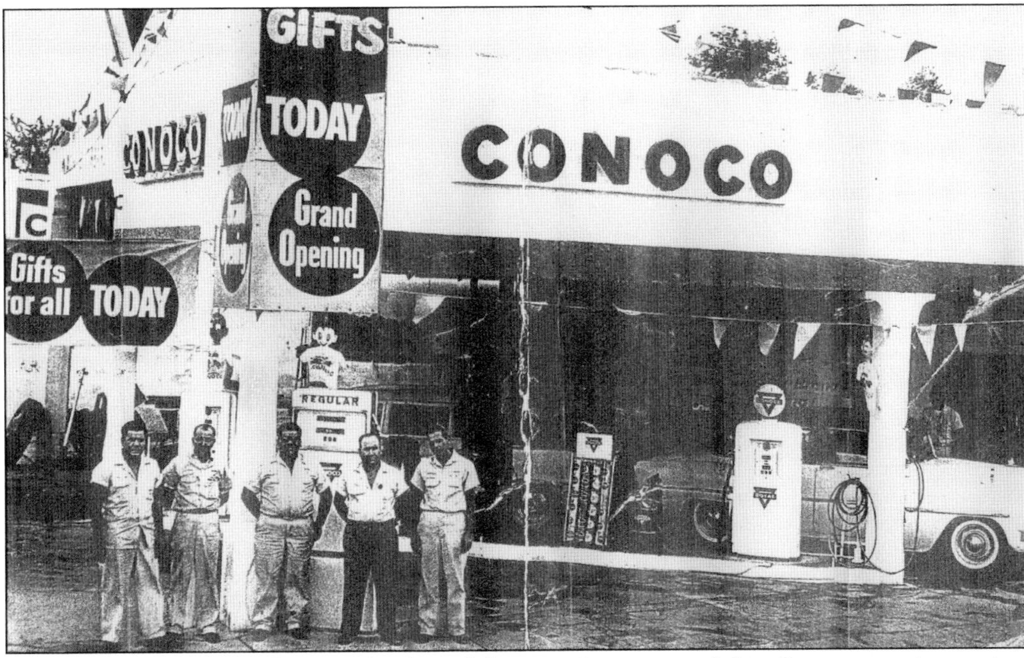

This photograph was taken on the day of the grand opening of this Conoco service station, sometime in the 1950s. This store was located on the corner of Aster Street and State Avenue. The men pictured are, from left to right, Gilberto Espinoza, Domingo Garza, Roberto Benavidez, Raul Espinoza, and Francisco "Panchito" Espinoza. (Courtesy of Ruben "Sepi" Rosales.)

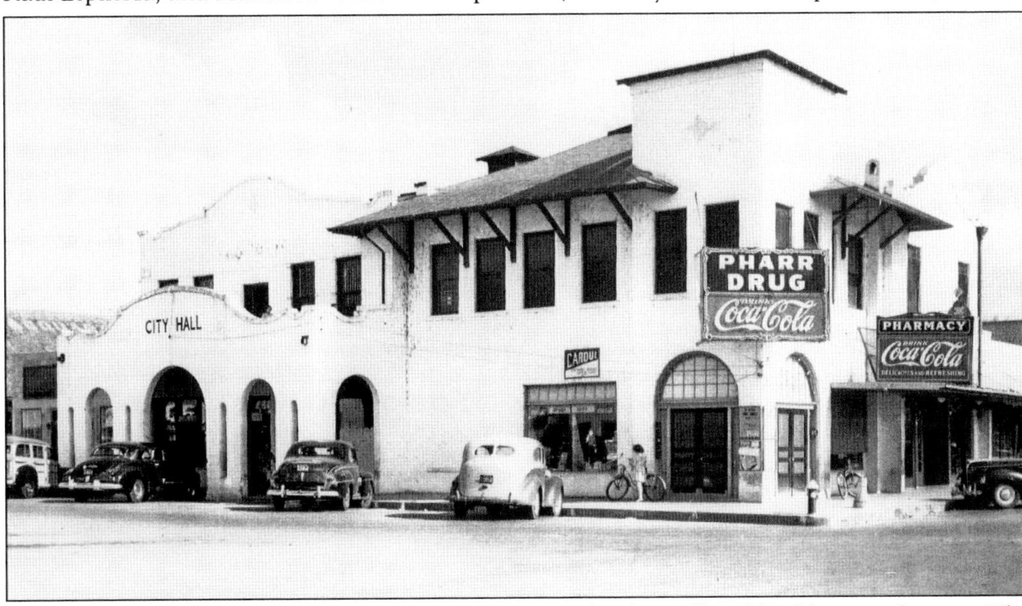

This 1950s downtown photograph of Pharr depicts the first official building in the city. The building underwent a transformation after the city's incorporation in 1916 and evolved from Pharr's city hall and First National Bank into the first drugstore for the city. The structure has remained relatively the same, but the building's proprietors have changed. It was managed and operated by a Mr. Crump, a Mr. Kelso, and Leo Sanchez in the 1950s. (Courtesy of the Museum of South Texas History.)

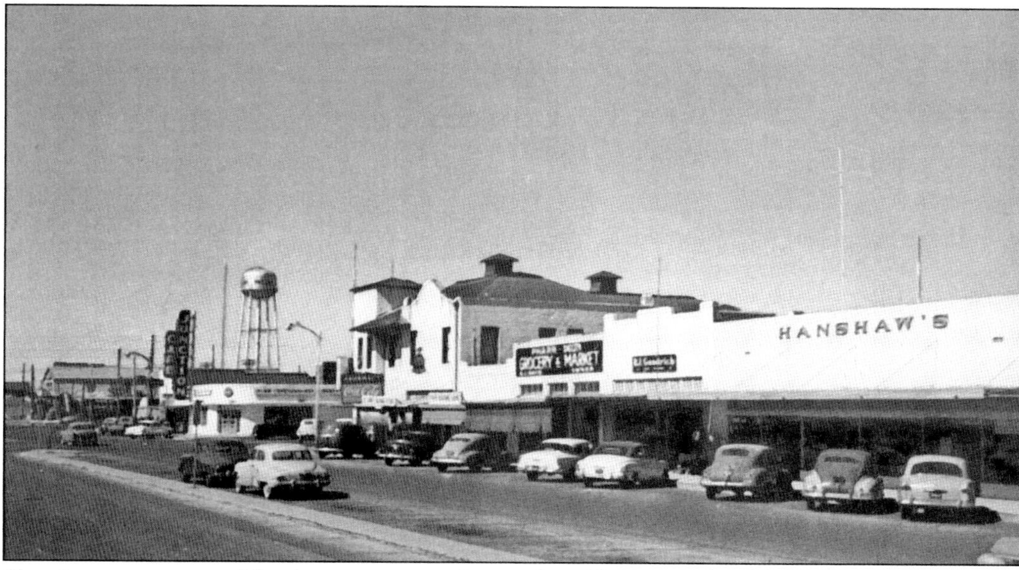

Here is a street scene of the downtown area during the 1950s. Many local businesses like Hanshaws could be found in this area. Hanshaws was a five-and-dime store, which sold a variety of things. In the distance, the Pharr water tower can be seen. The tower was painted entirely by Jose Saenz, who used to climb the tower with no rope or harness. The water tower no longer exists today. (Courtesy of the Pharr Memorial Library Archives.)

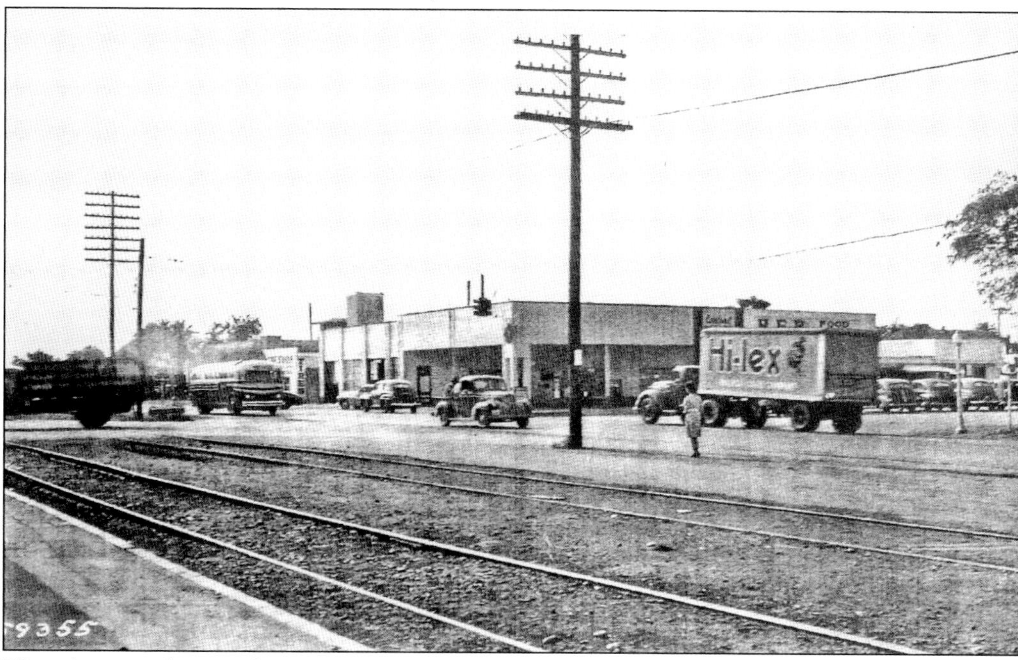

This photograph was taken just north of the railroad tracks on Business 83 and Cage Boulevard. Visible are several automobiles, a bus, and a small trailer making their way through town. By this time, traffic had picked up significantly in the downtown area as the population in Pharr had steadily increased every year. Barely visible is H-E-B grocery store, which has served the Rio Grande Valley since the 1950s. H-E-B has been relocated several times around town and is currently on Ridge Road and Cage Boulevard. (Courtesy of the Pharr Memorial Library Archives.)

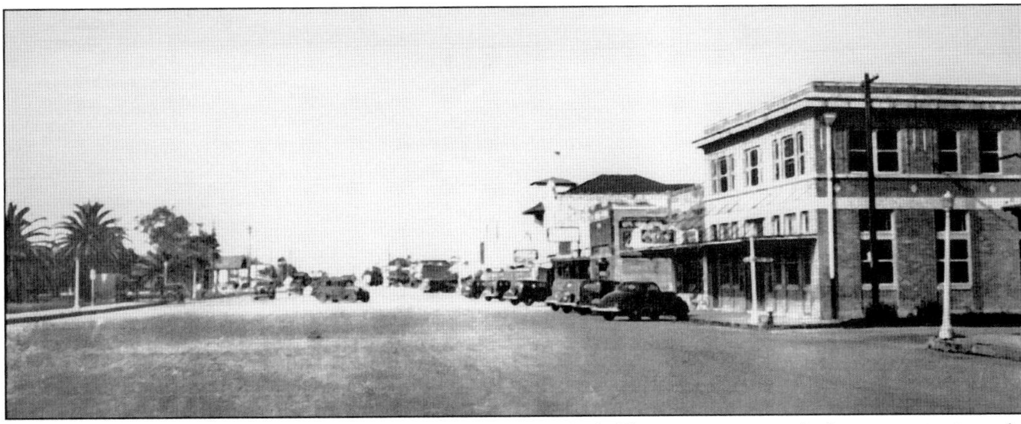

In just two decades since Pharr's incorporation in 1916, Pharr natives truly began enjoying the perks of a prosperous city. The wealth in the city remained mostly in the pockets of the white men and women who owned businesses or land. Riding around town on horseback was no longer the norm, as this picture shows. This 1930s photograph of Cage Boulevard shows how the city's streets had been paved, making traveling by car a lot better and a lot smoother. (Courtesy of the University of Texas–Pan American Library and Special Collections Department.)

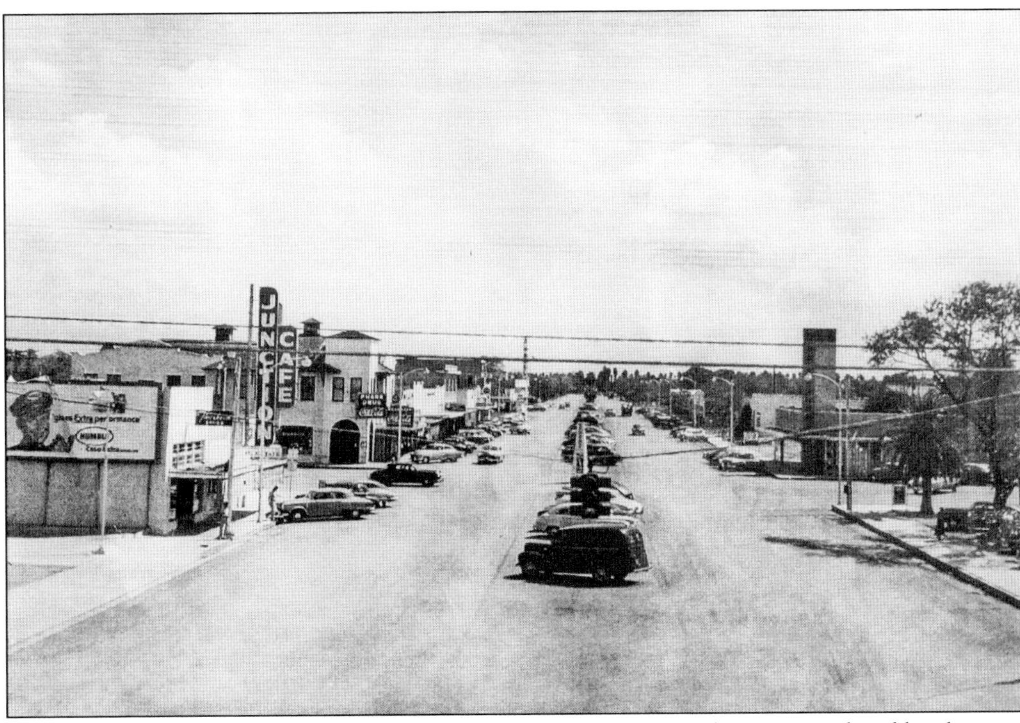

Cage Boulevard is the road that defines the city of Pharr. It is easily recognized and has been an economic hub throughout the city's history. This photograph of Cage Boulevard shows plenty of those businesses that were located there during the 1940s and 1950s. On the left is the Junction Café, which is still in operation today. In the distance is one of the most recognizable monuments in the city, the cowboy that stood above the Texan Hotel for a very long time. Pharr natives can look at this picture and say that the city has definitely changed but has also remained the same after all these years. (Courtesy of the Pharr Memorial Library Archives.)

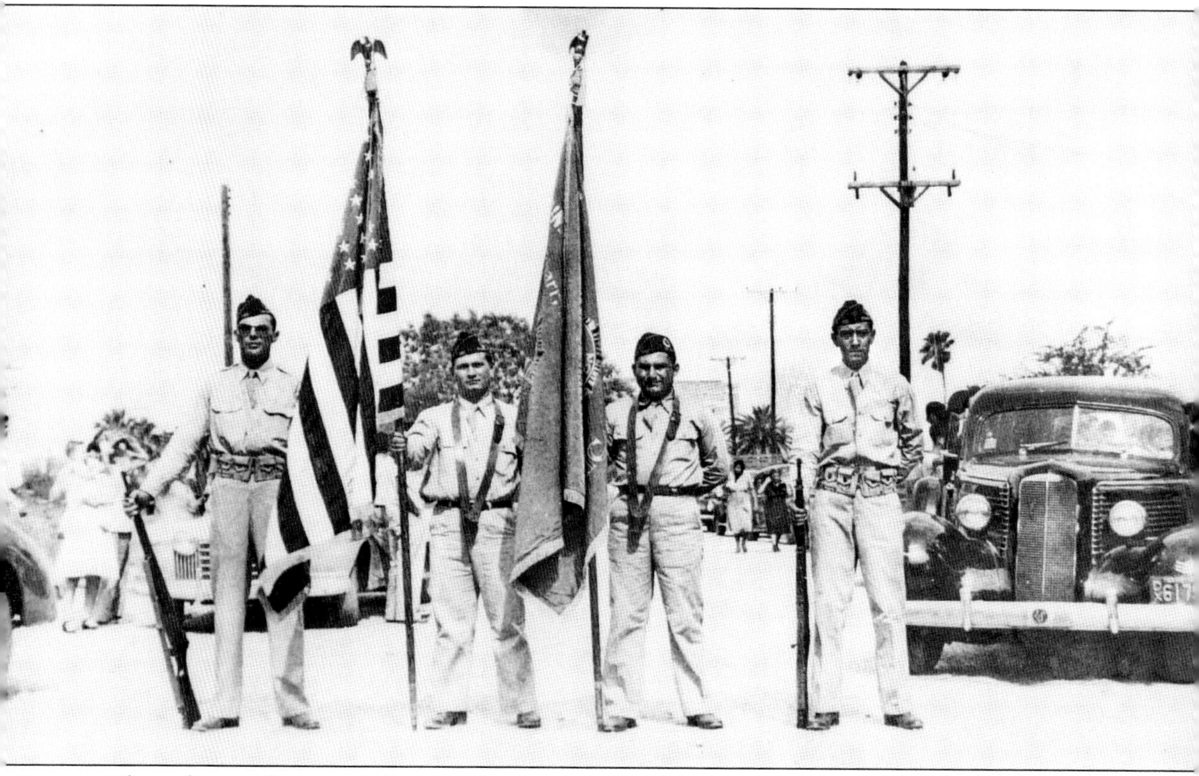

These four soldiers stand fast as someone takes a photograph of them. The flag holder on the right is local resident Tony Villegas, who was born in 1920 and is still alive today. The soldier standing on the far right is Celerino Castillo. His brother Juan Castillo was the first man from the city of Pharr to die in combat during World War II. Celerino himself served in the Philippine Islands as a point man and was wounded there. He survived and was able to come back home to play football for Pharr-San Juan High School due to him having one year of eligibility left to play. (Courtesy of Tony Villegas.)

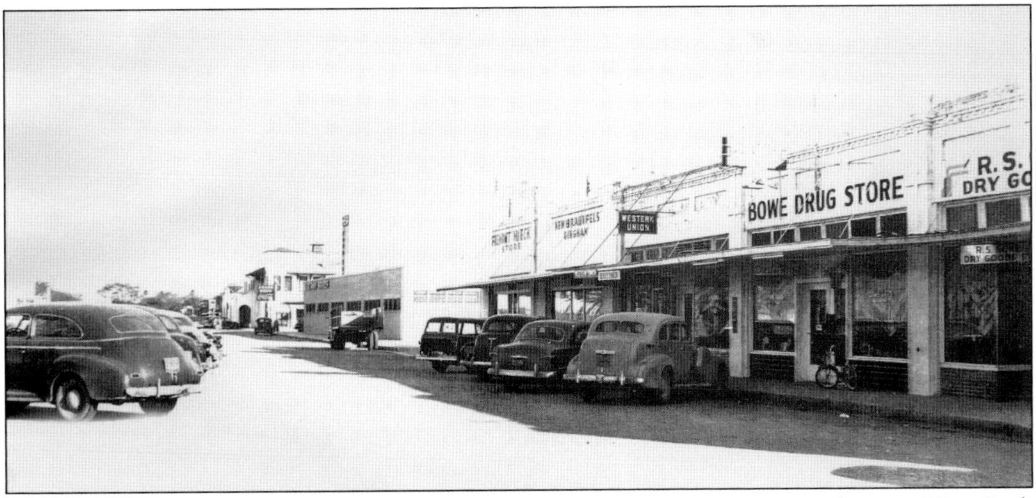

This 1950s street scene of downtown Pharr, with a view facing east, was taken on West Park Avenue. In the distance, Pharr Drug, the old city hall building, can be seen, as can H-E-B grocery store. On the right-hand side, Bowe Drugstore is visible. R.S. Bowe would later become mayor of the city of Pharr, and Bowe Drugstore later became Newcombe Pharmacy. Bowe was mayor until he was forced to resign in 1971. None of the businesses pictured here are around today except for H-E-B. (Courtesy of the University of Texas–Pan American Library and Special Collections Department.)

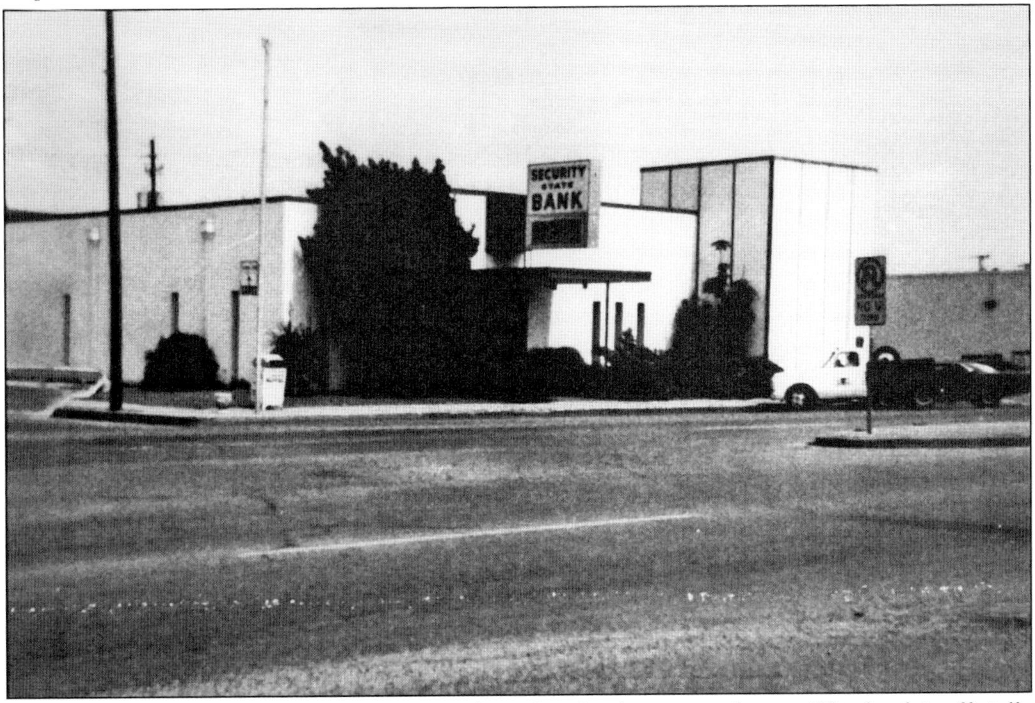

Security State Bank was located on Cage Boulevard in the downtown district. This bank is officially the only bank in the city of Pharr's entire history to be robbed at gunpoint. The robber entered through the back of the bank and tied up individuals who were handling the money. He made away with a large sum but was apprehended later that day. The bank no longer exists. (Courtesy of the University of Texas–Pan American Library and Special Collections Department.)

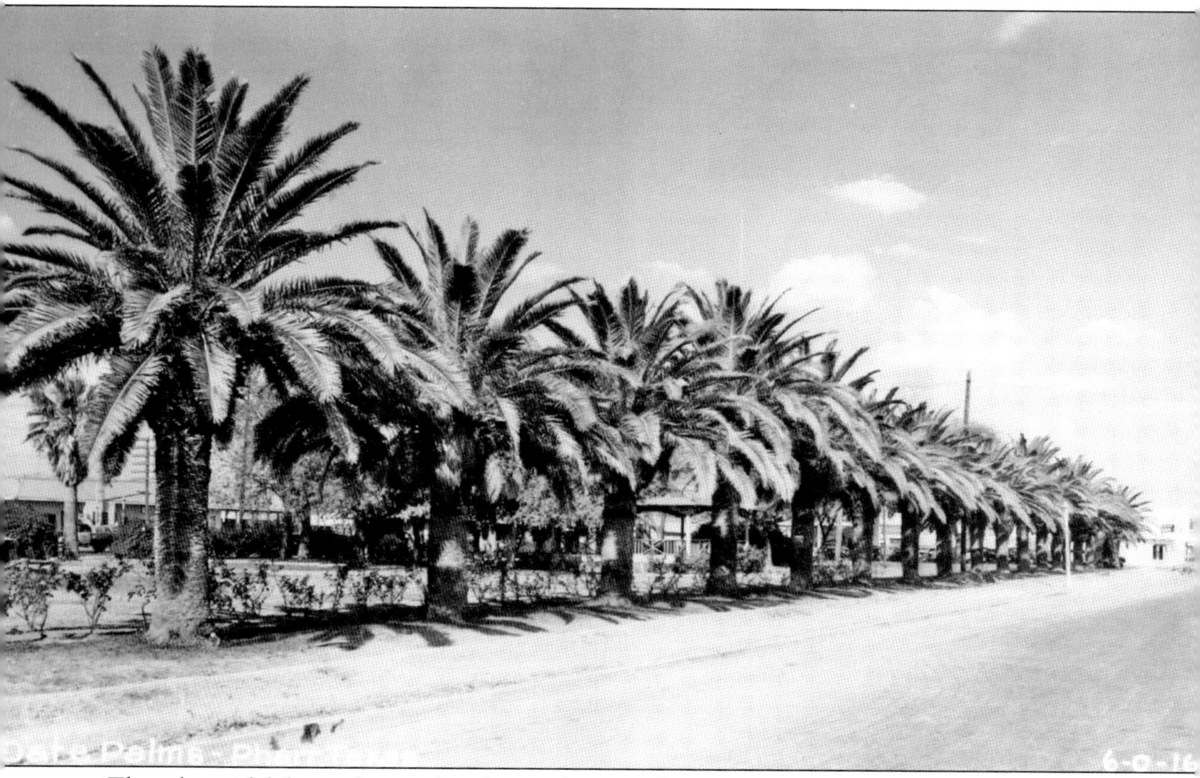

These beautiful date palms are lined up with meticulous precision along Park Avenue to give the city a tropical look. Local historians and botany experts believe palm trees were brought to the region in the early 1900s to make the valley appear more exotic and to attract more settlers to the land. The date palms were imported from Cuba, but most of them later died due to several freezes that swept across Pharr in the winter. (Courtesy of the Museum of South Texas History.)

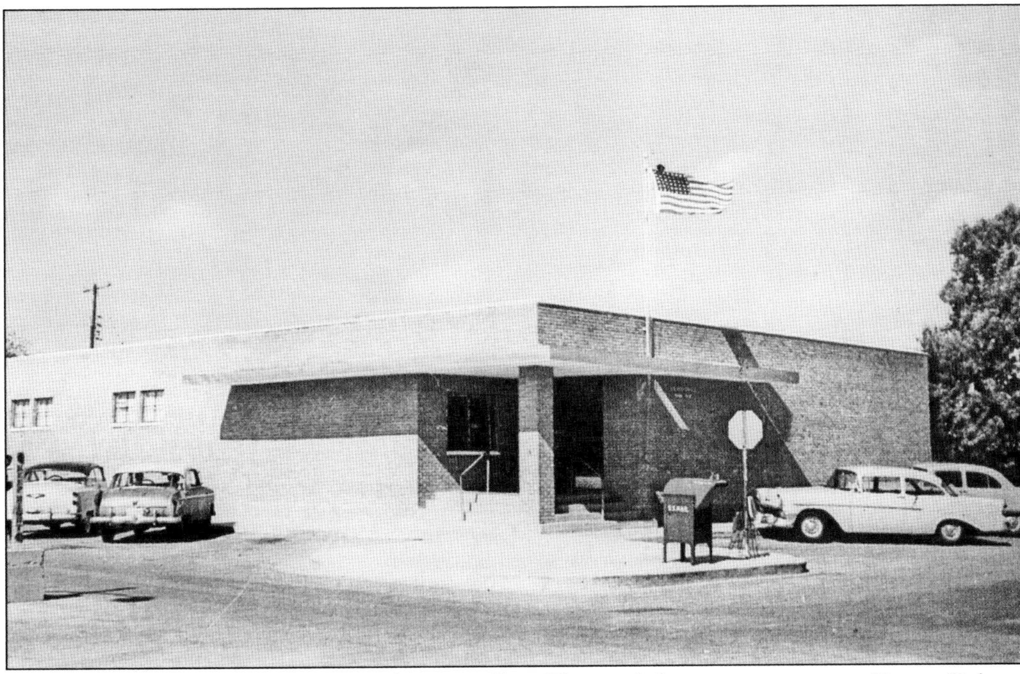

In 1911, the city of Pharr was granted a post office. The city's first postmaster was George Folsom. The Pharr Post Office has been relocated several times throughout its history. Pictured here in the 1960s is the post office located on the corner of West Park Avenue and South Bluebonnet Street. The post office has been located in this same area since 1957 and looks exactly the same today as it does in this picture. (Courtesy of the Pharr Memorial Library Archives.)

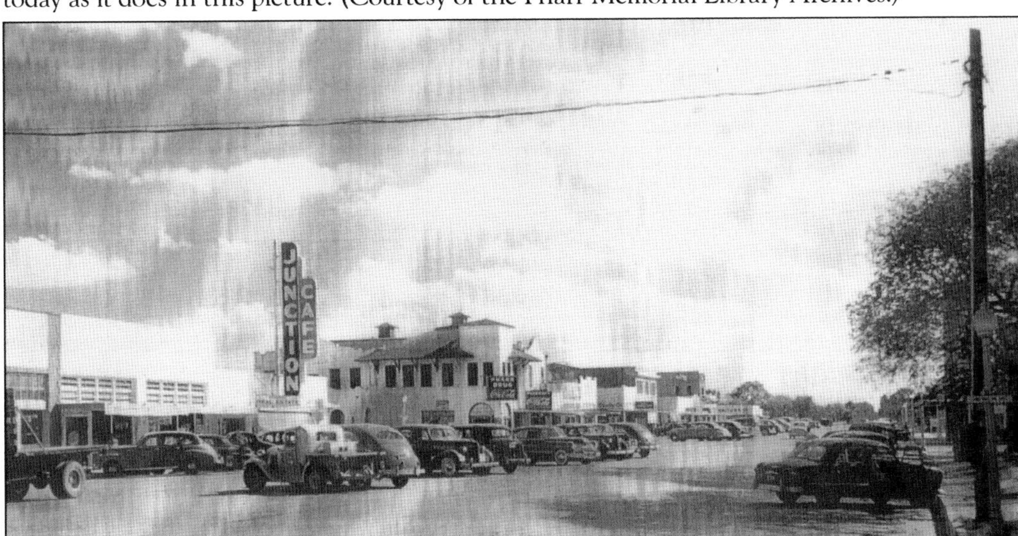

This picture of the downtown area of Pharr was taken from the corner of Cage Boulevard and Highway 83 sometime in the late 1940s or early 1950s. The photograph is rare because it shows plenty of cars parked in the middle of the street. When Pharr's population was not so large and traffic congestion was minimal, this was the norm. These days, however, it is no longer a possibility. Turning lanes have since replaced those parking spots. (Courtesy of the Pharr Memorial Library Archives.)

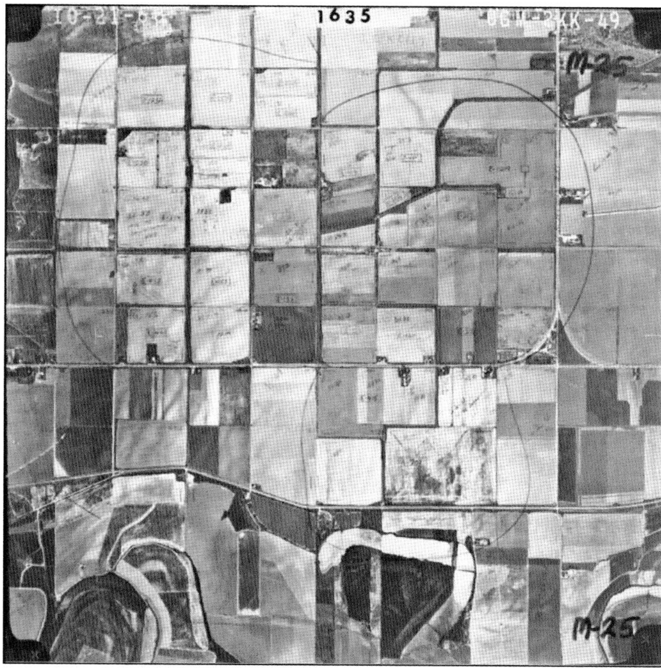

Old Military Road between Fort Brown in Brownsville, Texas, and Fort Ringgold in Rio Grande City, Texas, was originally built as a possible supply route for Zachary Taylor during the Mexican War. The road was only used, however, when the Rio Grande was low, making it impossible for steamboats to navigate. This 1968 aerial photograph of Pharr shows Military Highway (road running across about one inch from bottom of image), which is still used today. (Courtesy of the University of North Texas Libraries.)

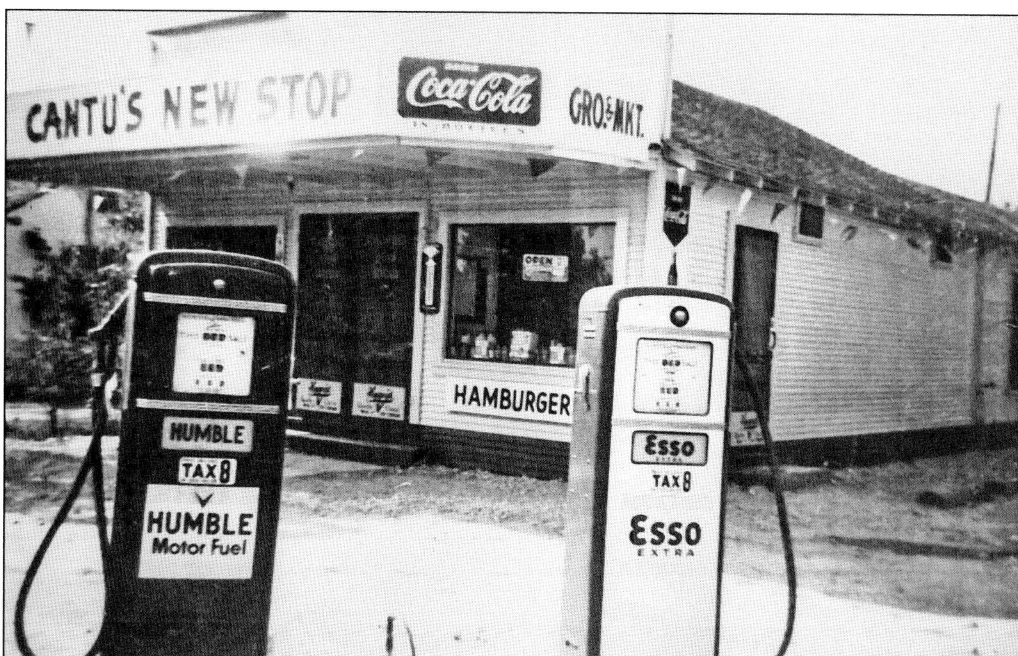

Cantu's New Stop store was located on the corner of State and Flag Streets. It was owned and operated by Carlos and Ercelia Cantu from when it was established in 1958 until recently, when they sold the business. The store still stands today and is operated by new owners. On January 6, 1999, local resident Manuel Salinas bought a $2 scratch-off lottery ticket, called Buck$ 'N Truck$, at Cantu's New Stop and won a 1998 Dodge Ram pickup. Throughout Texas, 50 trucks made especially for the Texas Lottery were given away. That was an exciting day for the store. (Courtesy of the University of Texas–Pan American Library and Special Collections Department.)

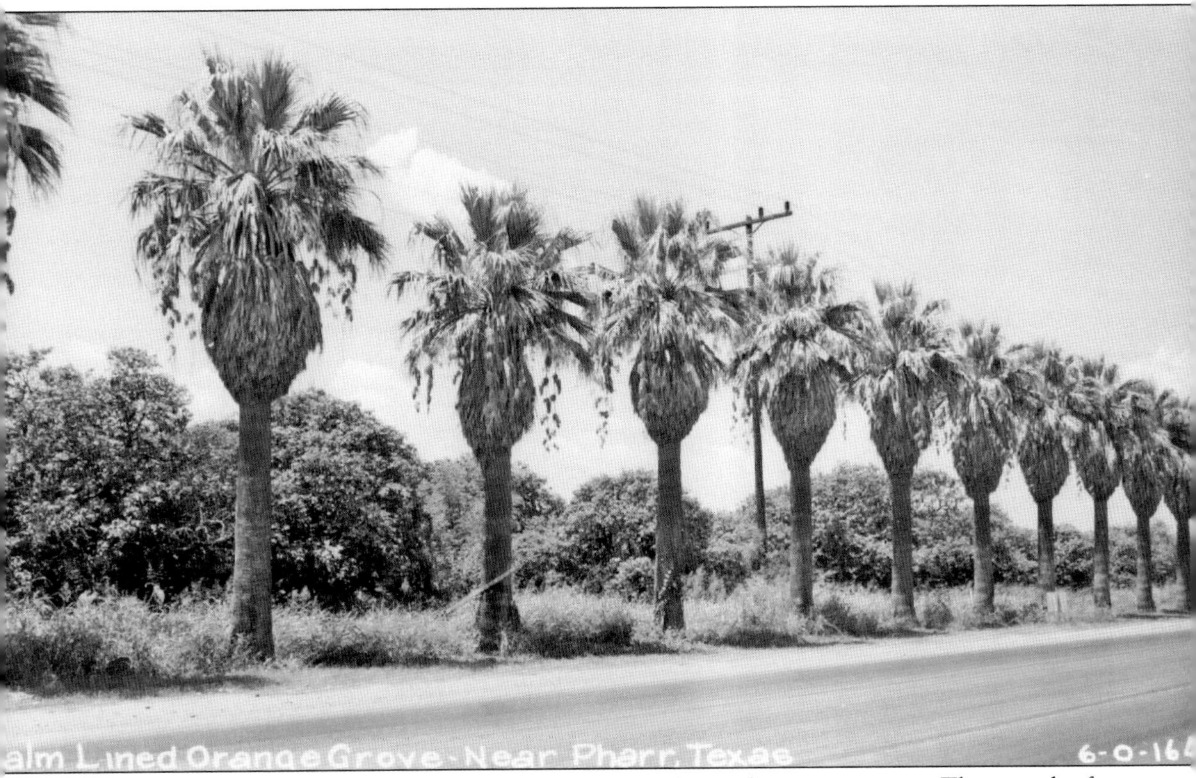

Pictured here are several palm trees perfectly lined up in front of an orange grove. The growth of citrus fruit in Pharr is said to have been started by Spaniards who, in the 18th century, planted seven orange trees on the Laguna Seca Ranch north of Edinburg. The Rio Grande Valley has the perfect climate for growing oranges. After peak harvests in 1947 and 1948, disastrous freezes in 1949 and 1951 killed seven million of the nine million trees that produced oranges and grapefruit. Several freezes continued to seriously effect citrus production, but it has never fully rendered it obsolete. (Courtesy of the Museum of South Texas History.)

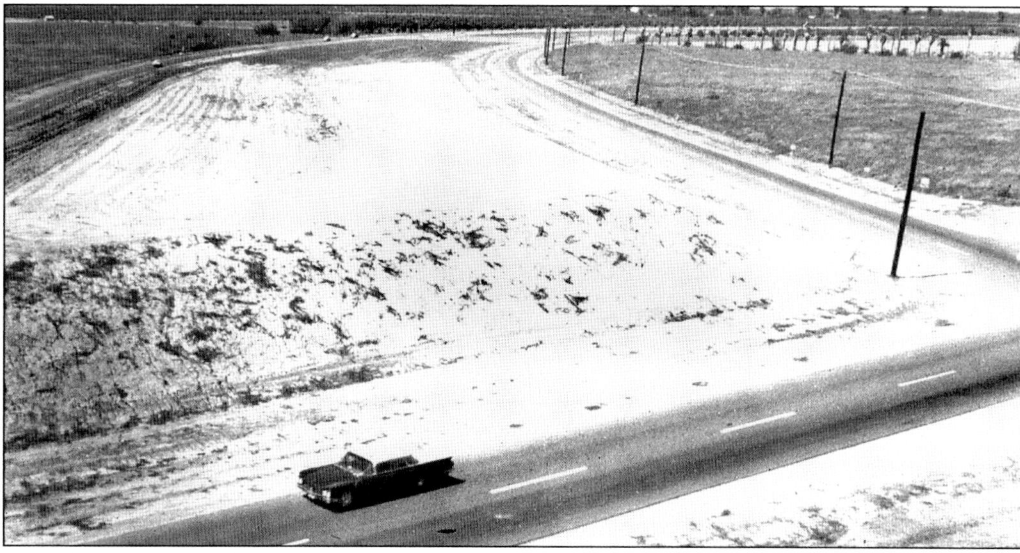

In 1963, construction began on an expressway overpass located on Jackson Road and Business 83. The Texas Highway Department (now the Texas Department of Transportation) hired a contractor to complete the work. Today, the finished overpass can still be seen and is surrounded by a plethora of businesses that include convenient stores, restaurants, and car dealerships. (Courtesy of the University of Texas–Pan American Library and Special Collections Department.)

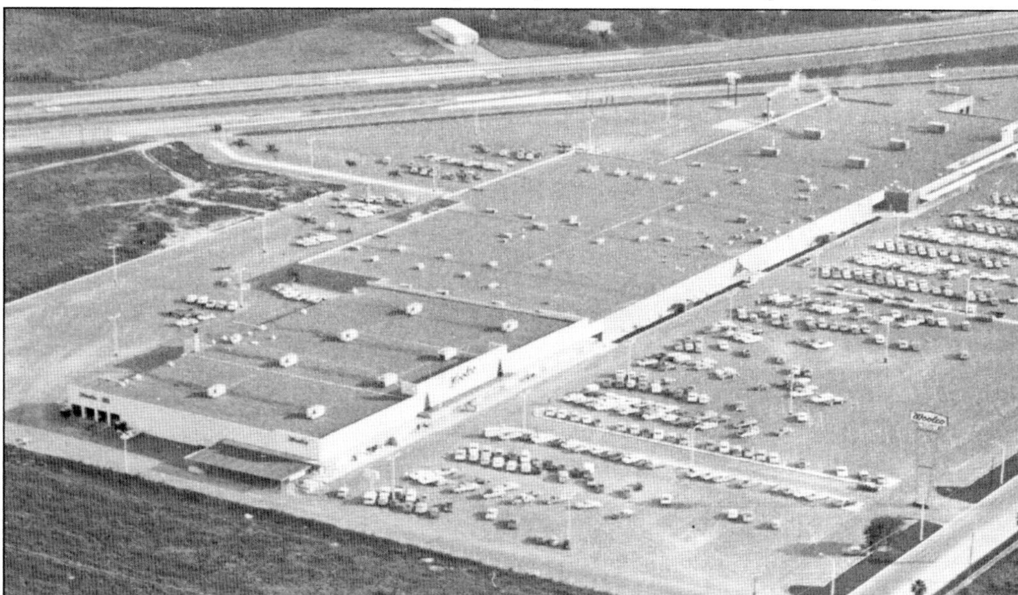

This 1970s aerial view shows El Centro Mall, which is located on Jackson Road. Over the years, El Centro Mall was home to a number of different stores like Woolco (in foreground). Woolco Woolco was a full-line discount department store that called Pharr home for several years until the chain went out of business nationwide in 1982. El Centro Mall is still located in the same location but has lost a lot of business to the much bigger La Plaza Mall, located in the neighboring city of McAllen. In 2013, the city announced that El Centro Mall will be demolished to make room for other businesses, including a Cinemark movie theater, which was open for business in early 2014. (Courtesy of the Museum of South Texas History.)

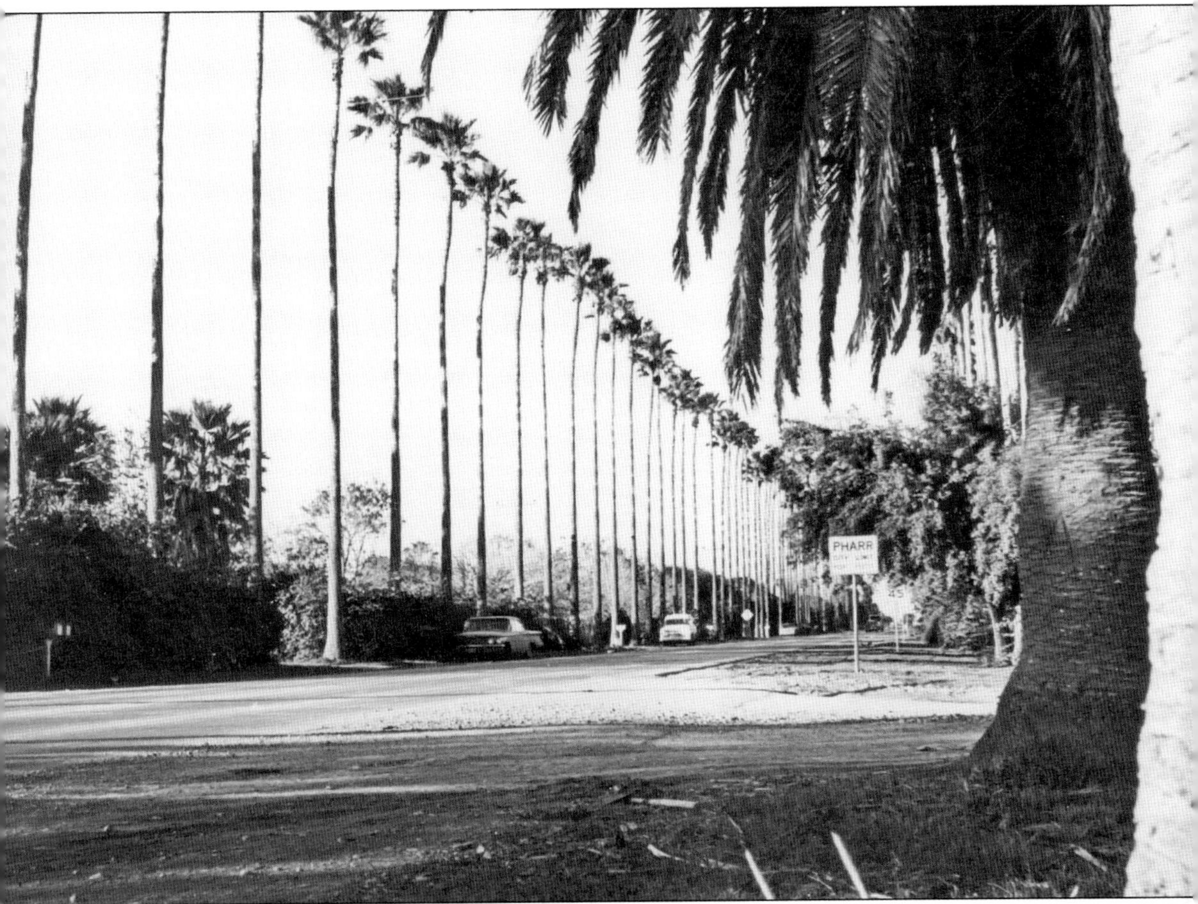

South Cage Boulevard was lined with beautiful palm trees and was quite a sight to see for Pharr community members. However, as beautiful as this area was, many people were known to have died along this stretch of road. Most of these deaths were caused by irresponsible driving and illegal racing that led to many car crashes and fatalities. Many of the palm trees have since been removed or died due to several winter freezes. (Courtesy of the Museum of South Texas History.)

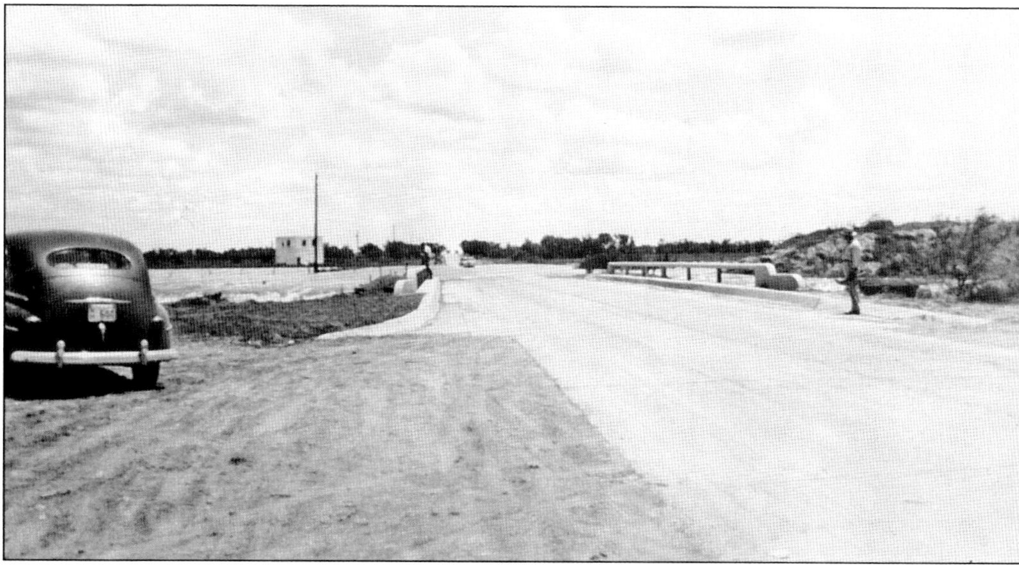

Pictured here in the 1950s or 1960s is a newly constructed bridge located on South US Route 281 (Interstate 69 today). The Texas Highway Department hired a contractor to complete the bridge as it supervised the construction. The contractor is unidentified. The bridge still stands today but is now a four-lane span that leads all the way to the Pharr-Reynosa International Bridge. (Courtesy of the University of Texas–Pan American Library and Special Collections Department.)

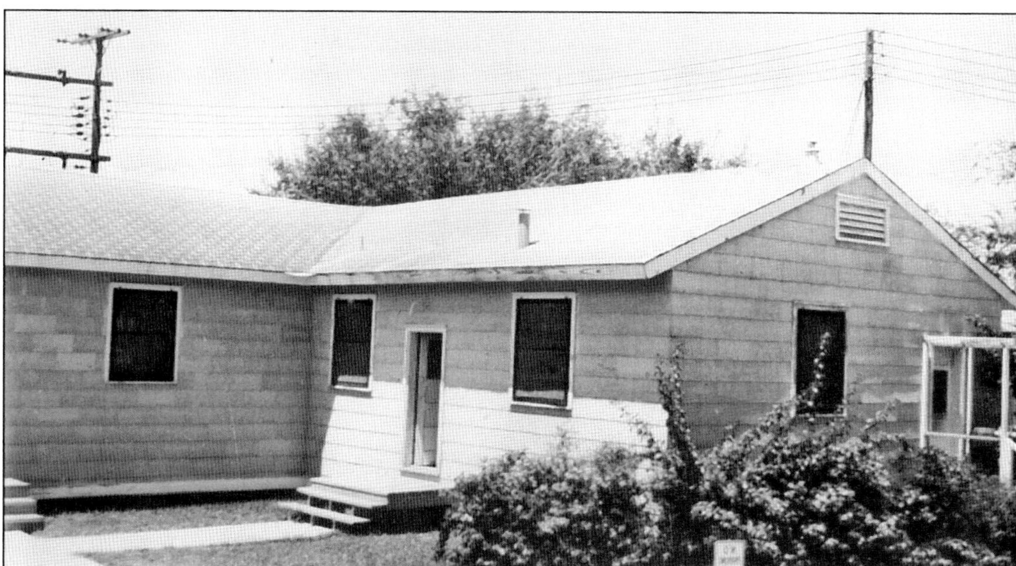

This small house was actually the engineering office and first district headquarters for the Texas Highway Department, now known as the Texas Department of Transportation. This photograph was taken in 1952. The headquarters was sold 17 years later, in 1969. Pharr District 21 is the main district for the Rio Grande Valley, and its office is now located at 600 West Expressway 83. (Courtesy of the University of Texas–Pan American Library and Special Collections Department.)

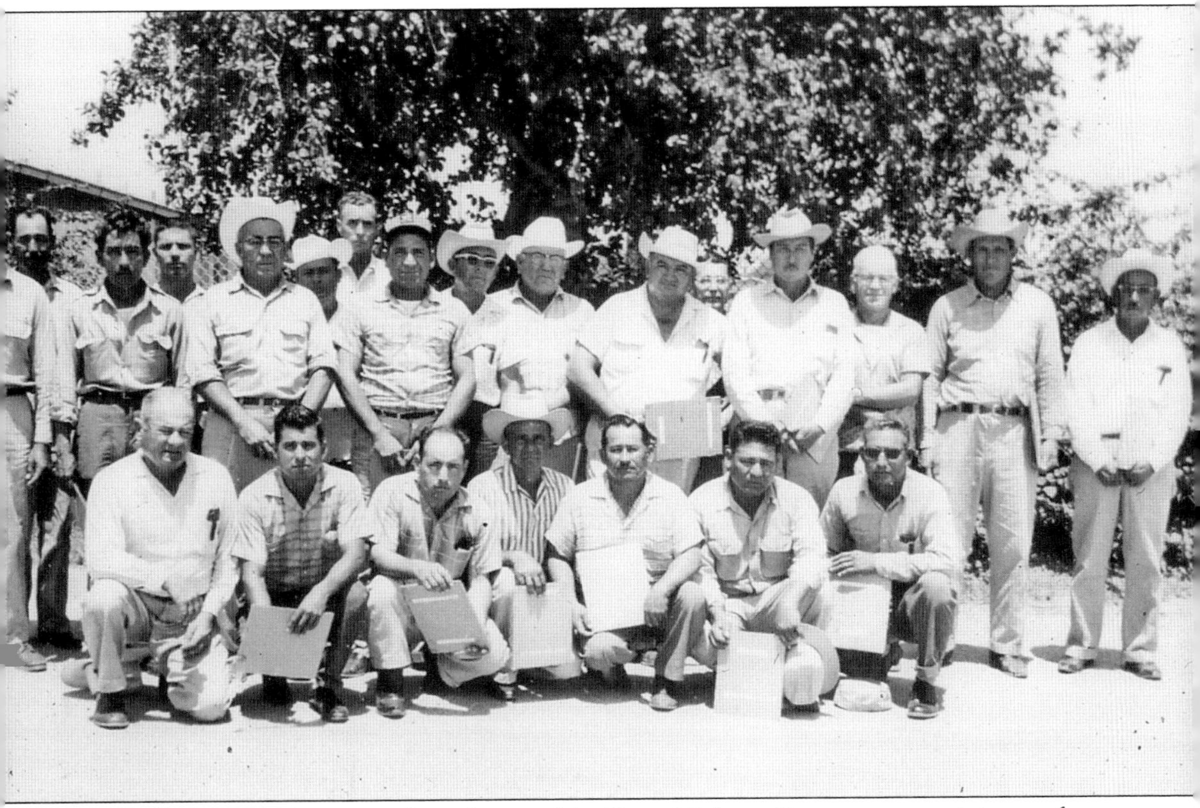

Pictured here in 1964 are several employees of the Texas Highway Department receiving a safety award. The Pharr District plans, designs, builds, operates, and maintains the state transportation system in Hidalgo, Brooks, Cameron, Jim Hogg, Kenedy, Starr, Willacy, and Zapata Counties. The district has been instrumental in the growth of the city. For the fiscal year 2012, the Texas Department of Transportation's combined construction-maintenance expenditures totaled a whopping $228,872,655.65. As of 2012, the Texas Department of Transportation Pharr District employed 125 construction employees and 156 maintenance employees. (Courtesy of the University of Texas–Pan American Library and Special Collections Department.)

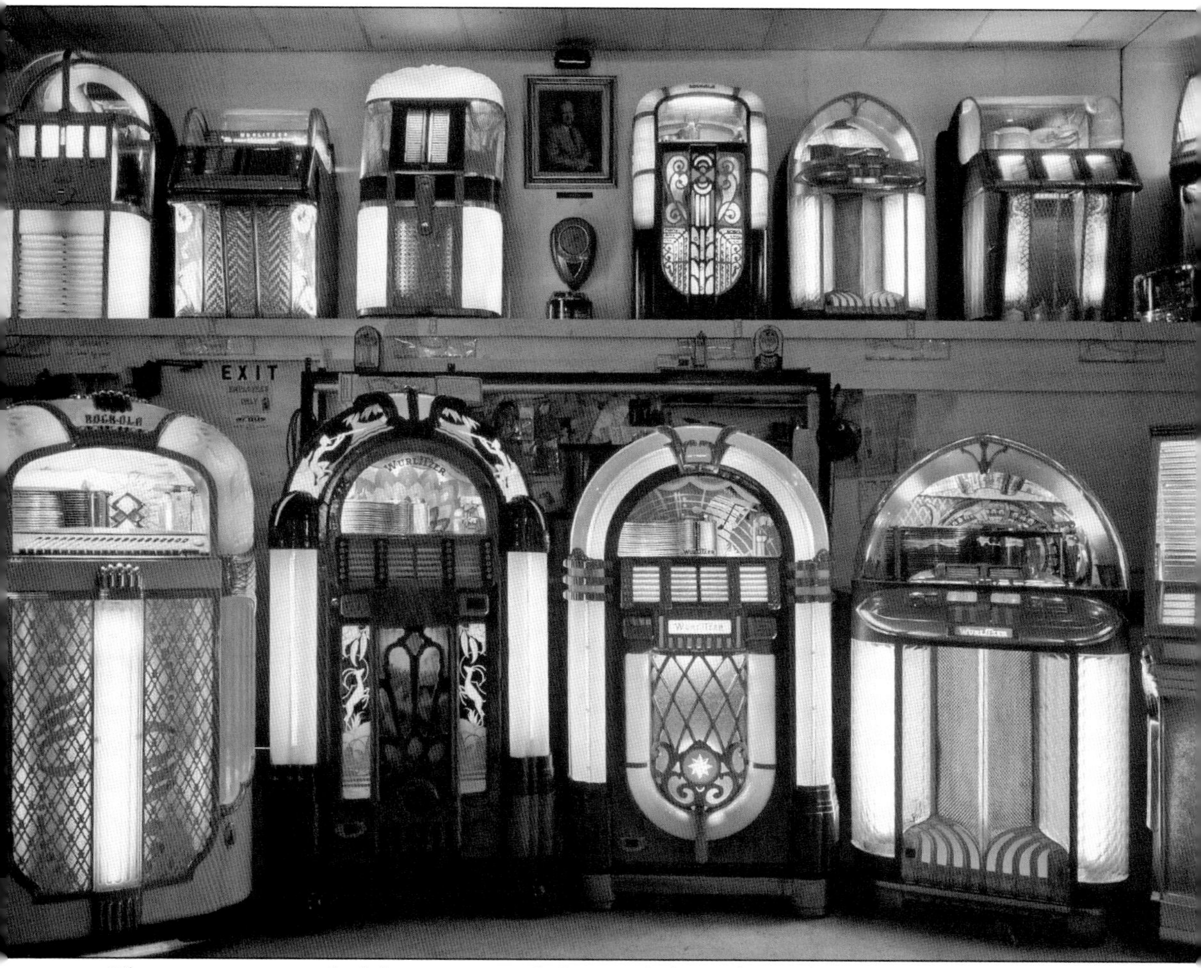

These are just several of the vintage and classic jukeboxes housed at Smitty's Jukebox Museum. The museum is located on West State Avenue and is currently operated by Leo "Smitty" Schmitt's son Leo "Junior" Schmitt. The museum houses a very impressive collection of Wurlitzers, Seeburgs, and Rock-Olas. Since there has been a major shift in the way music is heard and played, Smitty's is a great place to take a trip down memory lane. (Courtesy of the Library of Congress.)

This classic 1946 Wurlitzer 1015 jukebox can be seen at Smitty's Jukebox Museum. The Wurlitzer was an iconic jukebox during the big-band era. Wurlitzers became so popular that many people would refer to jukeboxes as Wurlitzers, when in fact there were many other companies that made jukeboxes. Many of these Wurlitzer jukeboxes are seen in Hollywood movies because of their unique and colorful light-up designs. (Courtesy of the Library of Congress.)

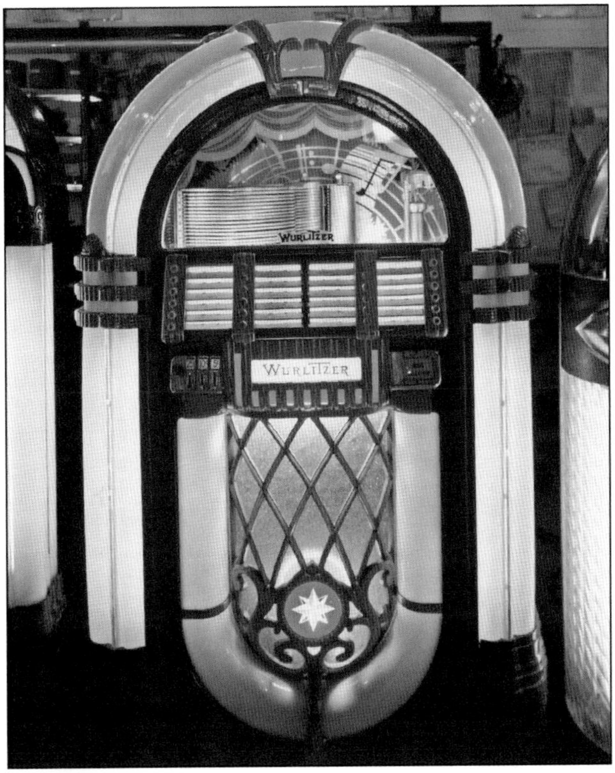

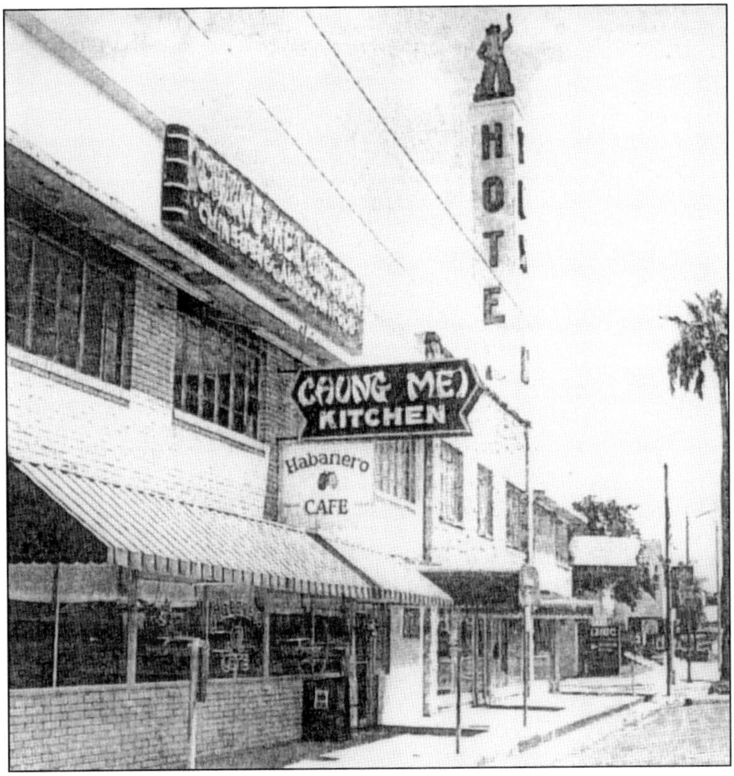

The Chung Mei Kitchen was owned and operated by Du Ong Lee, who was born in Canton, China, but moved to Brownville, Texas, at the age of 15. He ran the first Chung Mei Kitchen in Harlingen, Texas, until he moved in 1955 to Pharr, where he opened the second location. It was the first Chinese restaurant in the entire Rio Grande Valley and was in operation for 32 years from 1955 to 1987. On April 23, 2010, at the age of 94, Du Ong Lee passed away in McAllen, Texas. (Courtesy of the Pharr Memorial Library Archives.)

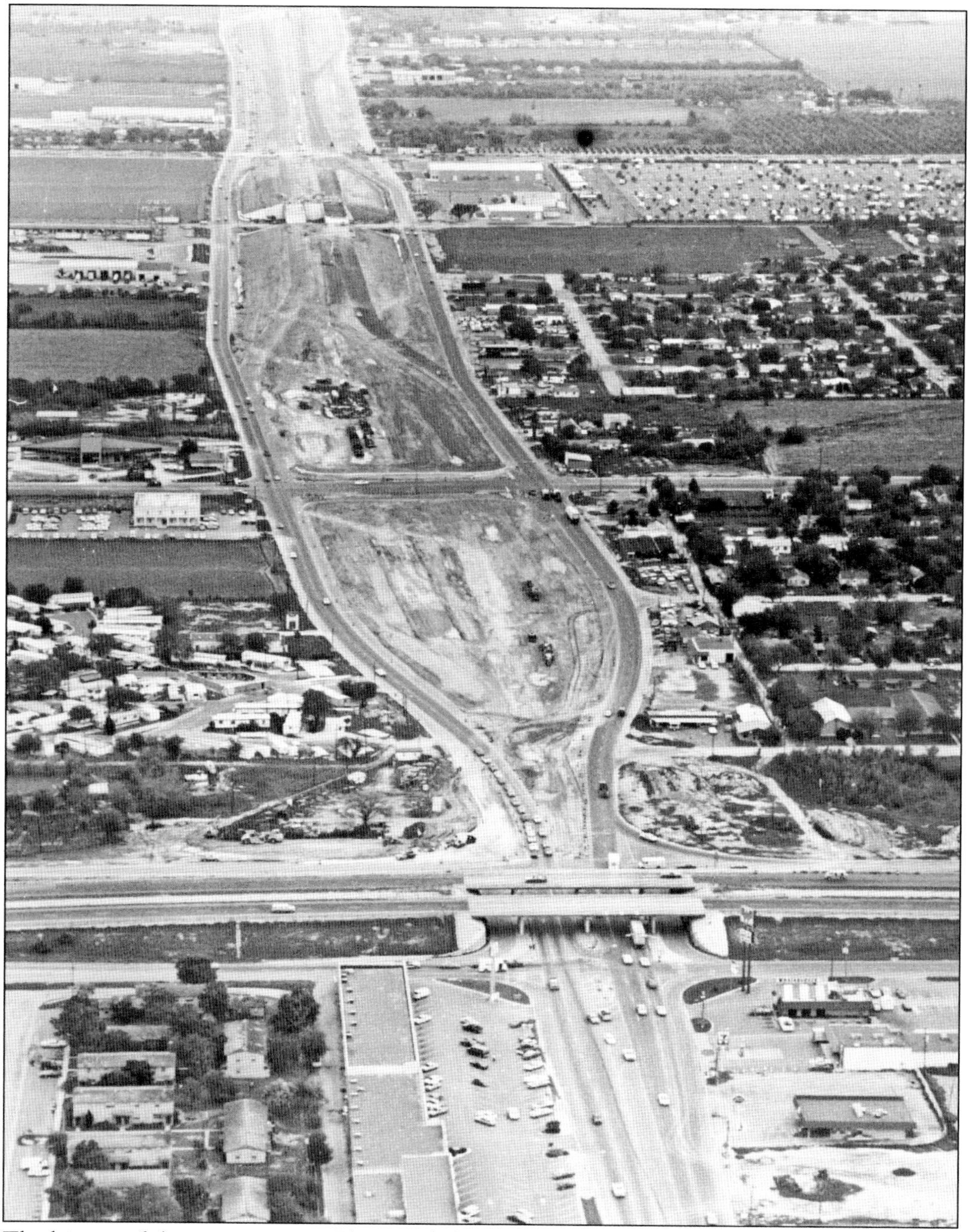

The history of the expressway in Pharr and the entire Rio Grande Valley was made possible by the Texas Highway Department's former district engineer Jimmy Snyder. Because of his efforts, the Rio Grande Valley went from having unimproved and unpaved roads to miles and miles of state-maintained highways. This early-1980s aerial view depicts Expressway 281 under construction. Snyder had died before this picture was taken, but it was his vision that made this expressway possible. Texas is known as the birthplace of fast-food chain Whataburger, one of which can be seen in the bottom right-hand corner of this photograph. (Courtesy of the Museum of South Texas History.)

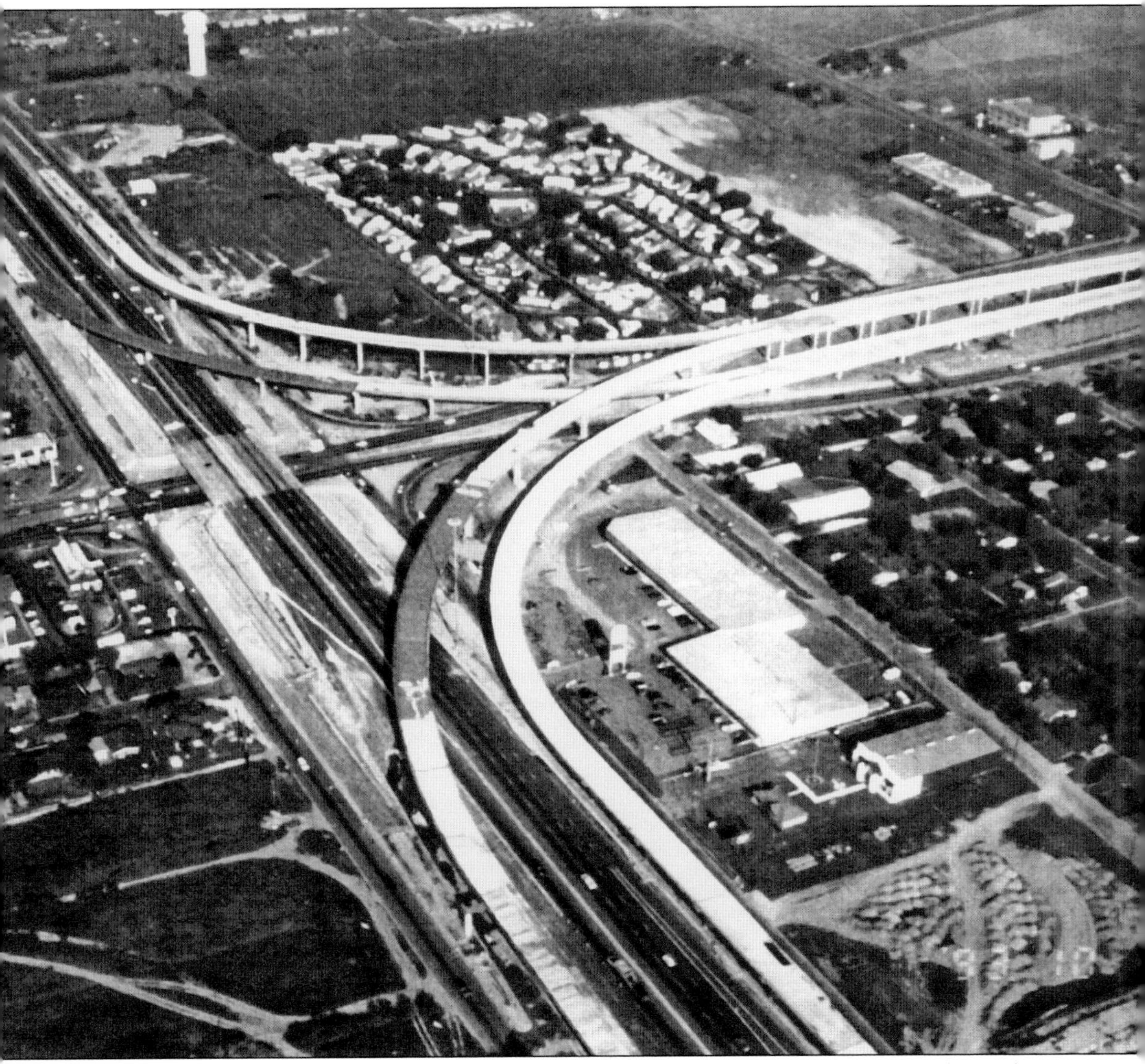

This 1993 aerial photograph captures the US Route 281 and US 83 interchange that is located in Pharr. At the time, this interchange seemed like a great idea, but nobody could have predicted the tremendous growth in Pharr, which has led to major traffic jams at this junction. Former Texas Department of Transportation District engineer Mario Jorge was the man in charge of designing this interchange. Eight different scenarios have been proposed to improve rush-hour traffic flow here. (Courtesy of the Museum of South Texas History.)

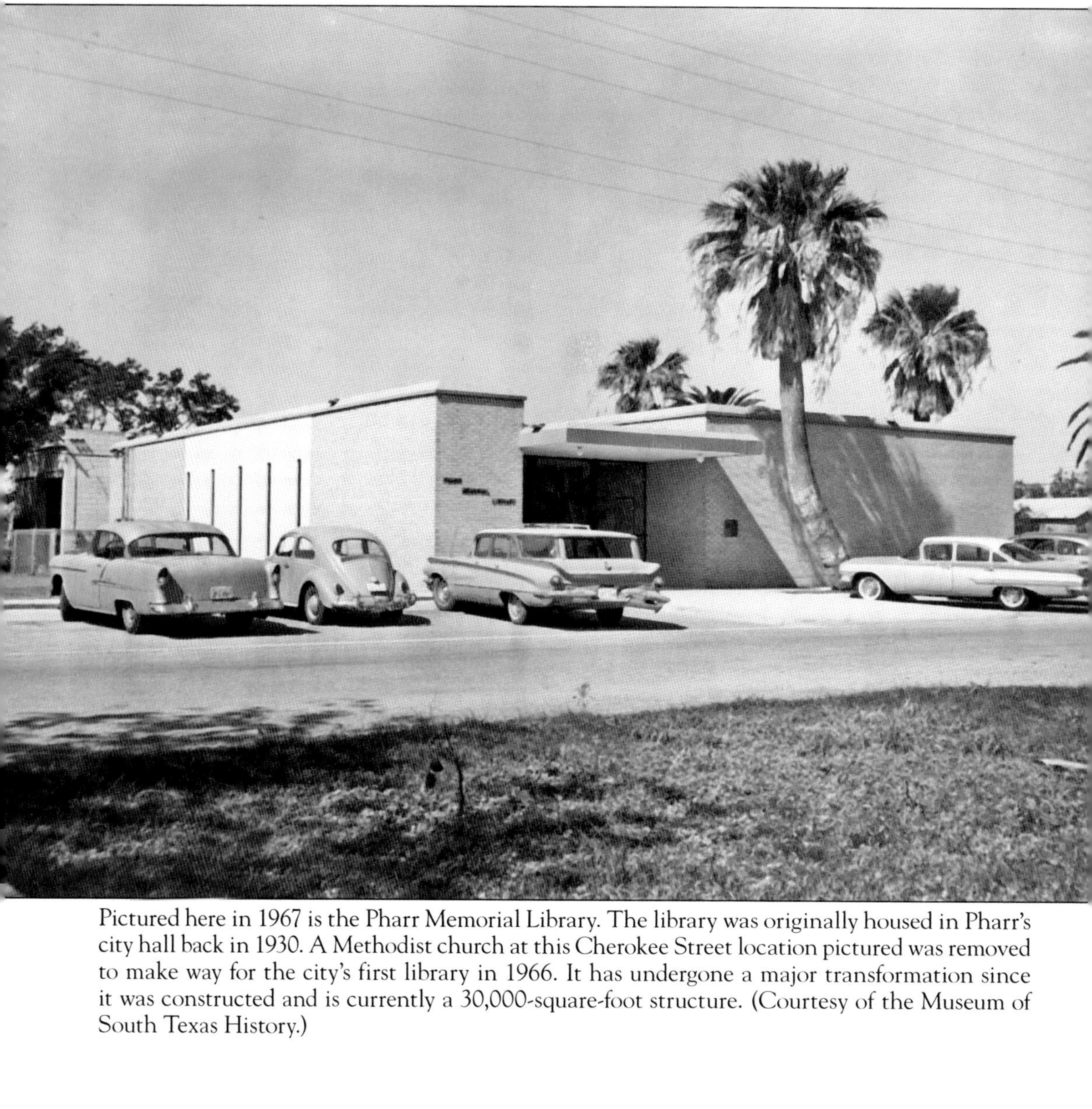

Pictured here in 1967 is the Pharr Memorial Library. The library was originally housed in Pharr's city hall back in 1930. A Methodist church at this Cherokee Street location pictured was removed to make way for the city's first library in 1966. It has undergone a major transformation since it was constructed and is currently a 30,000-square-foot structure. (Courtesy of the Museum of South Texas History.)

Five

THE LAW

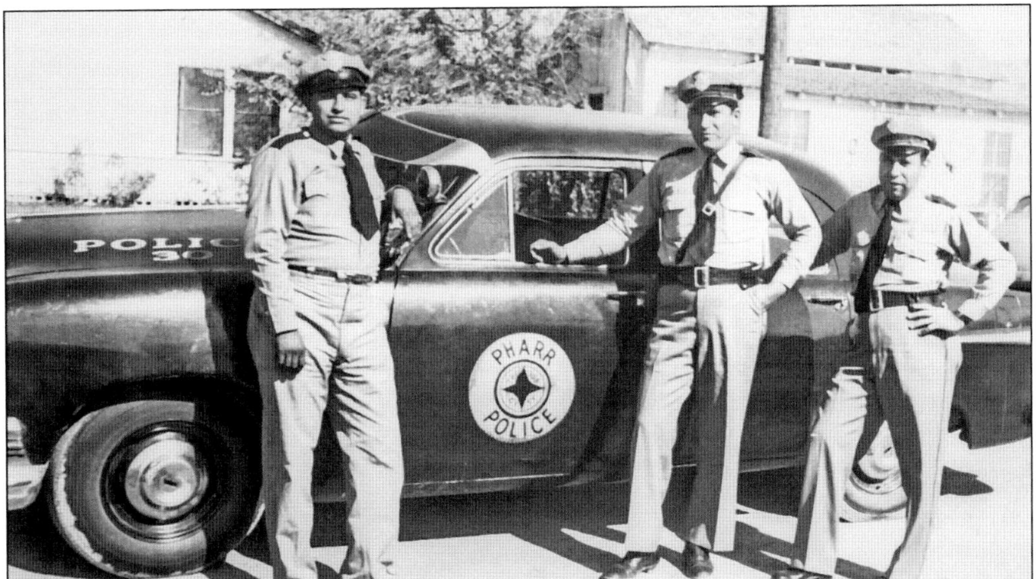

Pictured here are three Pharr police officers on duty. The man in the middle is Alfredo Ramirez. The other men are unidentified. Ramirez would later become chief of police and hold that position during one of the city's most trying times—the Pharr police riots. On February 6, 1971, local Mexican Americans began protesting over what they believed was police targeting and racial profiling by Pharr police officers. Alfonso Loredo Flores, a 20-year-old, was killed that day. (Courtesy of the Pharr Memorial Library Archives.)

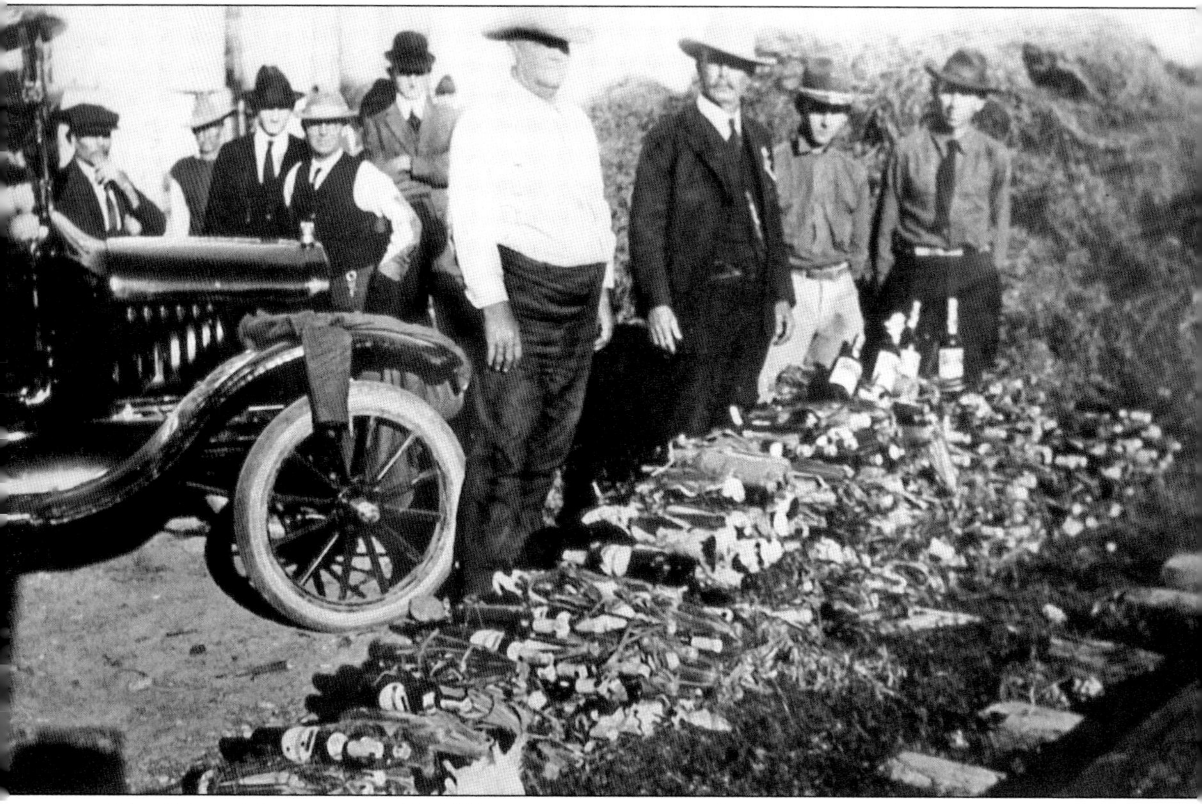

The Volstead Act was passed in 1919 to prevent the sale and consumption of intoxicating beverages, but this did not stop bootleggers from selling and making liquor. Prohibition lasted from 1920 until 1933, when ratification of the Twenty-first Amendment repealed it. Among those pictured here in 1921 are lawmen, from left to right, Marcus Hines, W.L. Wright, and L.C. McDuff, who confiscated a large amount of mescal (Mexican liquor) that was being bootlegged from Mexico to Pharr. (Courtesy of the University of Texas–Pan American Library and Special Collections Department.)

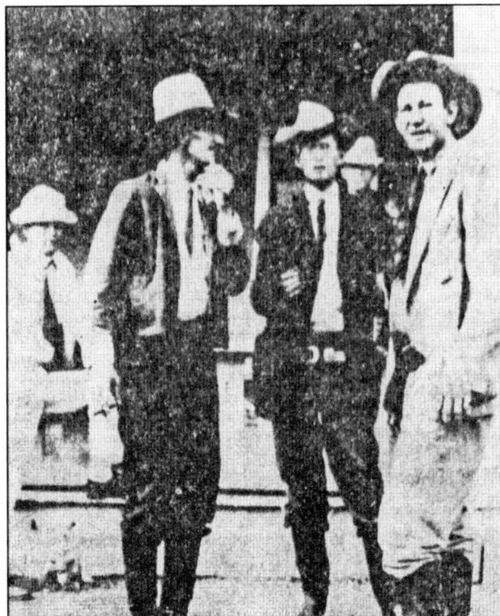

RANGERS IN PHARR IN 1916—At the peak of the bandit trouble, there were many Rangers in Pharr and other Valley towns. On the far left is L. J. Polk a young and coming attorney of that day. Others are Tom Mayfield, Special Ranger and Deputy Sheriff; Bill Sterling, Texas Ranger, later Captain of the force: and O. D. Cardwell, Ranger. (Picture furnished by Tom Mayfield)

During the Bandit War, many Rangers were stationed in Pharr to help defend against possible bandit raids. These Rangers are, from left to right, O.D. Cardwell, Bill Sterling, and Tom Mayfield. There is a story told that Mayfield once killed a Mexican American man near La Reynera Bakery because that man beat up Mayfield's brother-in-law. Witnesses to Rangers showing up to confront this man said they were told to leave and not come back. The following morning is when people found the man dead, but nobody said a word for fear they might end up dead too. (Courtesy of the Pharr Memorial Library Archives.)

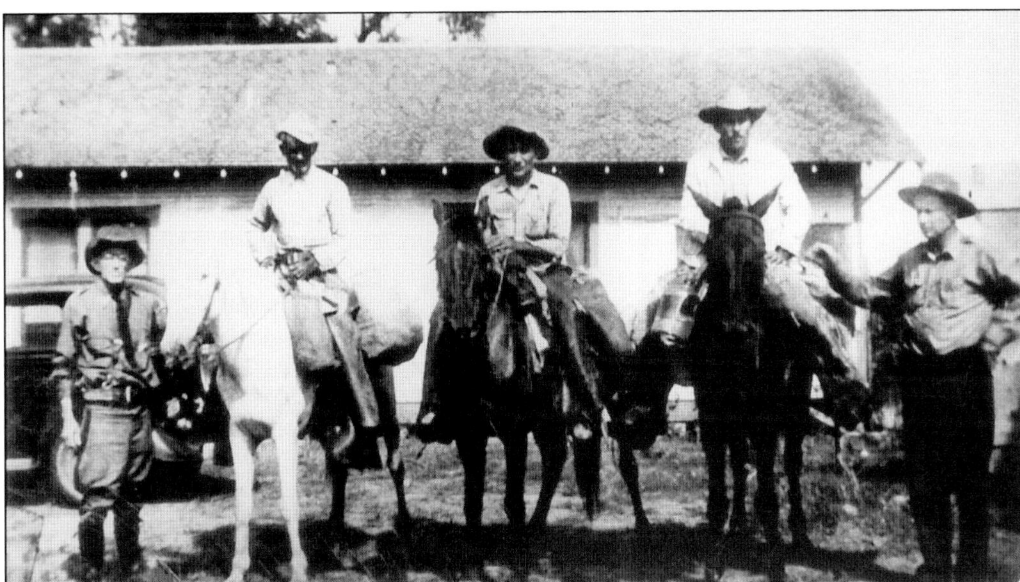

Pictured here in 1925 are captured bootleggers who were attempting to run liquor through Alcorn Ranch, which was situated just south of Pharr. Moonshining was often a popular family practice. Distinctive recipes and techniques were passed down from generation to generation. Transporting liquor from one place to another was easy when families and family friends worked together to relocate it. (Courtesy of the University of Texas–Pan American Library and Special Collections Department.)

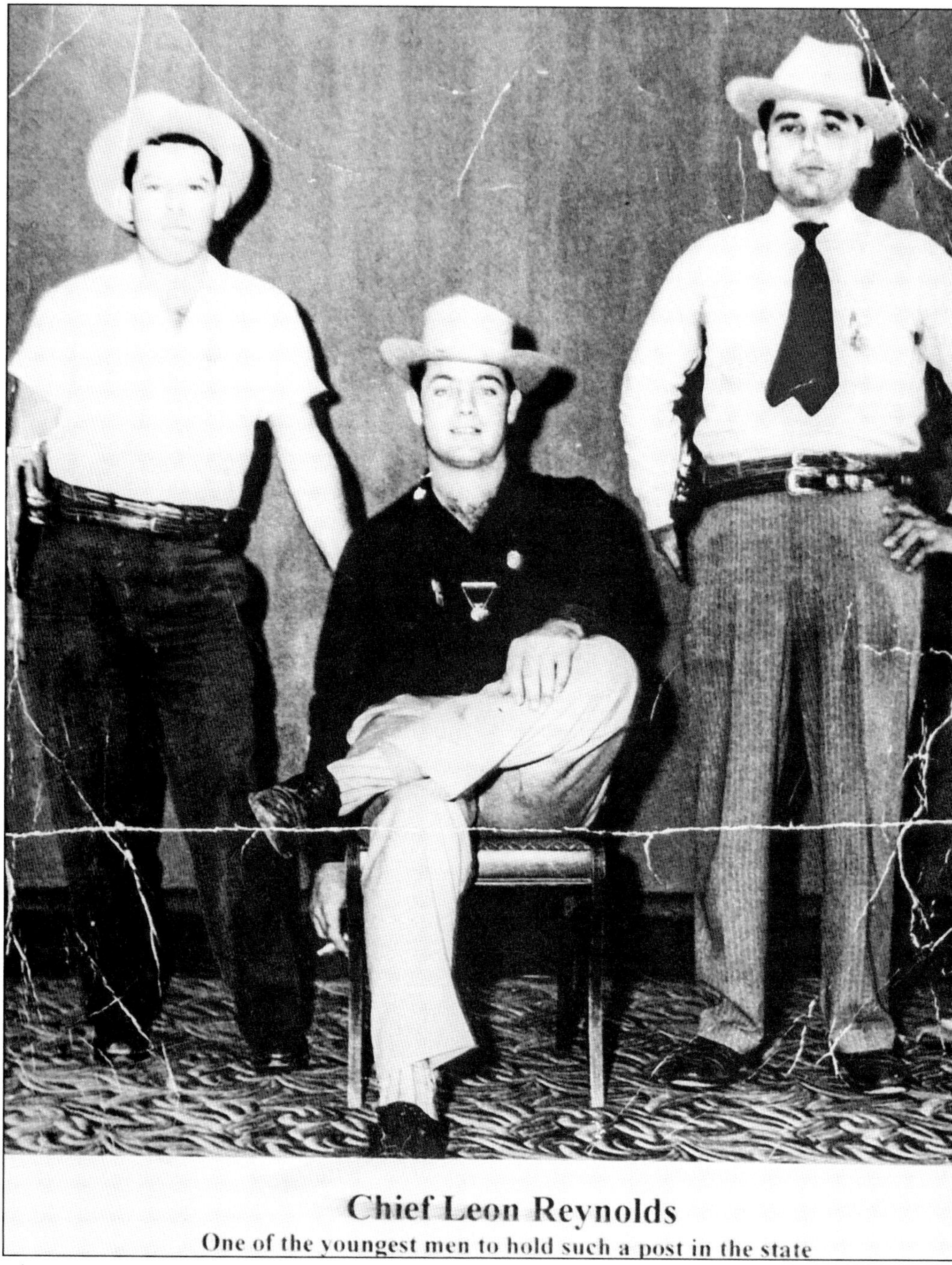

Chief Leon Reynolds

One of the youngest men to hold such a post in the state

The man sitting in the middle, casually holding a cigarette in his right hand, is Leon Reynolds. He was the chief of police of the Pharr Police Department. At the time of his posting as chief, Reynolds was one of the youngest men to hold that position in the state of Texas. He was a young man, but he definitely was not a short man. He was very tall and towered over many of his deputies and many of the residents in town. Standing beside him are unidentified deputies. (Courtesy of the Pharr Memorial Library Archives.)

Pictured here is Lazaro Garza. He was a police officer for the Pharr Police Department for quite some time. His work as a police officer began in the late 1940s or early 1950s. He is the uncle of another well-known former police officer, Alberto Gonzalez. (Courtesy of the Pharr Memorial Library Archives.)

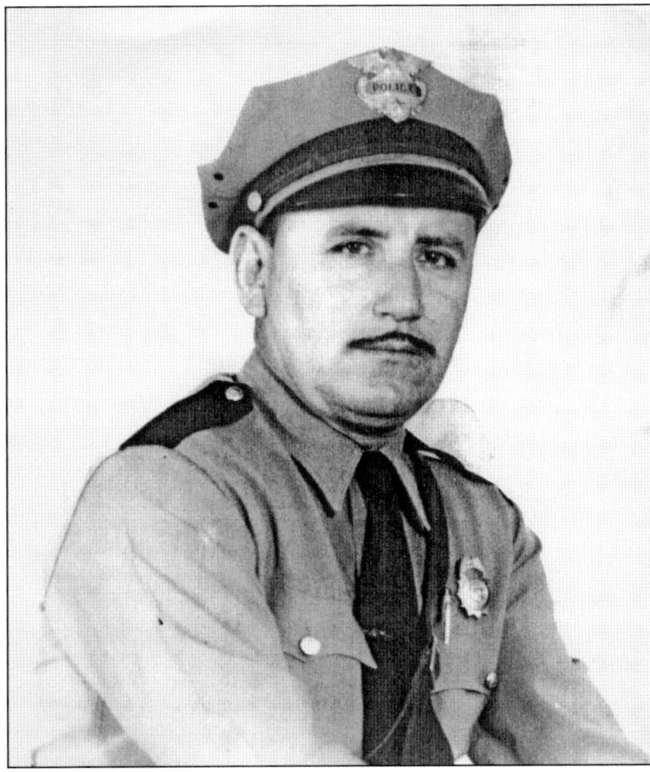

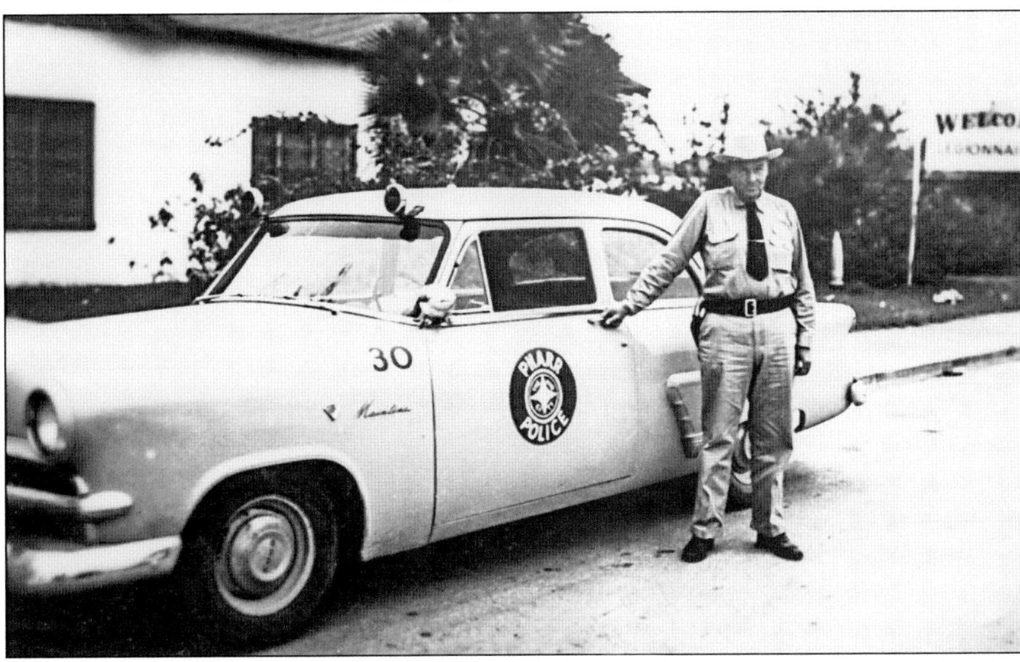

This police officer standing by his squad car is Chief Payton. The exact years he served as chief are unknown, but it was more than likely in the 1950s. By the time this photograph was taken, the Pharr Police Department was fortunate enough to patrol the city by car as opposed to on foot. (Courtesy of the Pharr Memorial Library Archives.)

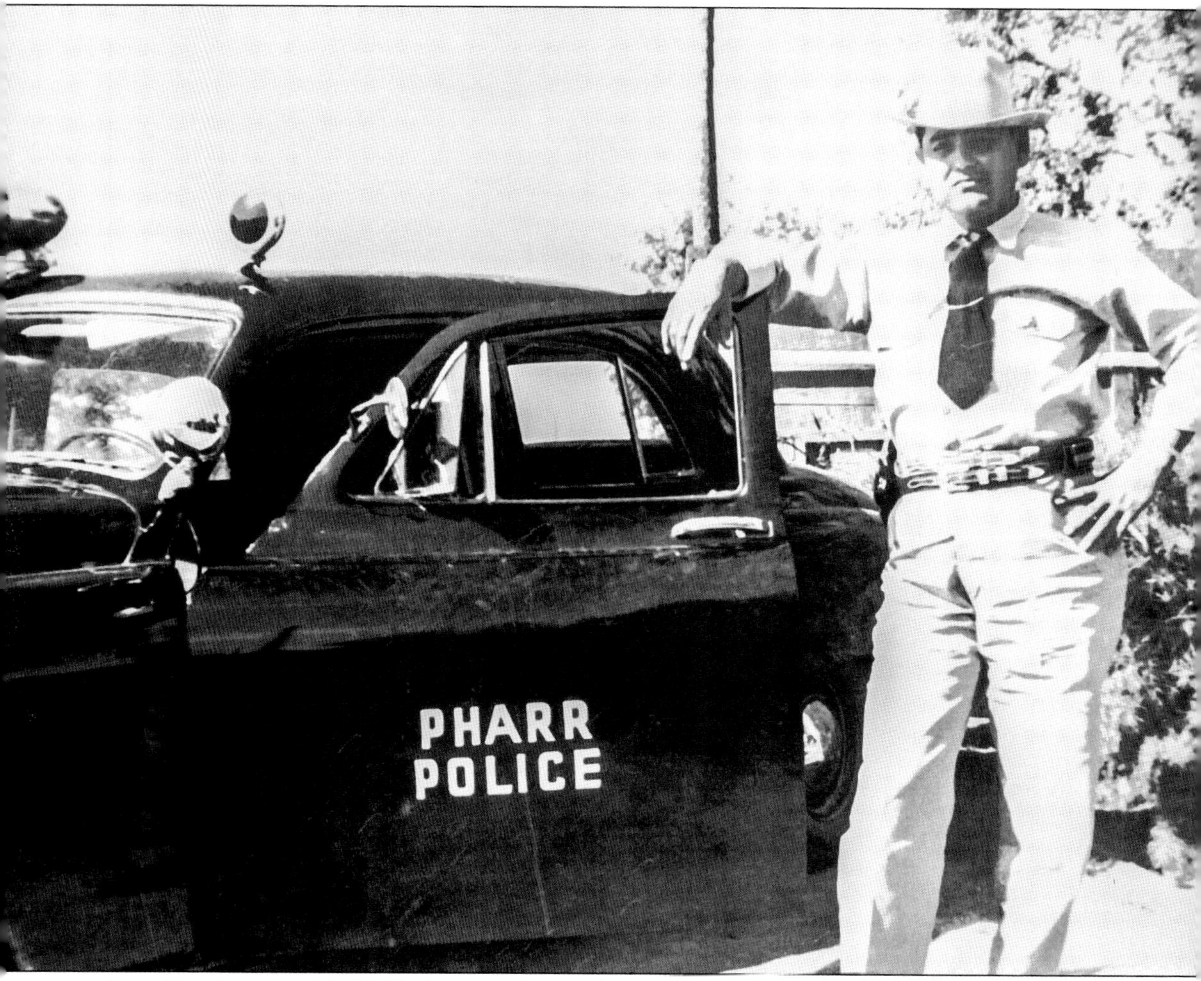

Standing here in this 1948 photograph is police officer Alberto Gonzalez. He happens to be standing next to the very first police car in the city of Pharr. This car was something the Pharr Police Department could be proud of. Today, the Pharr Police Department employs a staff that patrols on bikes, on all-terrain vehicles, and in police cars. (Courtesy of the Pharr Memorial Library Archives.)

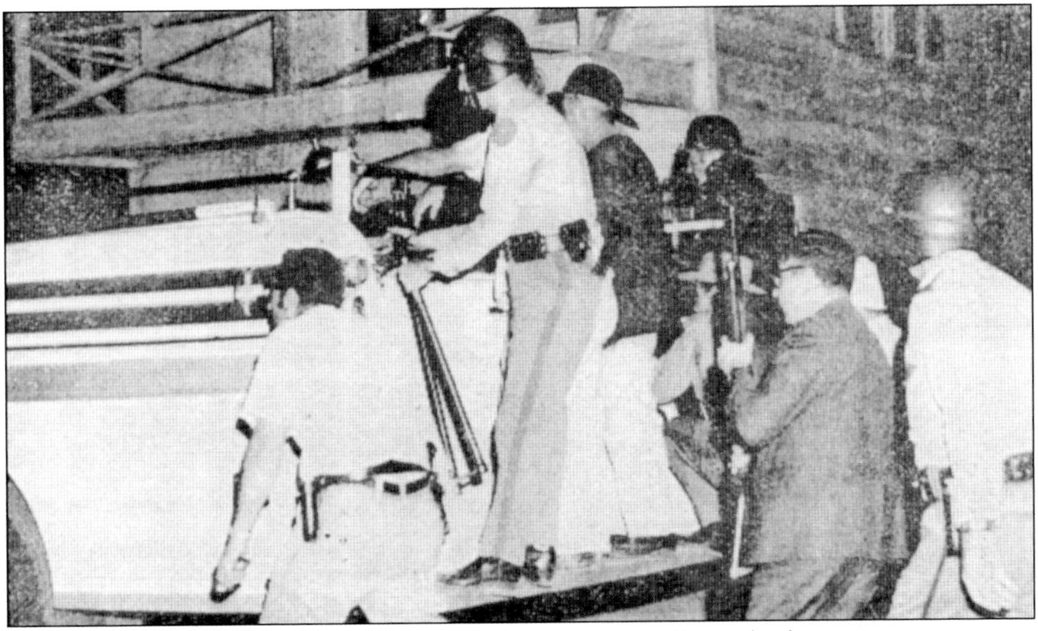

Pictured here in 1971 are several Pharr and Edinburg police officers slowly moving into position behind a rolling fire truck when the Pharr police riots are at their height near the Pharr Police Department Headquarters. The man with the shotgun and suit is believed to be then chief of police of Edinburg, Alfredo Gonzalez. Pharr chief of police Alfredo Ramirez was asked to leave the station after Mayor Bowe placed Edinburg chief Alfredo Gonzalez in charge. Chief Ramirez was not seen or heard from for days after being dismissed. (Courtesy of the Pharr Memorial Library Archives.)

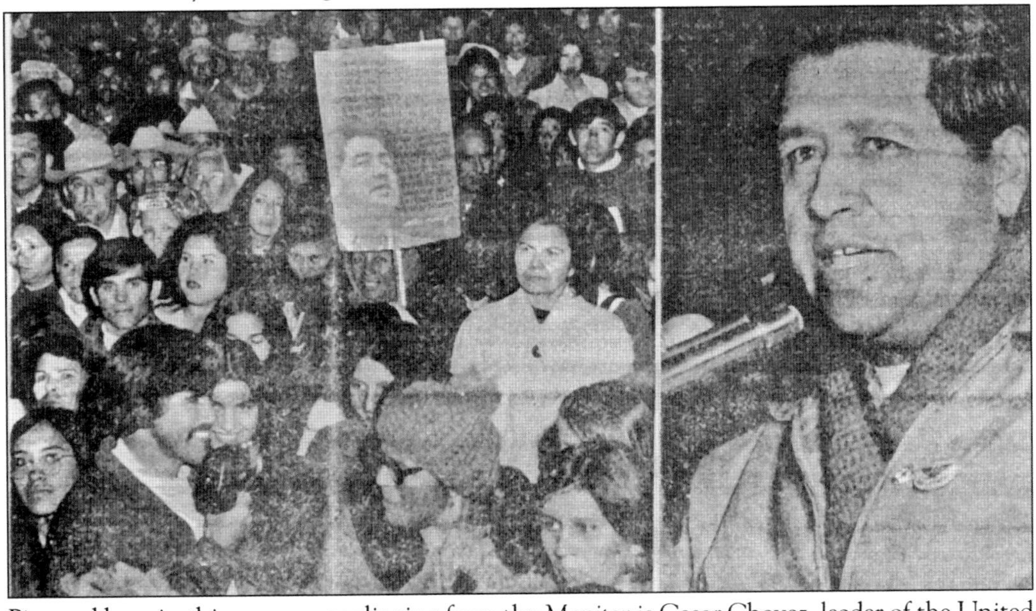

Pictured here in this newspaper clipping from the *Monitor* is Cesar Chavez, leader of the United Farm Workers of America organization. Chavez founded this organization in California in 1962. He came to visit the neighboring town of San Juan in 1971 to attend a rally at the San Juan Catholic Church. The event was held to honor Alfonso Flores, the one and only person killed during the Pharr police riots. (Courtesy of the Pharr Memorial Library Archives.)

FBI, DPS Both Investigating Violent Pharr Demonstration

2-9-71

PHARR — Both the Federal Bureau of Investigation and the Department of Public Safety were investigating a rock-throwing demonstration that left one young man shot to death.

District Attorney Oscar McInnis said Monday he has turned the investigation of the Saturday night incident over to the DPS and said he would recall the grand jury Feb. 18 to present the case.

U. S. Attorney Anthony J. P. Farris said in Houston he had received a request by Pharr Mayor R. S. Bowe for a Justice Department probe of the incident and events leading up to it.

It is underway," Farris said today. "The FBI is investigating allegations of police brutality. They are not just investigating the disturbance over the weekend, but the whole thing, starting with the police brutality charge.

"I imagine it will be two to three weeks before they finish their investigation and another week before they finish their report."

Farris said the investigation reports would go to the San Antonio FBI office and to the Civil Rights Division of the Justice Department in Washington, "and a copy is sent to me."

Farris said the statues involved, if in fact there were any cases of police maltreatment of defendants or prisoners, was 18 U.S. Code 242, which he said protects a citizen from violation of rights by a person or persons acting under the "color of the law."

The 31 adults charged in the incident remained free on $200 personal recognizance bonds. Eight to 10 juveniles also were arrested when 60 lawmen armed with riot guns helped Pharr police disperse an angry crowd protesting alleged police brutality.

Fatally wounded by a shot fired by an unknown person was Alfonso Laredo Flores, 20.

McInnis sought postponement Monday afternoon of proceedings leading to a possible trial on disorderly conduct charges in Justice of the Peace Jim Wilson's court at Franburg.

Wilson agreed to postpone the case nearly two weeks while the DPS investigates. McInnis said the delay was to insure "that justice be done to all parties — the accused as well as the accusers."

"This is a situation we don't want to skip over hurriedly. There may be some charges in this (Justice of the Peace) court, (Hidalgo) County Court-at-Law and district court," McInnis said.

(See PROBE, Page 3)

Probe--

(Continued from Page 1)

The Saturday night protest began as a peaceful demonstration in front of the Pharr police station. But when the crowd began shouting insults at the police a fire unit was called in. When rocks started hitting firemen and vehicles, the firemen doused the crowd with water.

The crowd reponded with a hail of rocks and bottles, whereupon the officers sallied forth firing riot guns in the air and bursting a few canisters of tear gas.

Flores was found afterwards lying wounded on the city's main avenue, Cage Street. He died Sunday night. It has not been determined who fired the shot that killed Flores and an autopsy has not revealed the caliber of bullet.

Firemen who sprayed the protesters said shots were being fired at the authorities.

All those arrested were released soon afterward and told by Wilson, who arraigned them on charges of disorderly conduct by enticing a riot, to stay at home or face contempt charges.

Wilson reversed that ruling Monday and allowed those arrested to attend a rally Monday night for Cesar Chavez, farm labor organizer and founder of the United Farm Workers Organizing Committee.

Chavez' appearance at San Juan was turned into a brief memorial service for Flores.

The Pharr police riots drew national attention—so much so that the Federal Bureau of Investigation (FBI) and Texas Department of Public Safety both investigated allegations of police brutality. US attorney Anthony Farris, along with district attorney Oscar McInnis, turned the investigation over to the San Antonio, Texas, FBI office and to the civil rights division of the Justice Department in Washington, DC. This negative attention led to the resignation of Mayor Bowe and several Pharr police officers. This newspaper clipping from February 9, 1971, sheds some light on the investigation. (Courtesy of the Pharr Memorial Library Archives.)

Six

Education and Religion

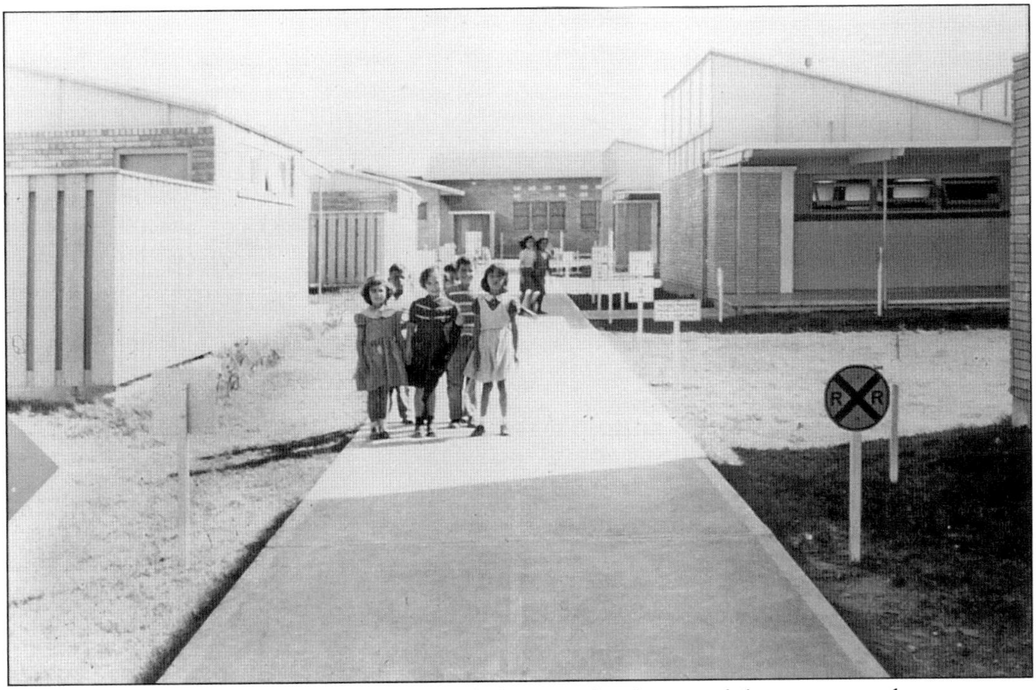

The Texas Highway Department would regularly visit schools around the city to conduct programs on street safety. Pictured here on an unknown date are several students from Napper Elementary School who participated in street-safety activities during school hours. Napper Elementary School still exists today and is located at 903 North Flag Street. (Courtesy of the University of Texas–Pan American Library and Special Collections Department.)

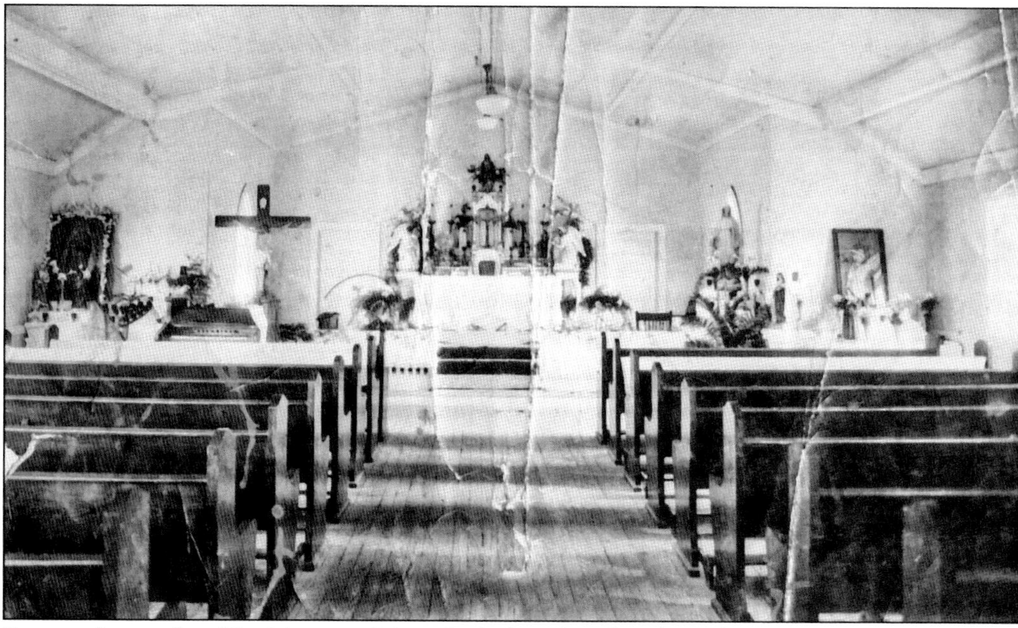

Seen is the inside of St. Margaret Mary Catholic Church. Throughout the years, St. Margaret Mary has undergone a major transformation as its many priests have continued to make changes to the church as they see fit. The church has served the community for nearly 100 years and continues to do so today. (Courtesy of the Pharr Memorial Library Archives.)

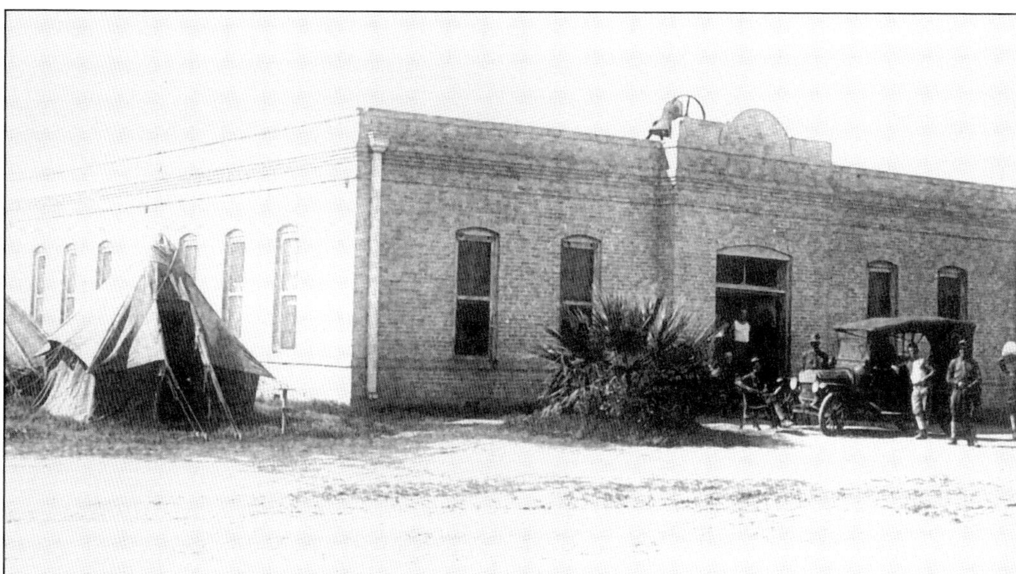

One of the oldest buildings in the city of Pharr still stands on the corner of Cherokee and South Athol Streets. This building served as the first school building and was constructed by the Pharr Townsite Company, costing some $6,000. The building had many duties: It served as a school building on weekdays, a community church on Sundays, and also as a headquarters for soldiers who were stationed in Pharr to protect the border during the bandit era in 1915–1916. (Courtesy of the University of Texas–Pan American Library and Special Collections Department.)

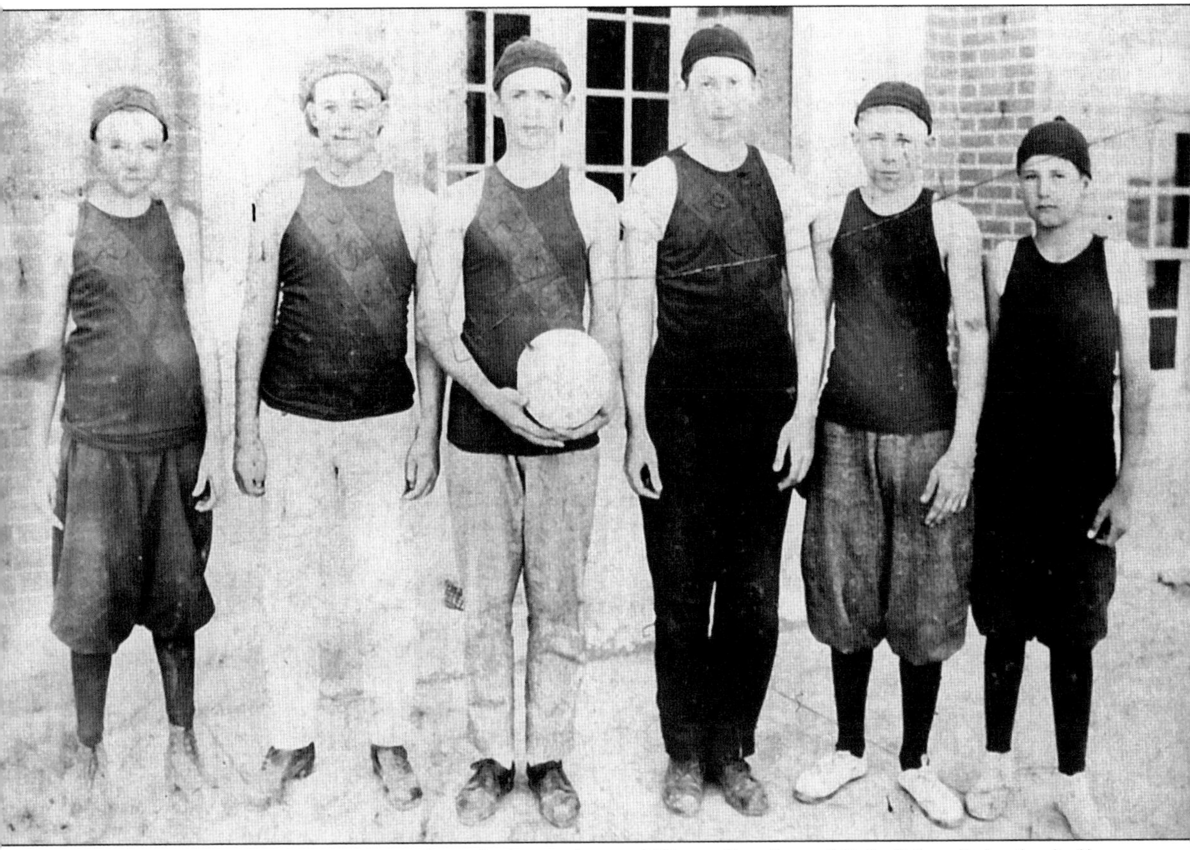

Pictured here in 1917 are six unidentified members of Pharr-San Juan High School's basketball team. When this picture was taken, the game of basketball was only 26 years old. Compared to the game uniforms worn today, the attire the young men are wearing might seem more appropriate for a pickup game. Also, the ball the young man in the middle is holding is much smaller than a regulation basketball. (Courtesy of the University of Texas–Pan American Library and Special Collections Department.)

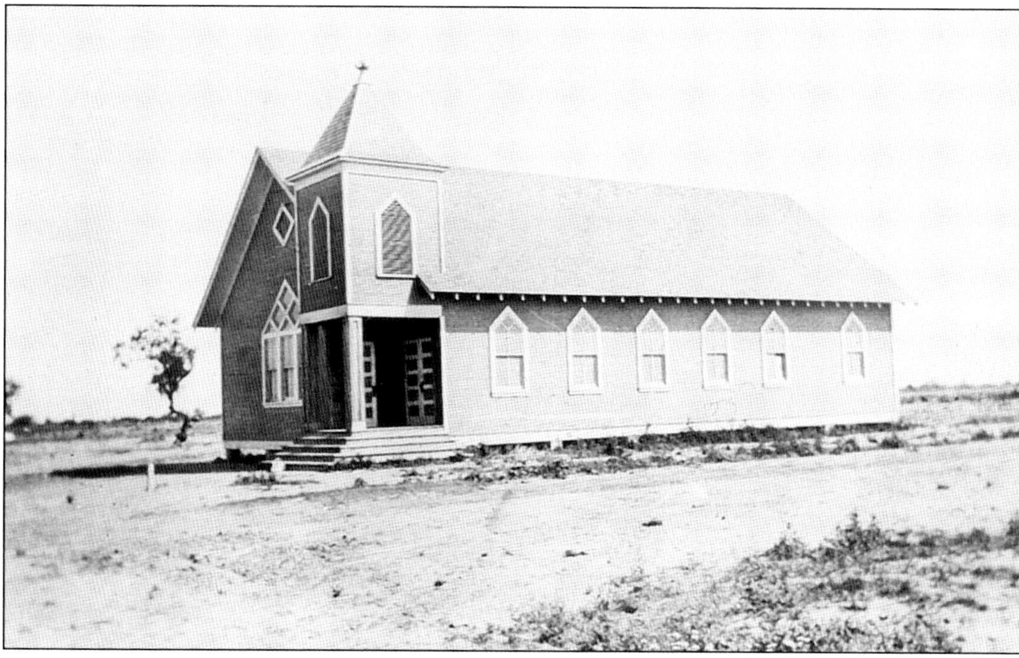

Pictured here is an early church in Pharr. This photograph was taken right before a major storm, more than likely a hurricane, made landfall in 1914. The church was isolated on a large, empty tract of land with no structures to shield the structure from strong winds. (Courtesy of the University of Texas–Pan American Library and Special Collections Department.)

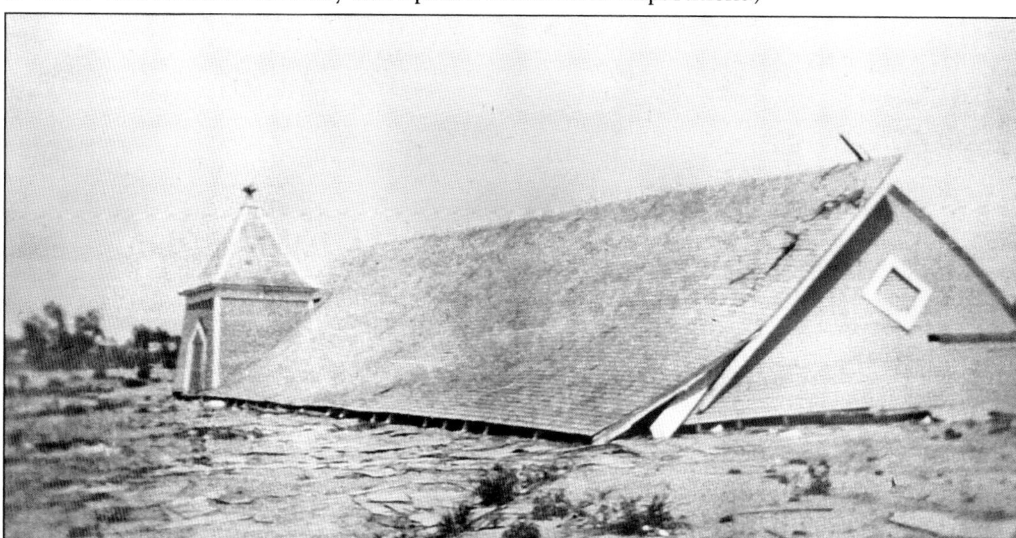

This photograph of the same church shows the aftermath of a storm that made its way through Pharr in 1914. It is said that a strong hurricane was responsible for the damage. Pharr is located only about 70 miles inland from South Padre Island. Hurricanes do not occur often, but they have struck Pharr before. Hurricane Beulah hit Pharr in 1967 and caused severe flooding and damage. At the time, it was the second-costliest hurricane on record, amassing roughly $1 billion worth of damages. (Courtesy of the University of Texas–Pan American Library and Special Collections Department.)

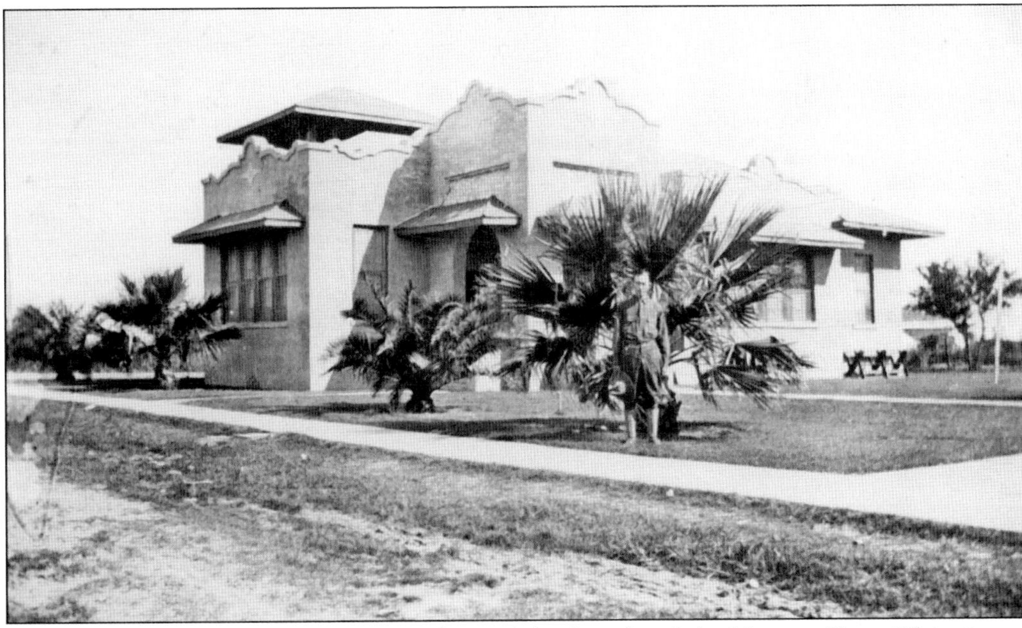

This unidentified soldier is standing in front of the first church building in Pharr. This picture, taken around 1916, is the oldest known photograph of this structure. It served as a community church in 1911 and was than a Methodist church for the next four decades. In 1963, the building was demolished in order to make way for the city library. (Courtesy of the Museum of South Texas History.)

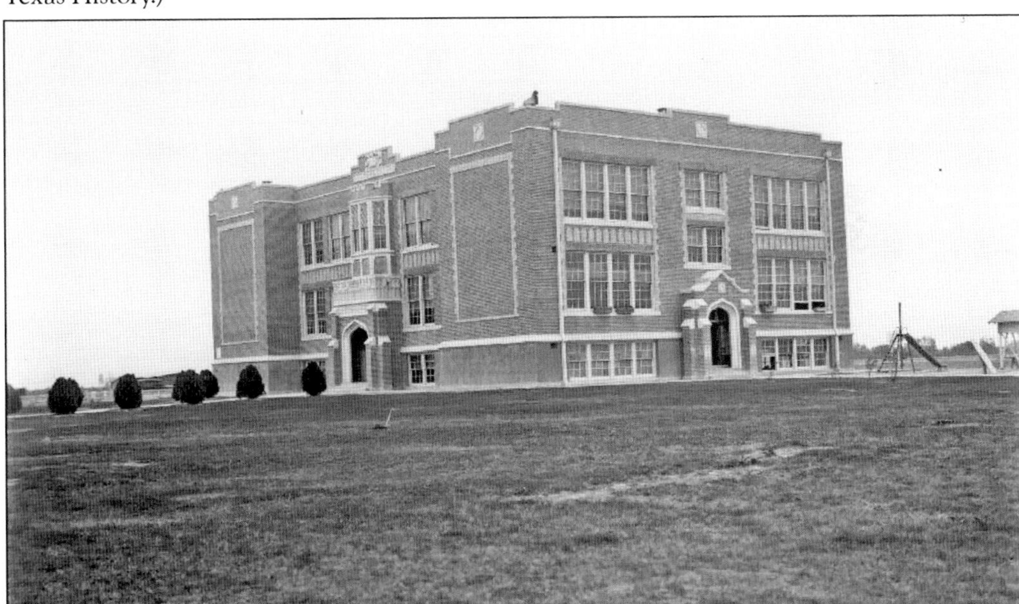

The Common School District of Pharr and San Juan began construction of this school in 1915. First used for the 1916–1917 school year, its enrollment was 143, with 12 teachers and a graduating class of 9. The name was changed in 1919 to Pharr-San Juan Independent School District. It eventually became Pharr-San Juan-Alamo School District when the neighboring city of Alamo was added in 1959. The building still stands today. (Courtesy of the Library of Congress.)

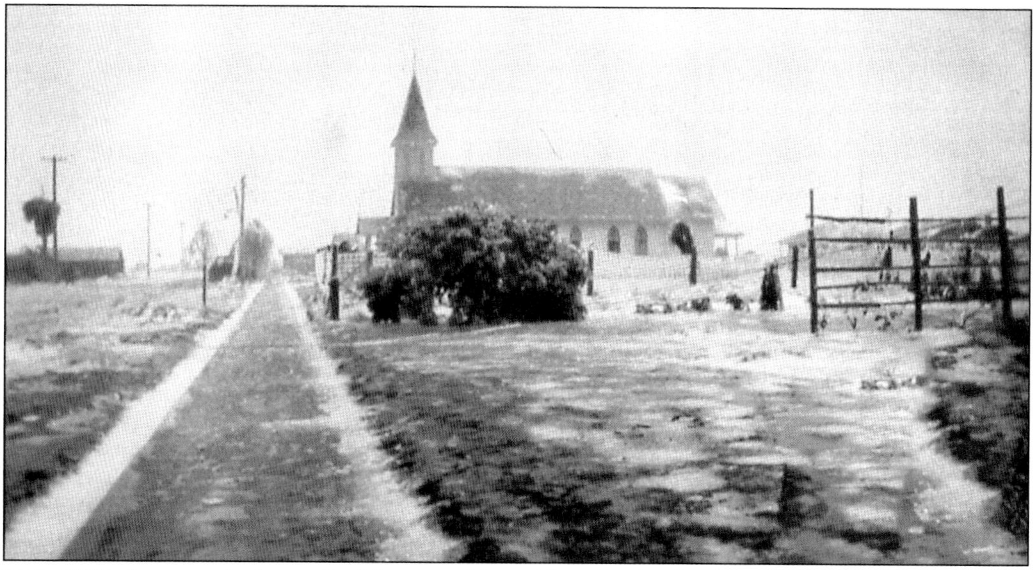

This 1919 photograph shows St. Margaret Mary Church, the first Catholic church in town. It was located on the corner of Bluebonnet and Cherokee Streets until it was moved to its current location on West Hawk Street. Throughout the years, the church has undergone some drastic changes and continues to transform today. St. Margaret Mary has served the city of Pharr for nearly 100 years. (Courtesy of the University of Texas–Pan American Library and Special Collections Department.)

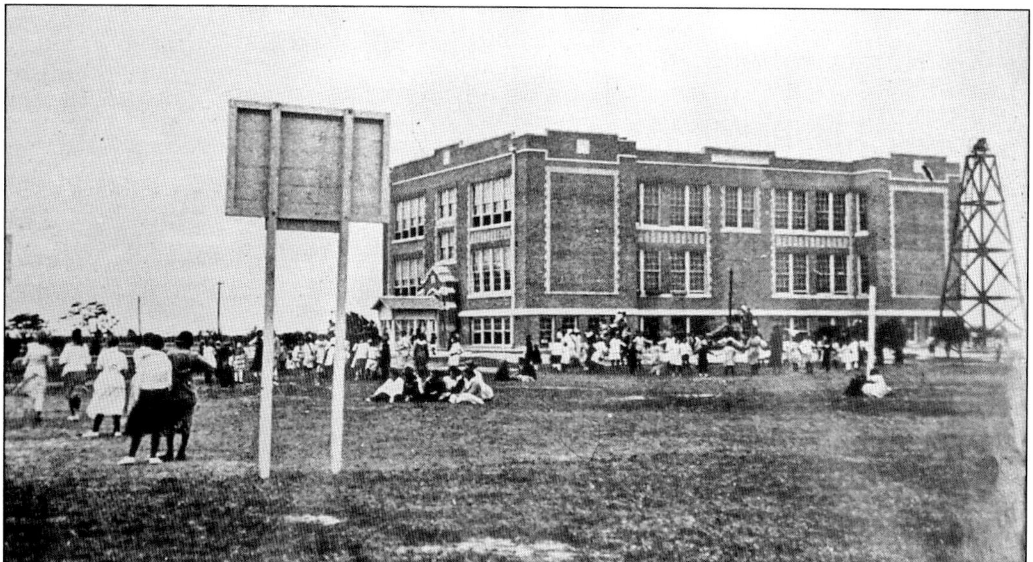

Pictured here in the all-female playground at Pharr-San Juan High School in 1919 are a number of young women, of all different age groups, utilizing recreation time. In 1906, the Playground Association of America dictated that an ideal, proper playground would have separate play sections and athletic fields for boys and girls. Playgrounds were not free-form in the early 1900s; trained instructors supervised recreation time. (Courtesy of the University of Texas–Pan American Library and Special Collections Department.)

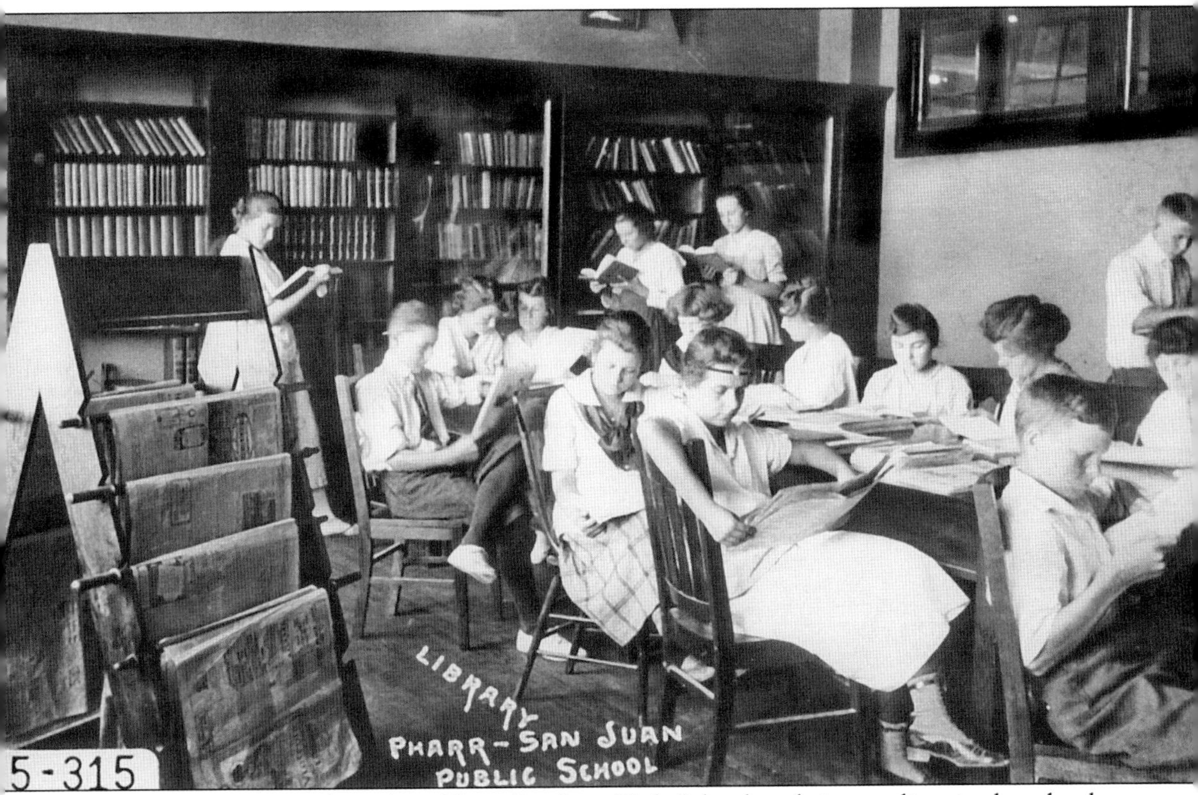

In this 1919 picture, students from Pharr-San Juan High School are being studious in the school library and reading to sharpen up their education. The library is said to have been originally located on the basement level of the school but was later relocated to an area on the first floor. All the students enrolled at this school were white. Mexican Americans suffered from segregation and were not included in much around town concerning education until 1927, when Buell School was built to serve Mexican American children. (Courtesy of the University of Texas–Pan American Library and Special Collections Department.)

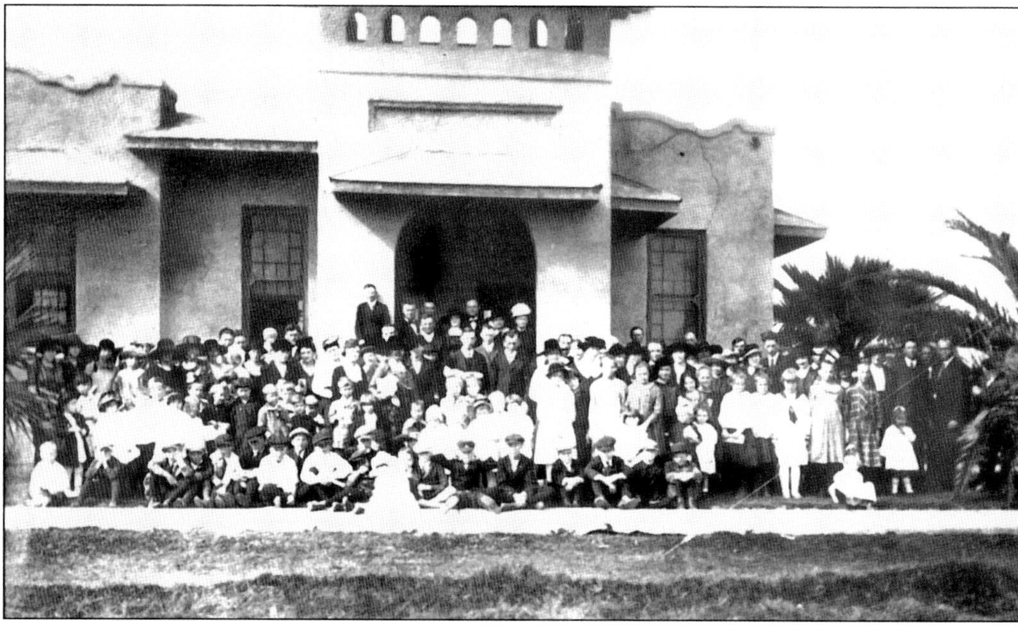

In this image taken around 1920, the individuals are all members of Pharr's first Methodist church. After a Sunday morning service, dressed in their Sunday's best, every member stuck around so this photograph could be taken. The church had a unique Spanish-style look to it. The building does not exist today. (Courtesy of the University of Texas–Pan American Library and Special Collections Department.)

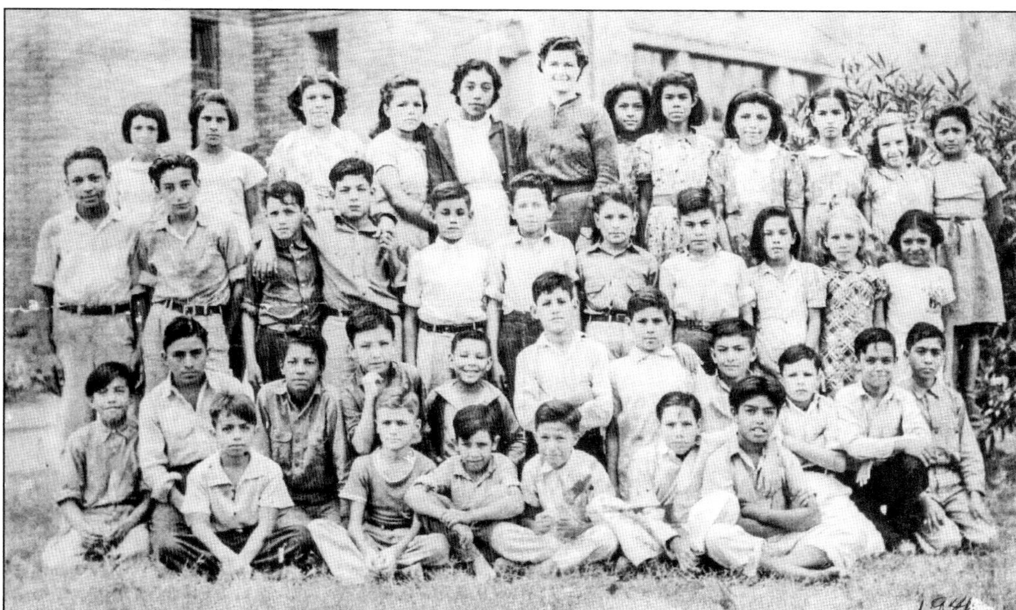

Pictured here in 1941 at Buell School are students and a teacher (tall woman in the center of the back row). They are, in no particular order, Luis Gonzalez, Maria Mendoza, Humberto Garcia, Roy Rutledge, Romeo Escobar, Lupe Hinojosa, Nick Elizondo, Raul Rosales, Pedro Flores, Speedy Flores, Katherine Coronado, Nellie Pantel, Emma Benavidez, Esperanza Vargas, and Julia Martinez. (Courtesy of the Pharr Memorial Library Archives.)

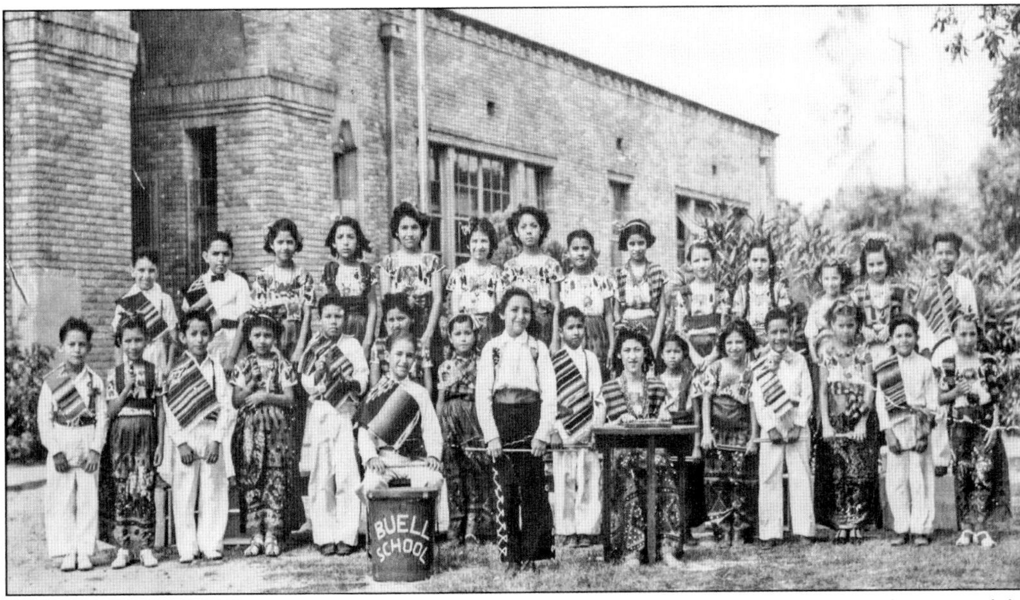

Pictured here in front of Buell School in 1941 are members of the Buell rhythm band. Some of the children pictured here are Alicia Ramos, Irma Zuniga, Olivia Cruz, Norma Garza, Dahlia Peña, Elva Benavidez, Guadalupe Gonzalez, Jose Gonzalez, Daniel Peña, Hilda Ramirez, Mary Alice Ramos, Lamberto Balli, Julia Rivera, Macedonio Balli, Julia Navarro, Clemente Cruz, Elena De Los Santos, Oscar Sanchez, Nora Gonzalez, Andrea Serda, Armando Ortiz, Belia Elizondo, and Elizabeth Bernal. (Courtesy of Reyes and Anita Vela.)

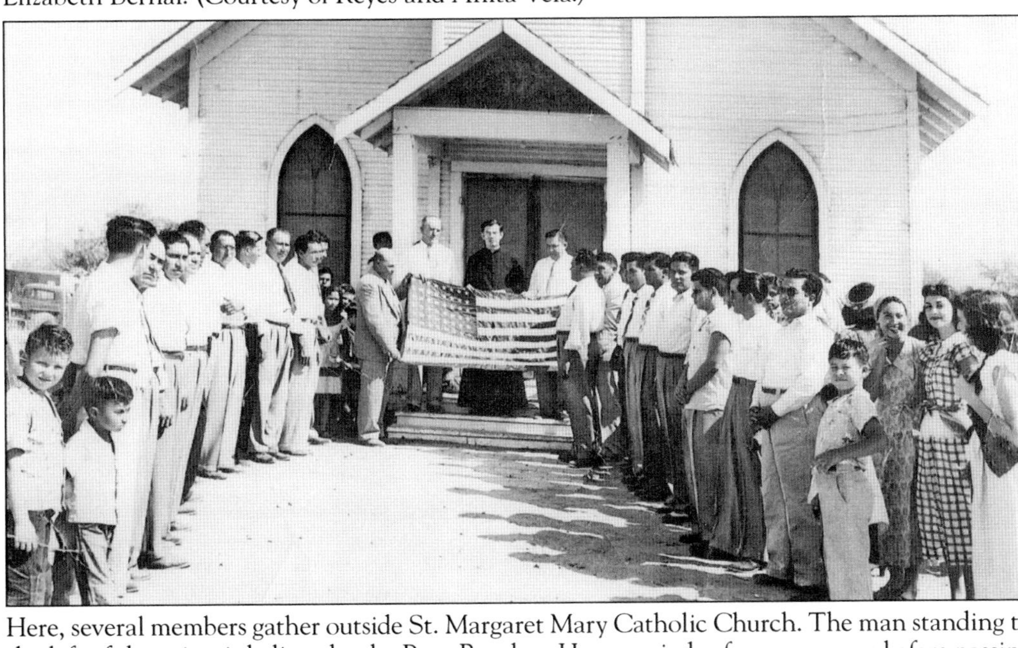

Here, several members gather outside St. Margaret Mary Catholic Church. The man standing to the left of the priest is believed to be Pepe Rendon. He was a judge for many years before passing away at a young age. Of the three women standing on the far right in the photograph, two are identified: the woman second from right, in the gingham dress, is Dora Lopez, and the woman on the far right is Hermelinda Saenz. Note a US flag is being presented to the church. (Courtesy of the Pharr Memorial Library Archives.)

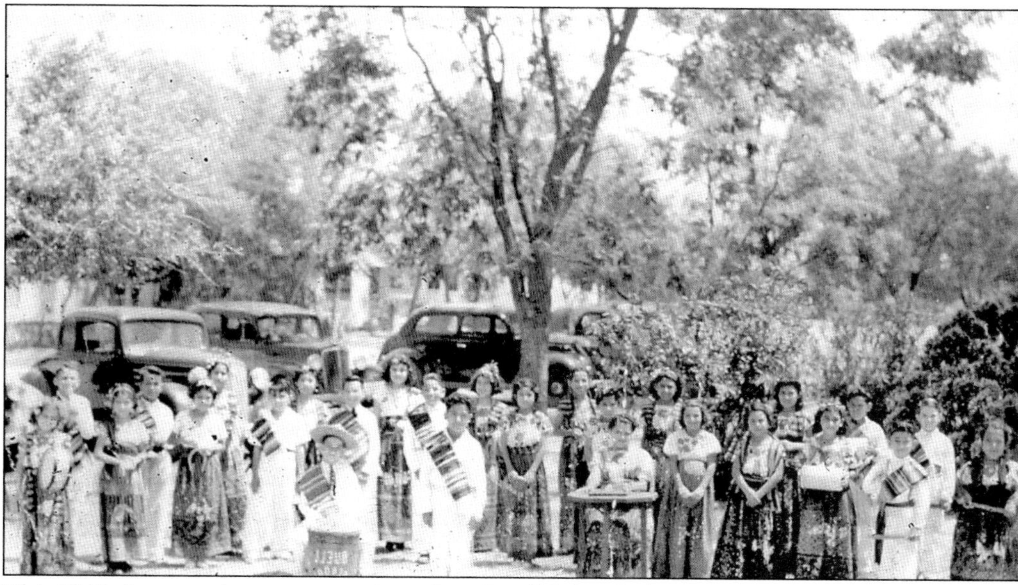

This 1940 photograph captures students from Buell School who are part of Buell's Mexican band. The members are dressed up in *folklórico* (folk) attire. Regardless of segregation and racial issues, being part of this Mexican band was something these kids could be proud of. (Courtesy of the University of Texas–Pan American Library and Special Collections Department.)

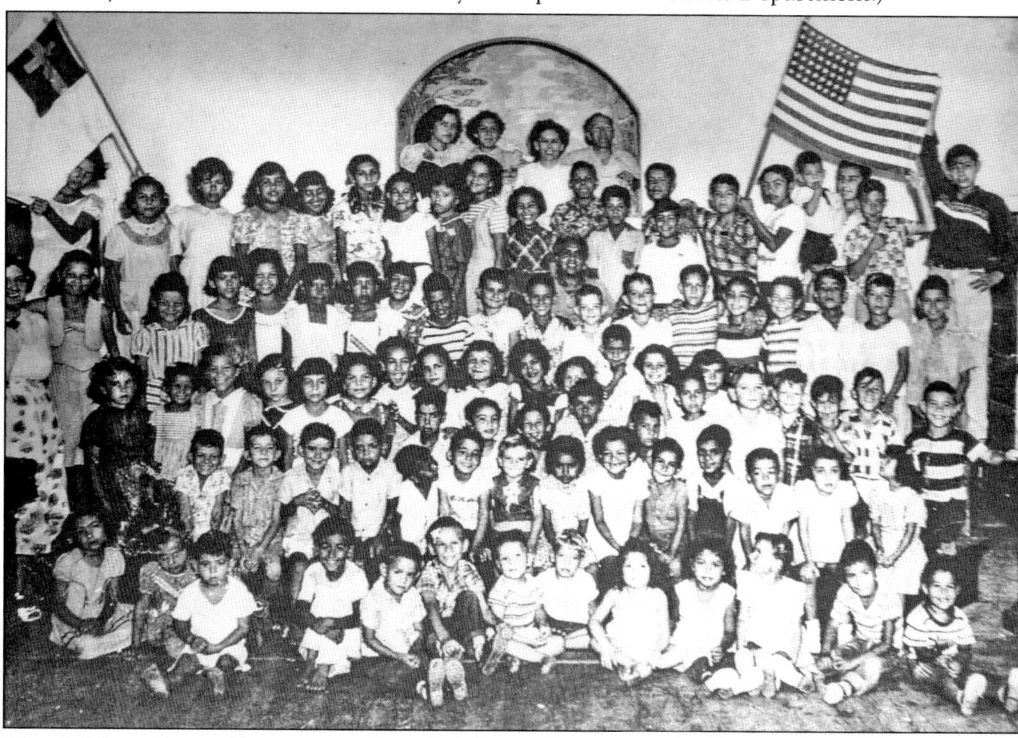

The children pictured here are unidentified. Several sitting on the floor are not wearing shoes, as some local families simply could not afford to buy shoes for their children. Hidalgo County, where Pharr is located, is listed as one of the lowest-income counties in the United States. (Courtesy of the Pharr Memorial Library Archives.)

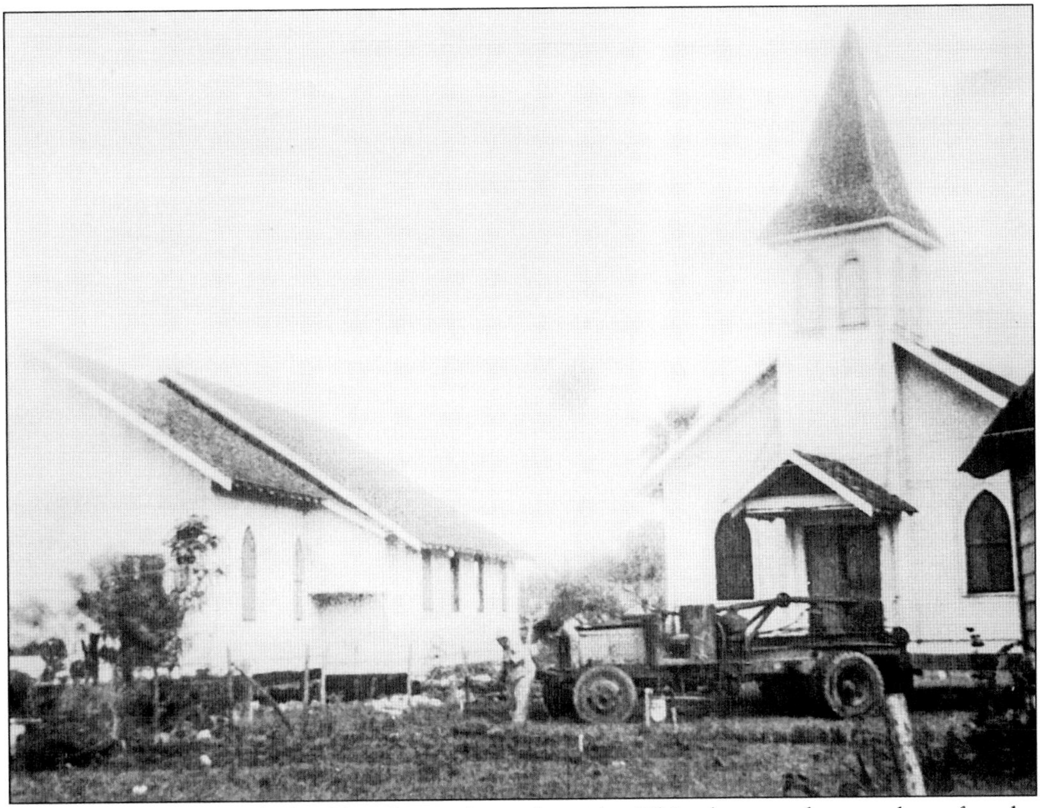

St. Margaret Mary Catholic Church stands on the right. This photograph was taken after the church was moved from the corner of Bluebonnet and Cherokee Streets to West Hawk Avenue. St. Margaret Mary Church is still located on West Hawk Avenue, but it no longer looks the way it does in this photograph. It is one of the oldest congregations in the entire city. (Courtesy of the Pharr Memorial Library Archives.)

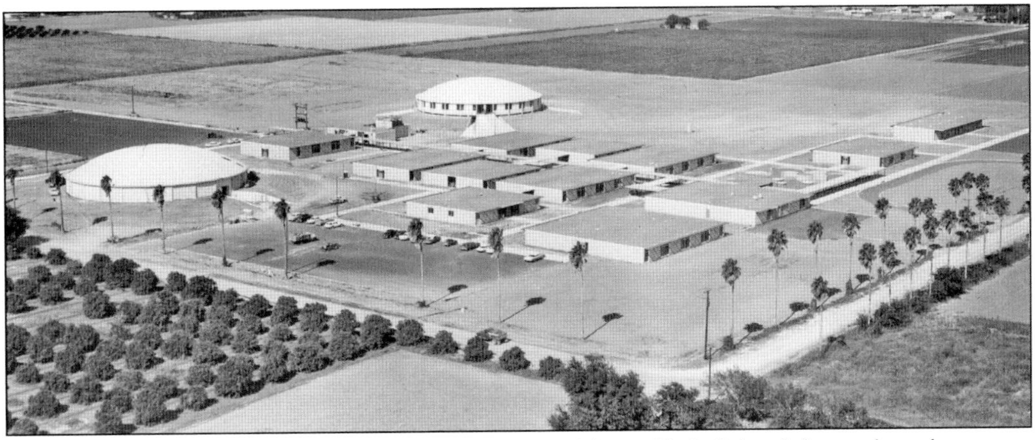

This is a 1960s aerial photograph of Pharr-San Juan-Alamo High School, located on the corner of I Road (Veterans Boulevard) and Ridge Road. The original high school was built in 1915 and was located on Business 83. Today, the current high school is located across the street (south) from where this photograph was taken. The school in this picture has since become a middle school. (Courtesy of the Museum of South Texas History.)

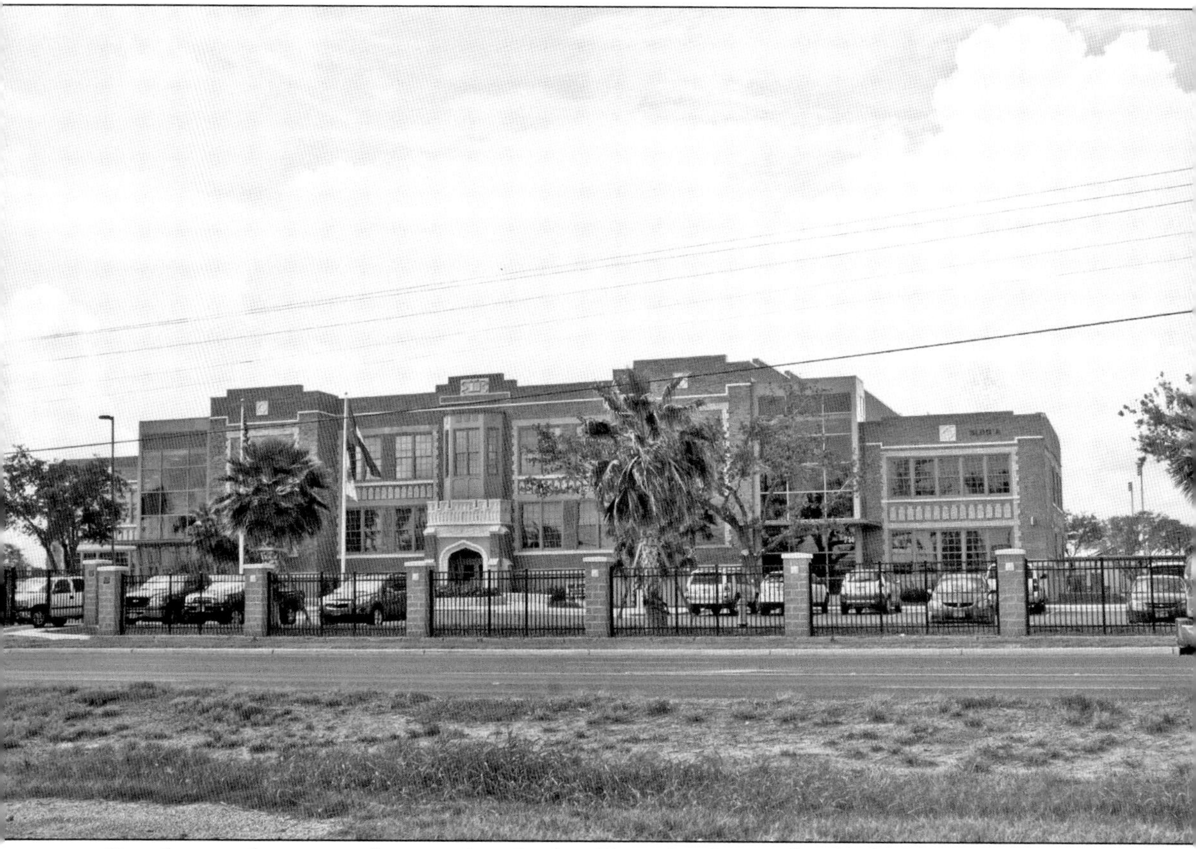

Seen here in this recent photograph is the first Pharr-San Juan School, which was erected in 1915. It was first used in the 1916–1917 school year with an enrollment of 143. Today, the school is still located in the same spot. It has undergone a transformation, but only to restore it and preserve it as a historical landmark. Today, the school is operating as PSJA Thomas Jefferson T-STEM Early College High School. (Courtesy of Julio Enriquez.)

Seven

Social Life and Entertainment

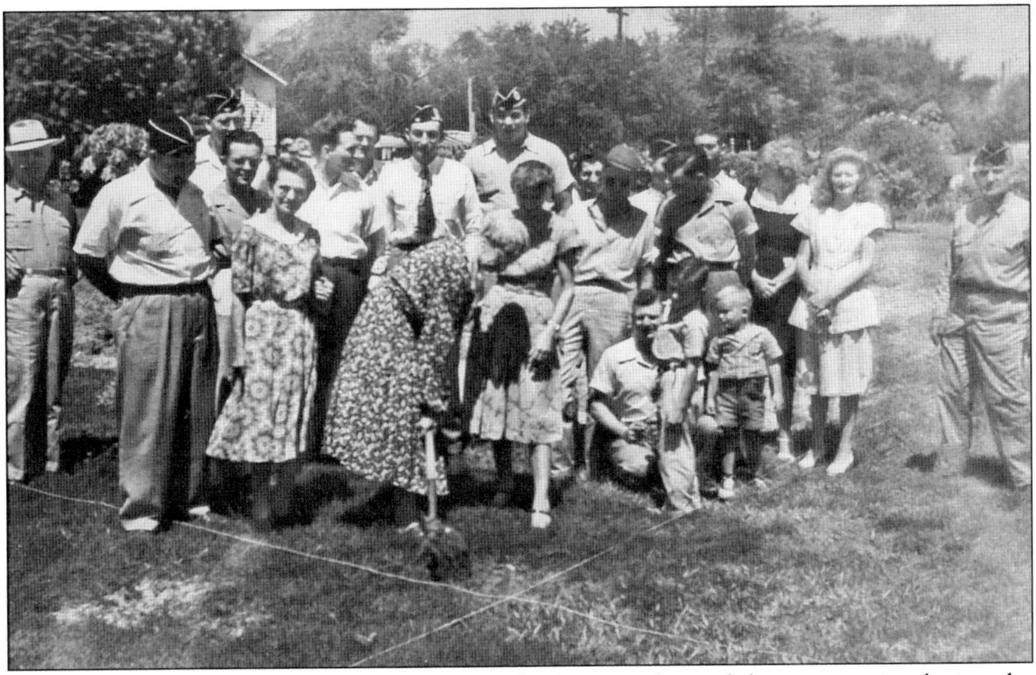

Pictured here in 1951 are several veterans and other members of the community during the ground-breaking ceremony for the American Legion Post No. 101. The building is located on Cage Boulevard just south of Kelly Avenue. The American Legion is a social and mutual-aid veterans' organization that includes members of the armed forces. Plenty of veterans from Pharr are known to frequently visit the Legion hall. In 2004, the building suffered structural damage due to a kitchen fire but did not burn down completely. (Courtesy of the University of Texas–Pan American Library and Special Collections Department.)

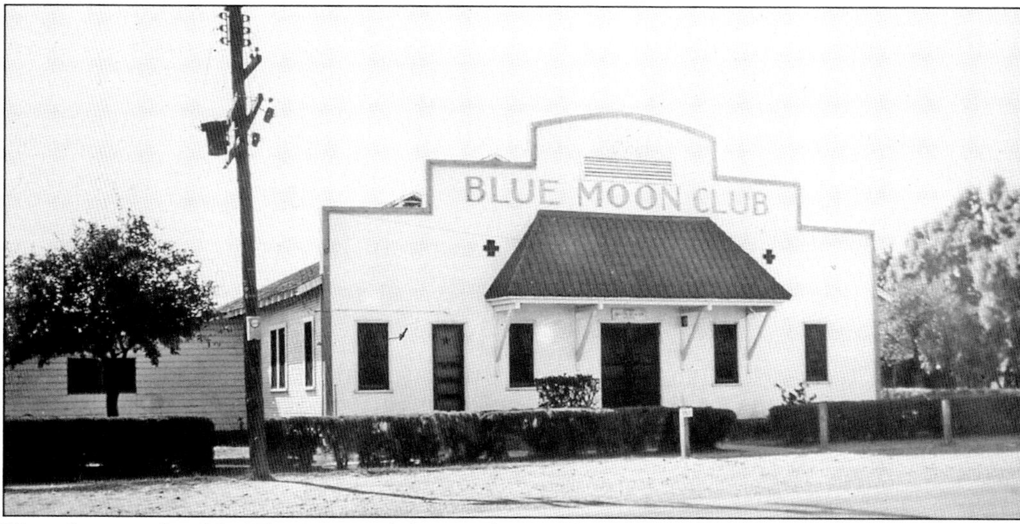

This photograph of the Blue Moon Club was taken in the late 1930s after it was completed. Homer and Juanita Bentley originally owned the club, but Joe and Gloria Vera bought the building in 1960 after they began promoting dances there in 1959. Before being purchased by the Veras, the club catered to whites only. However, that all changed, as the Veras turned it into a place of entertainment for Mexican Americans in the 1960s. The club was located on Business 83 not too far from the Cactus Drive-in. (Courtesy of the University of Texas–Pan American Library and Special Collections Department.)

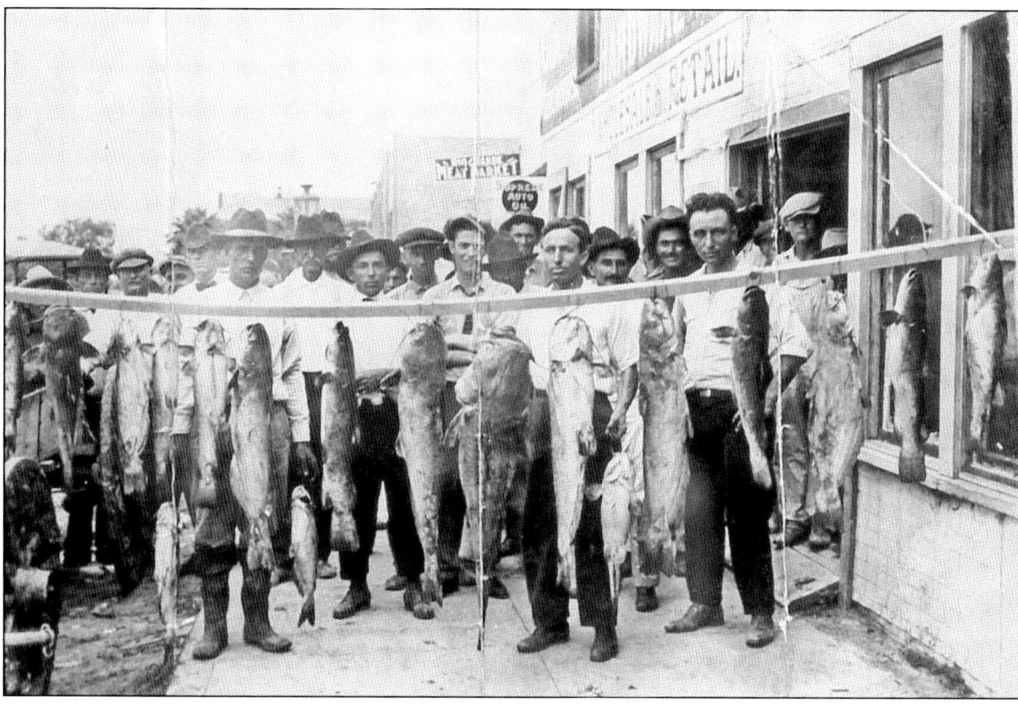

On an unknown day in 1923, many of the anglers in town celebrated their day's catch of nearly 20 catfish with a party and fish fry at the city market. Where the men were fishing exactly is unknown, but the likely site is the Rio Grande, located approximately eight miles south of Pharr. (Courtesy of the University of Texas–Pan American Library and Special Collections Department.)

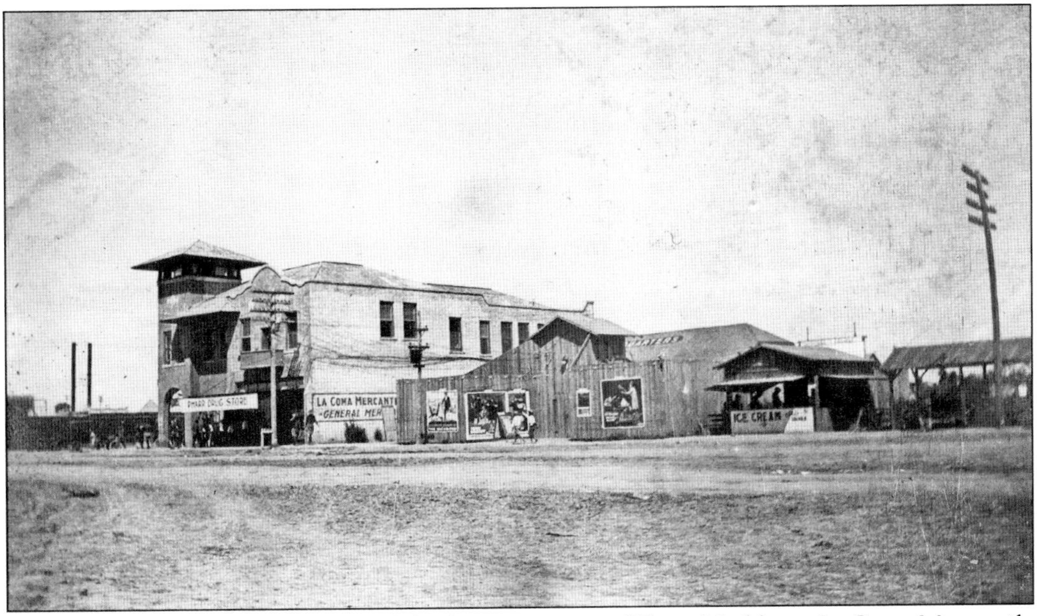

In 1916, this photograph was taken of the downtown area of Pharr. Visible are La Coma Mercantile Company, Pharr's city hall, Pharr's drugstore, and the old picture house, which had no roof. There are quite a few posters for Harry Houdini serials posted on the walls of the old picture house that can be seen. (Courtesy of the Museum of South Texas history.)

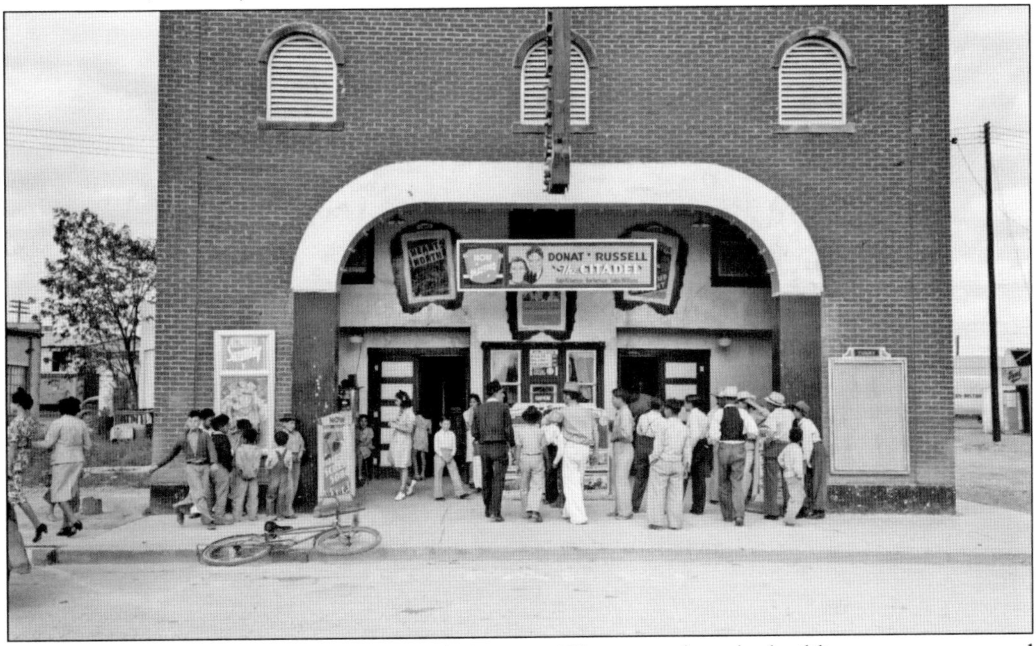

The Texas Theater is located on East Park Avenue. The exact date the building was constructed is unknown, but the theater served as a place for family fun and entertainment until the 1970s, when it ceased operations. By the 1930s, the Texas Theater owners began allowing Mexicans to enter their theater to watch movies and purchase snacks at the concession stand. Unlike today, one could see a movie in the late 1940s for 9¢ and buy an assortment of treats for less than 25¢. The building still stands in 2014. (Courtesy of the Library of Congress.)

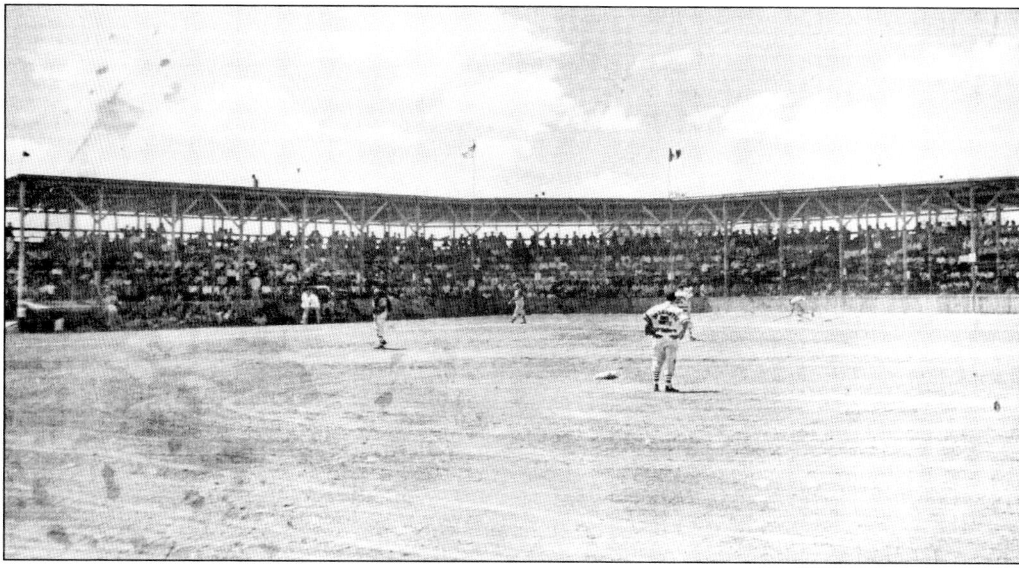

This unique view from center field shows the old Pharr Merchants Baseball Park, which was located in south Pharr just outside of the city limits. Member of the Pharr Merchants baseball team can be seen standing on the field, waiting for play to resume. Playing in front of large crowds became the norm for the team, which was named Pharr Merchants because city merchants bought jerseys and equipment when the players could not afford the needed gear for themselves. (Courtesy of the Pharr Memorial Library Archives.)

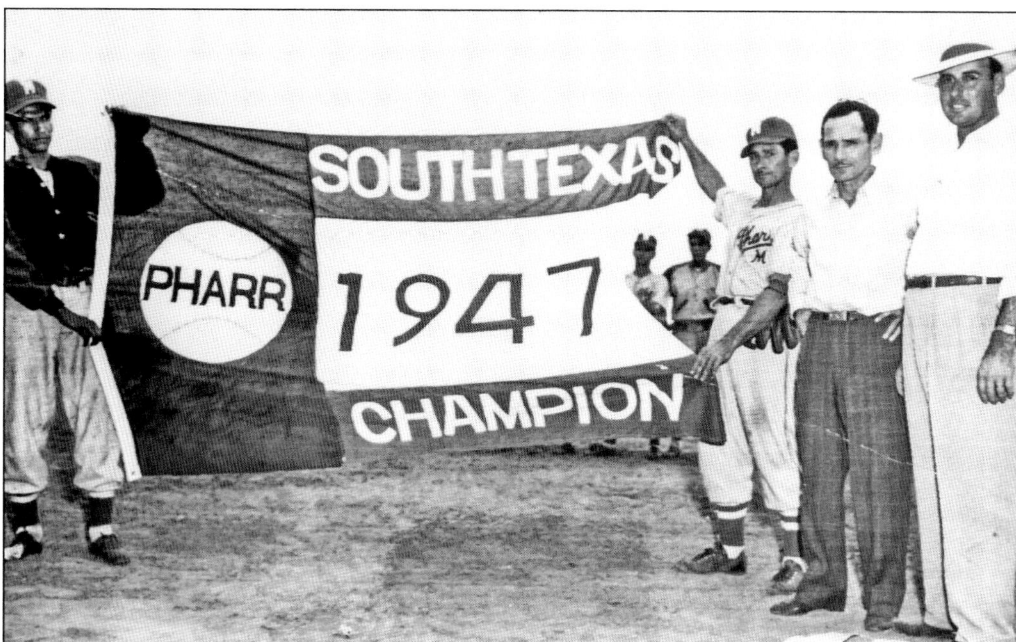

Members of the Pharr Merchants baseball team are pictured here holding up their 1947 South Texas Champions banner. Manager Loreto Treviño is standing on the far right. Two of the more popular players on the team were "Chano" and Nacho Gonzalez. Fans would give up their Sunday afternoons to watch these two men and the rest of the Merchants play ball. (Courtesy of the Pharr Memorial Library Archives.)

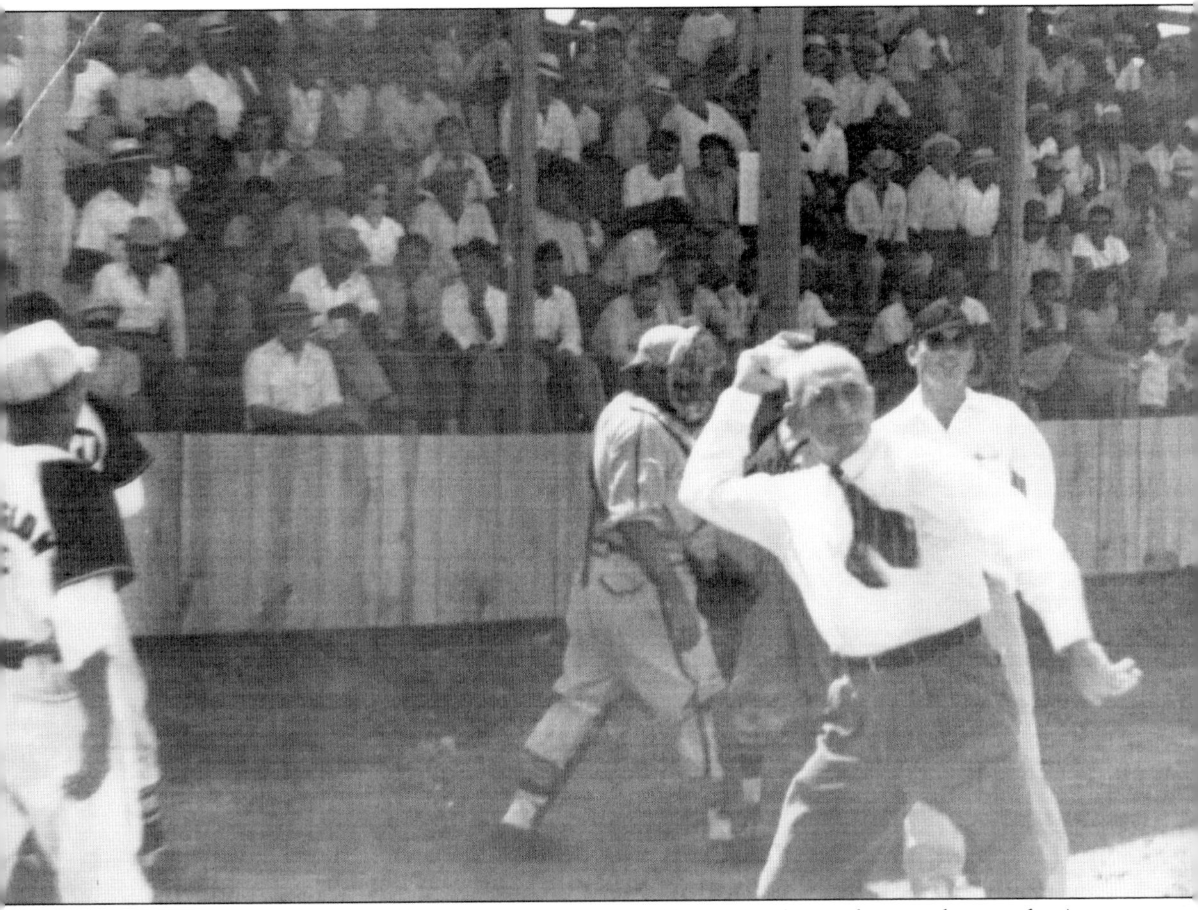

Taken in the late 1940s, this photograph shows a few Pharr Merchants fans in the stands. An opposing manager throwing a baseball and a few players can also be seen in this picture. After World War II ended in 1945, watching and playing baseball was a way for many to kick back and relax. (Courtesy of the Pharr Memorial Library Archives.)

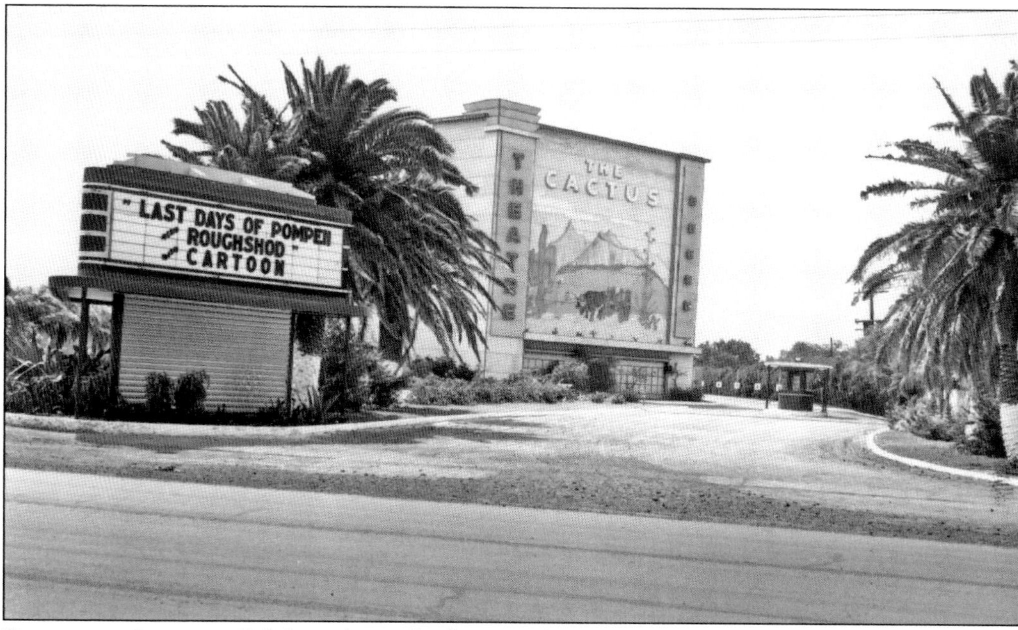

Since many homes still did not have the luxury of possessing a television, the Cactus Drive-in Theater was a favorite getaway spot for families and youngsters. The theater was located on East Highway 83 just south of the railroad tracks. It was built sometime in the 1940s and was demolished in 1974. This photograph was taken in the late 1950s. (Courtesy of the Museum of South Texas History.)

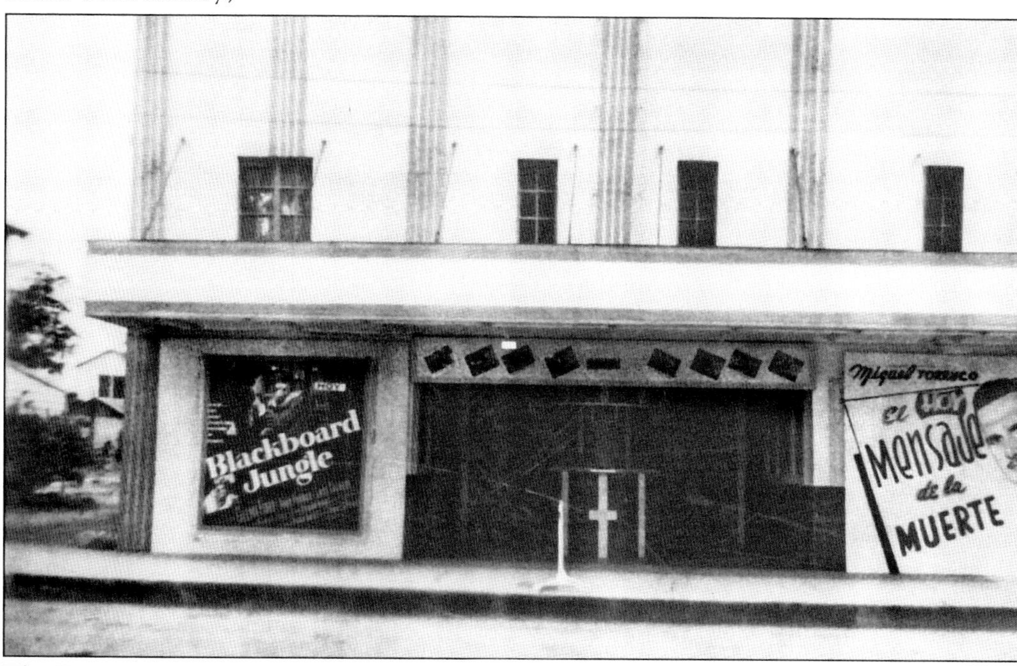

The Teatro España (Spain Theater) was built by Don Antonio Saeta in the early 1930s. He gave it the name España because he hailed from Spain. This was the only theater in town that showed Mexican movies. Saeta was one of the wealthiest people in Pharr. (Courtesy of the Pharr Memorial Archives.)

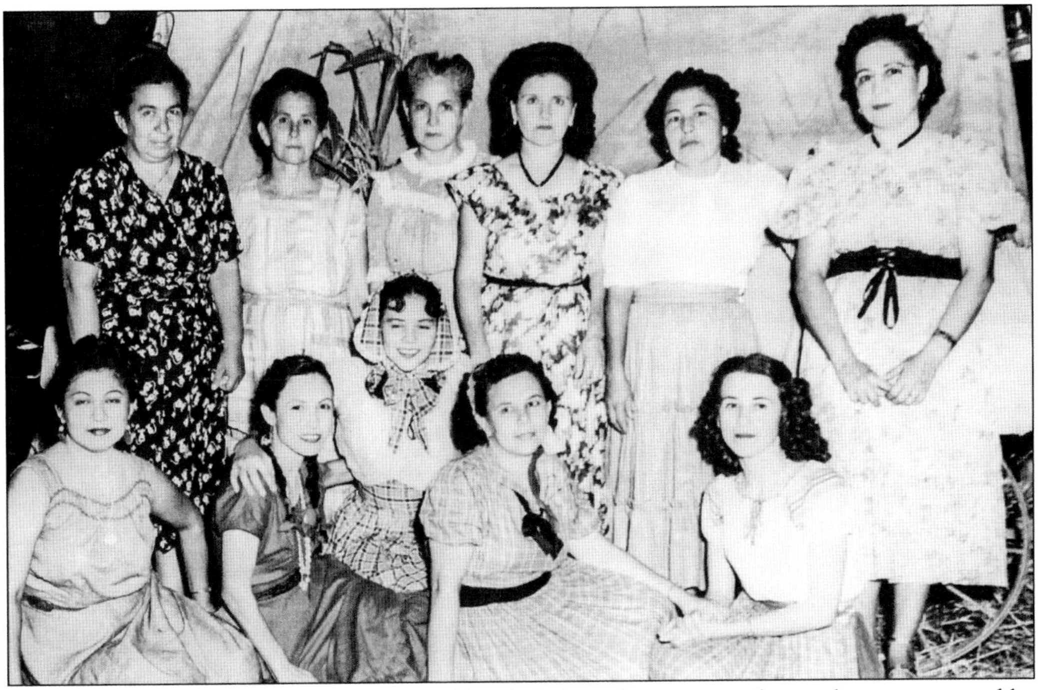

Pictured here on July 11, 1948, are several lovely ladies who are attending a dance sponsored by the Asociación Latino Americana (Latin American Association). Some of the women pictured are Raquel Gonzalez, Lupe "Panchita" Garcia, Fortino Godinez, Criselda Cantu, Raquel Godinez, and Eliza Rendon. (Courtesy of the Pharr Memorial Library Archives.)

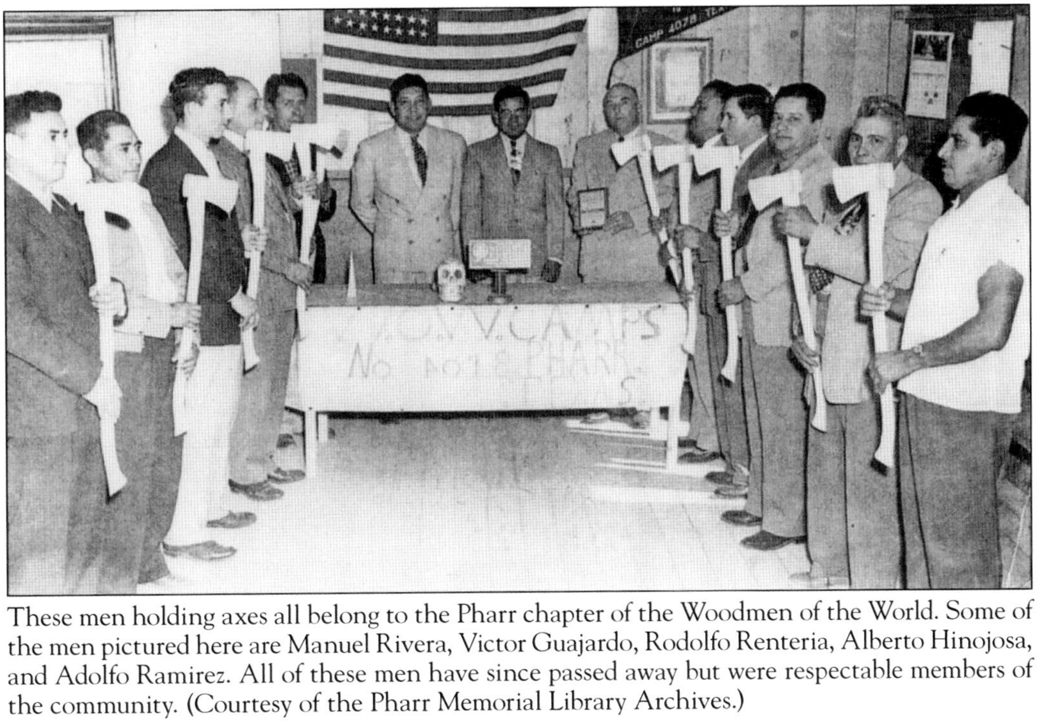

These men holding axes all belong to the Pharr chapter of the Woodmen of the World. Some of the men pictured here are Manuel Rivera, Victor Guajardo, Rodolfo Renteria, Alberto Hinojosa, and Adolfo Ramirez. All of these men have since passed away but were respectable members of the community. (Courtesy of the Pharr Memorial Library Archives.)

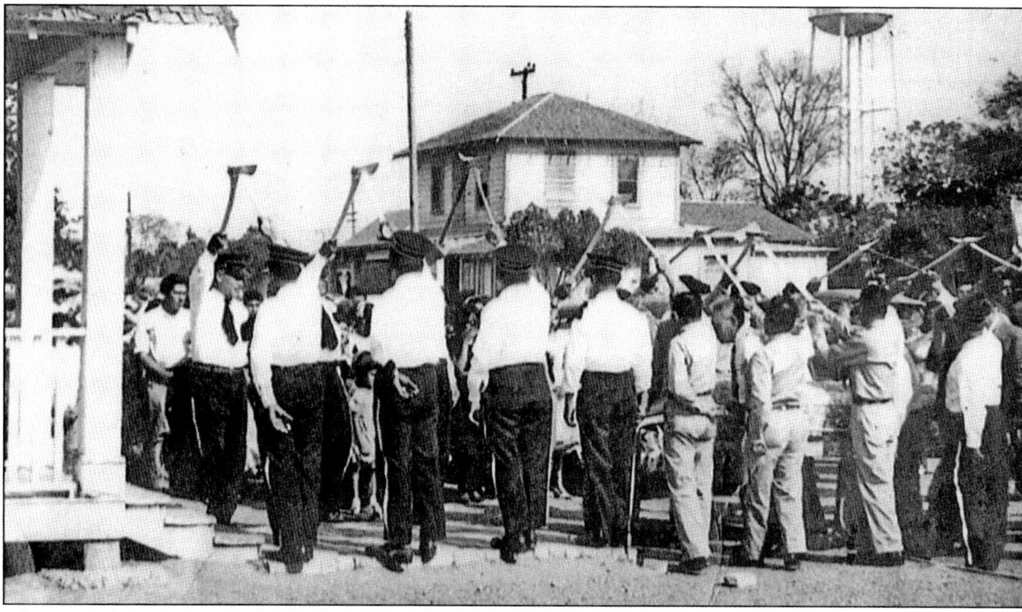

The Woodmen of the World is a fraternal (now insurance) organization whose history dates back to 1890 in Omaha, Nebraska. Pictured here are members of the Pharr chapter of the Woodmen of the World; they are honoring a member who passed away. These men are raising their axes as a traditional sign of respect. In Pharr, they were known as *hacheros*, meaning "lumberjack" or "logger" in English. The two-story home in the background belonged to Santos Ramirez. It is said that many games of chalupa, the Mexican version of bingo, were played on that front porch. (Courtesy of the Pharr Memorial Library Archives.)

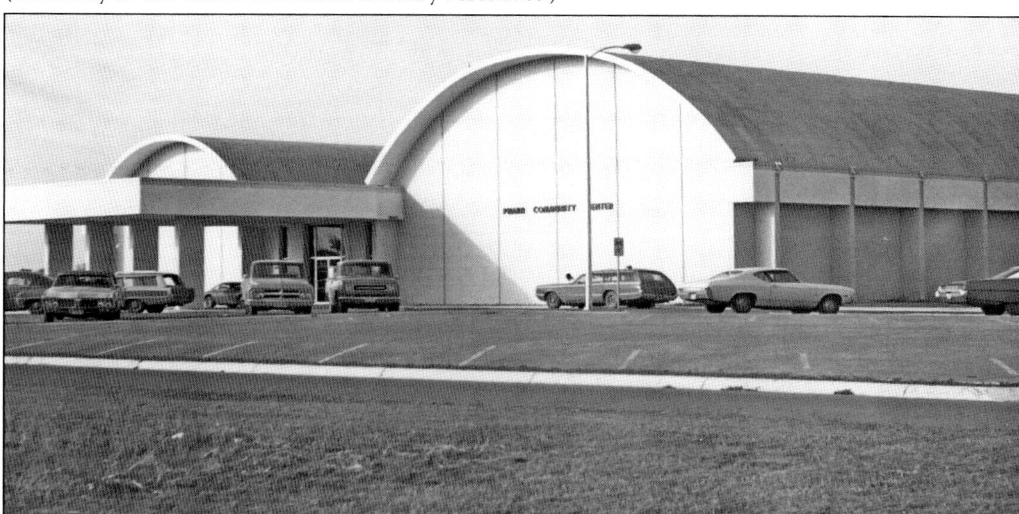

Since it was built, the Pharr Community Center was primarily utilized for intimate receptions such as luncheons and small dances, but small concerts and weddings have also taken place there. This 1971 photograph shows a south-facing view of the community center, which is located on West Kelly Avenue, with a few cars parked outside. Any Pharr resident will say that the center looks the same today as it did in this photograph. In 2003, the building was renamed the Jose "Pepe" Salinas Memorial Civic Center in memory of one of the city's most beloved citizens. (Courtesy of the Museum of South Texas History.)

Eight

PRESENT-DAY PHARR

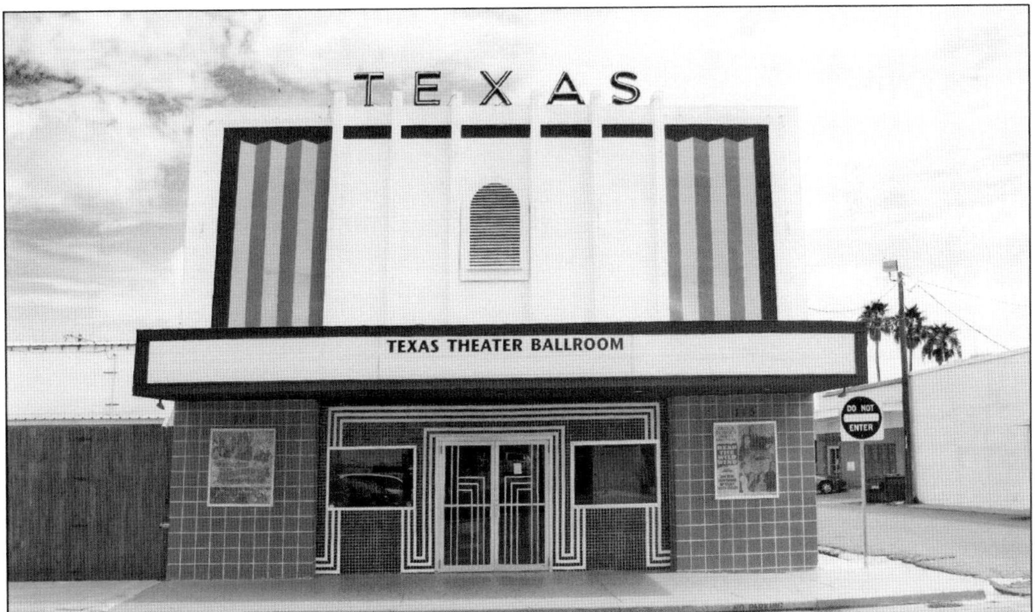

This photograph of the Texas Theater shows just how it looks in 2014. The theater has undergone a transformation two times in its history, and this is the end result. An old John Wayne movie poster still hangs out in front. The theater ceased operations in the 1970s, but is a local landmark for the community and serves as a reminder of Pharr's amazing history. (Courtesy of Julio Enriquez.)

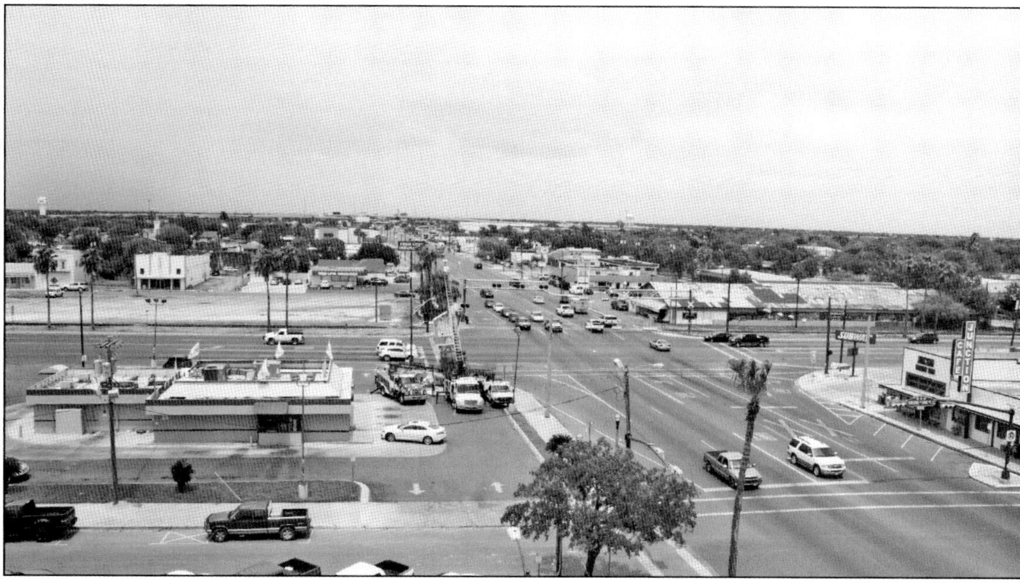

This photograph was taken atop the current city hall building in Pharr. The image captures the intersection of Cage Boulevard and Business 83 facing north. Visible below on the right-hand corner is Junction Café, which has served the community for over 50 years. Also visible, in the distance on the left-hand side, is Smitty's Jukebox Museum. This area of the city has grown tremendously over the years and continues to enjoy growth. (Courtesy of Julio Enriquez.)

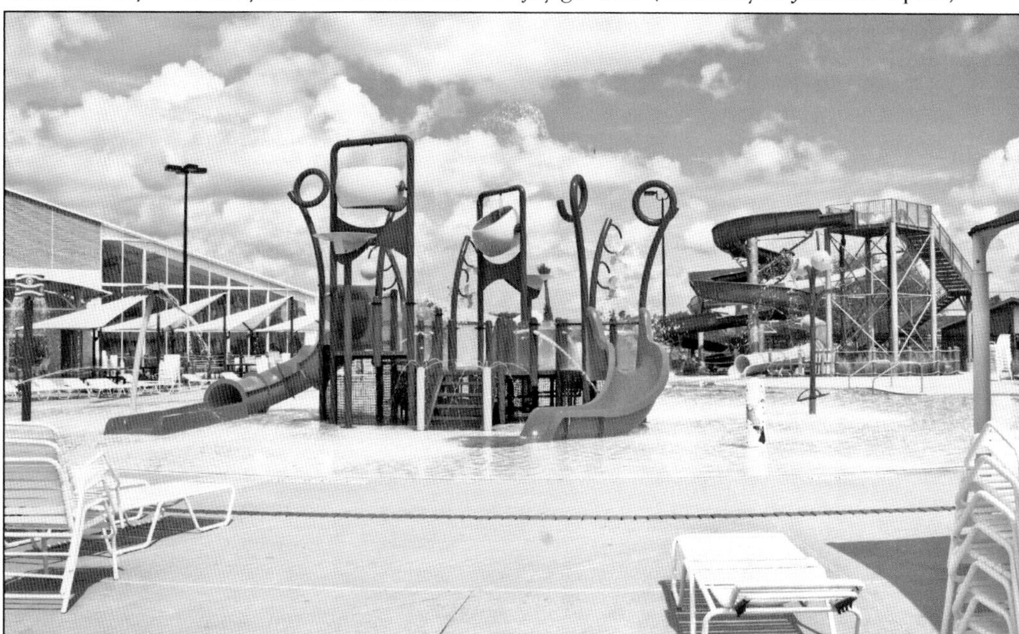

This amazing photograph captures the Pharr Aquatic Center, which is located at 1000 South Fir Street. The grand opening was July 4, 2013, and the center serves the community with plenty of family fun. It features a lazy river, water slides, and a toddler area. It is a two-acre $10 million park. It also includes a natatorium with 10 lanes and a diving board. The Pharr-San Juan-Alamo School District uses the pool for swim team training. (Courtesy of Julio Enriquez.)

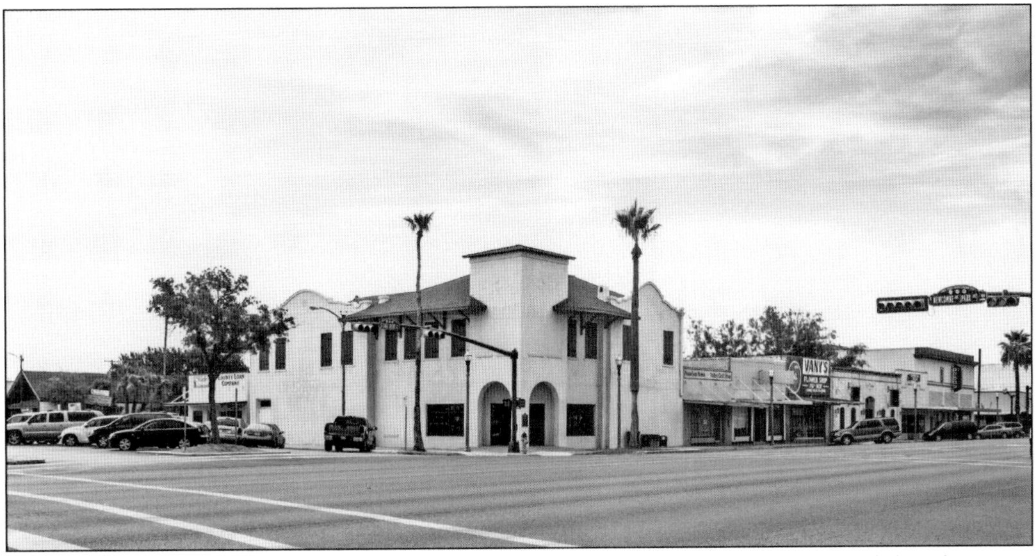

Pictured here is the old Pharr City Hall. The building looks exactly the same as it did in the 1940s and 1950s. It is a historical landmark and is owned today by Romeo Escobar. This photograph was taken from the corner of Cage Boulevard and Park Avenue. (Courtesy of Julio Enriquez.)

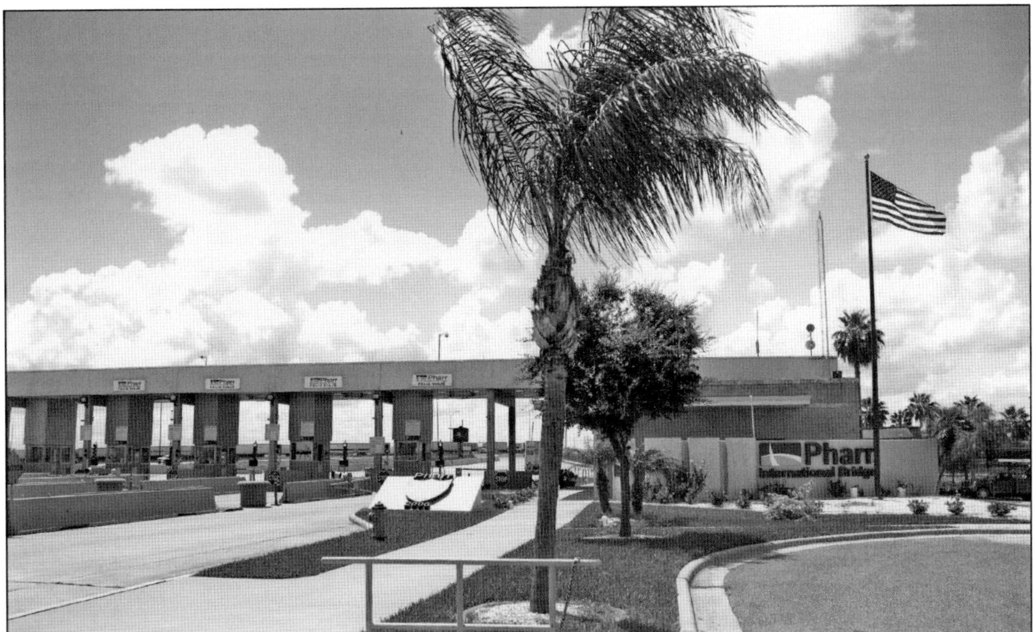

Pictured here is the office of the Pharr-Reynosa International Bridge. The bridge operates by using four lanes to cross and a toll fee that varies from car to truck, depending on the number of axles. The total revenue for the Pharr-Reynosa International Bridge totaled $978,290 for the month of July in the fiscal year 2012–2013. This is a very important and busy bridge. (Courtesy of Julio Enriquez.)

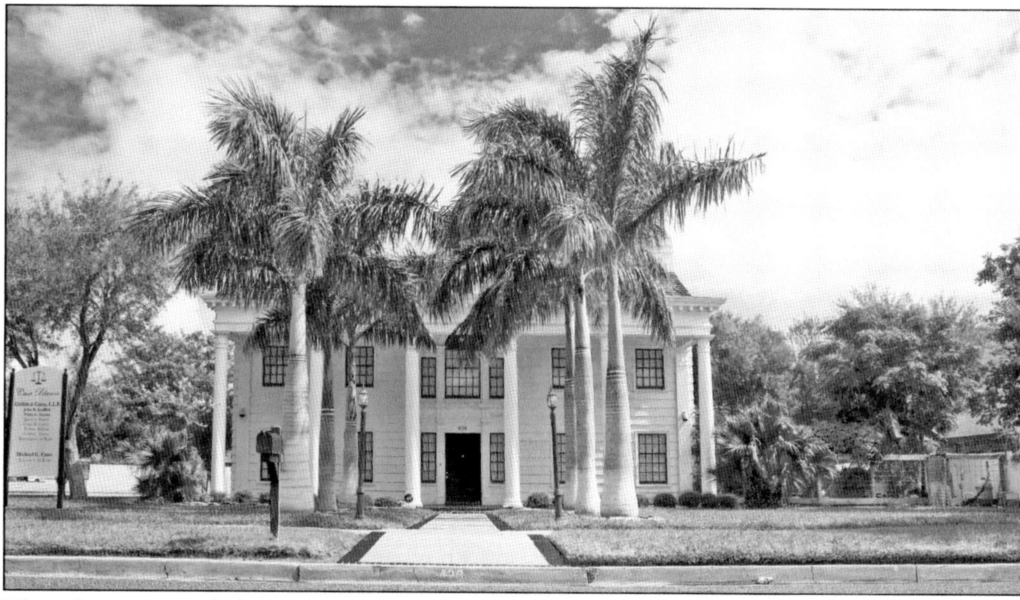

This plantation-style house at 426 West Caffery Street is one of the most amazing structures in the city. It was originally home to a family, whose name is not known at this time, but was later sold and converted to Skinner Funeral Home. The owners of the funeral home eventually changed locations, leaving the house vacant. Today, the structure serves as offices for a law firm. (Courtesy of Julio Enriquez.)

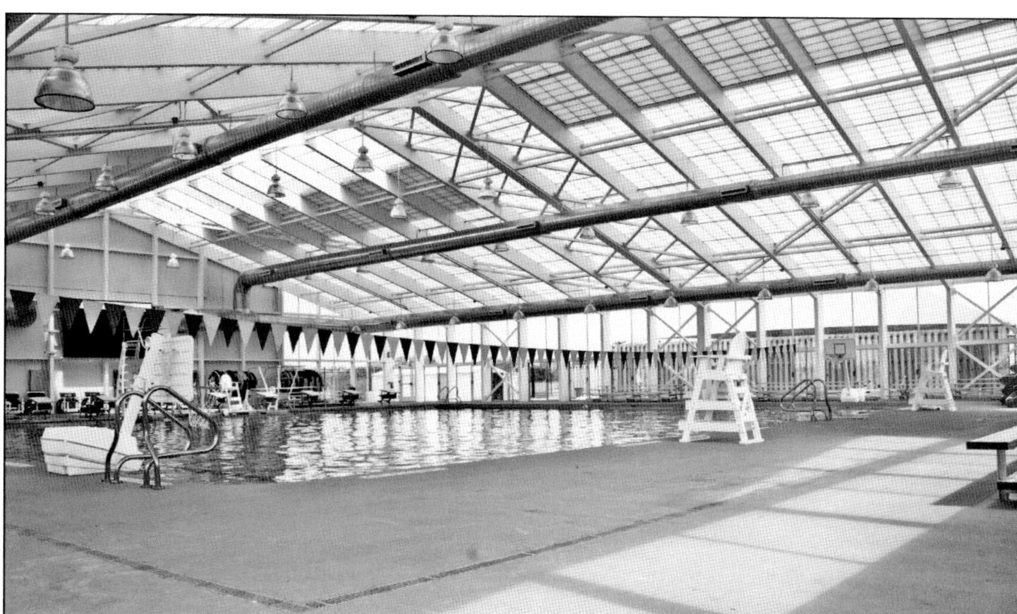

The Pharr Aquatic Center is not only a place for family entertainment. Pictured here is the natatorium, located on the same grounds as the aquatic center. This indoor pool is equipped with 10 lanes and a diving board. Since the Pharr-San Juan-Alamo Independent School District uses the pool, the district chipped in nearly half of the total funding for the aquatic center to pay for this natatorium structure. (Courtesy of Julio Enriquez.)

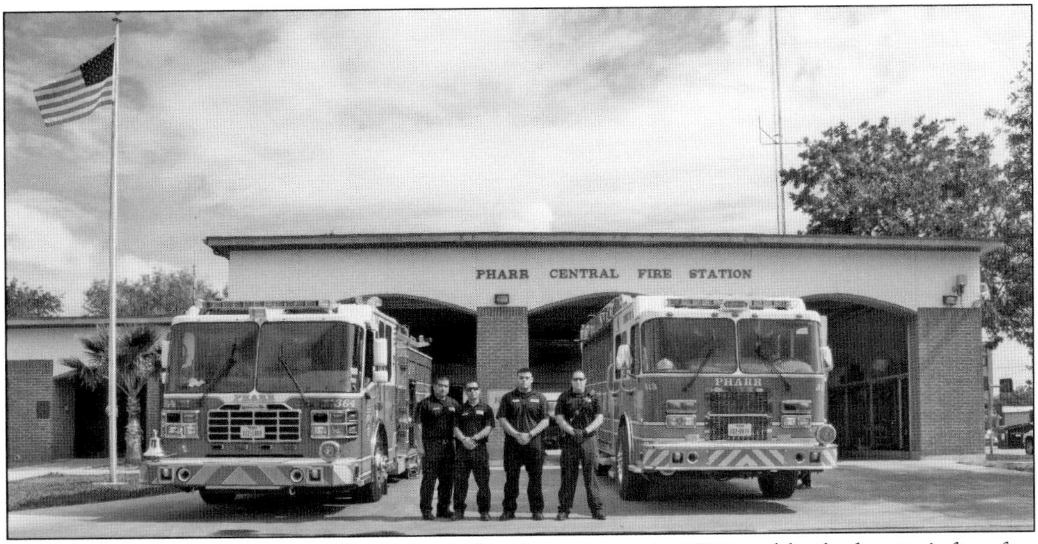

The city officially formed an all-volunteer fire department in 1921 and built the city's first fire station in 1928. Pharr has come a long way since then. Pictured here is station No. 2, which is located on 120 West Cherokee Street, right next to the original fire station. There are two other fire stations in the city. Station No. 1 is located on 1901 North Fir Street and station No. 3 is located on 7107 South Cage Boulevard. The firemen pictured are, from left to right, Santos Baez, Santos Vallejo, David Martinez, and Mike Navarro.

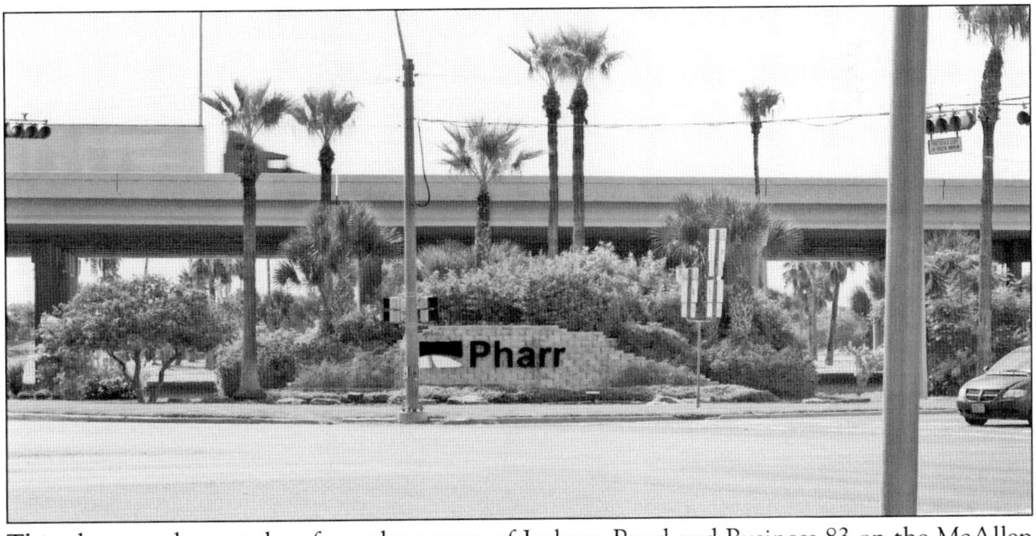

This photograph was taken from the corner of Jackson Road and Business 83 on the McAllen side. Visible is a small sign that welcomes travelers to the city of Pharr. Behind it is the overpass which is under construction in the 1963 photograph on page 76. This intersection sees heavy traffic on a daily basis as Pharr and McAllen connect here. (Courtesy of Julio Enriquez.)

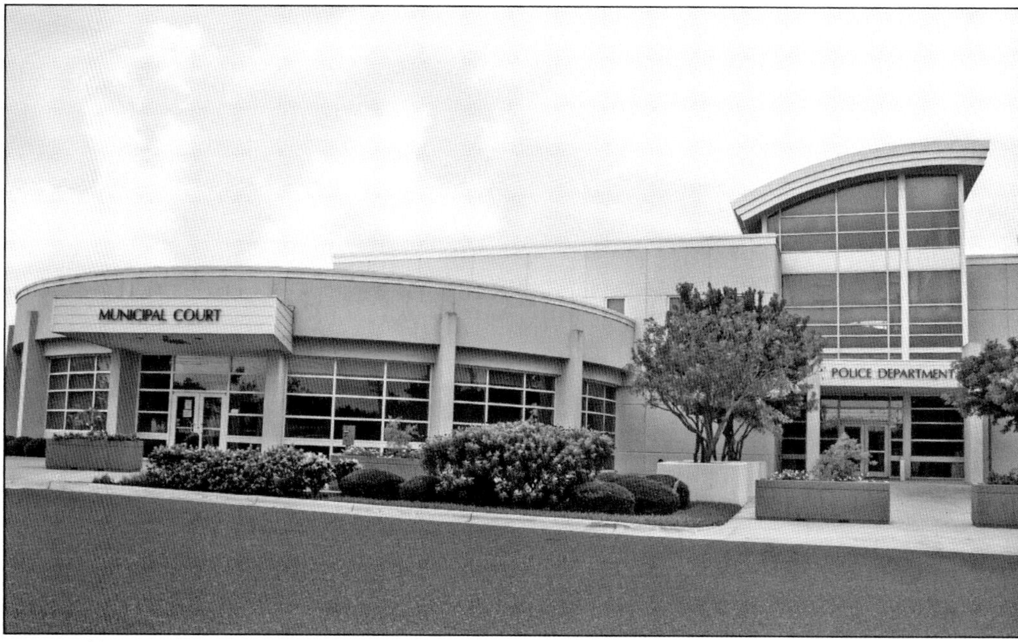

Pictured here is the Pharr Police Department, which is located on South Cage Boulevard. For a long time, the department was located in a small building on East Clark Street, until the current home was built approximately 10 years ago. The new department is a 46,000-square-foot structure that cost $6.8 million to build. The Pharr Police Department has almost 200 employees. (Courtesy of Julio Enriquez.)

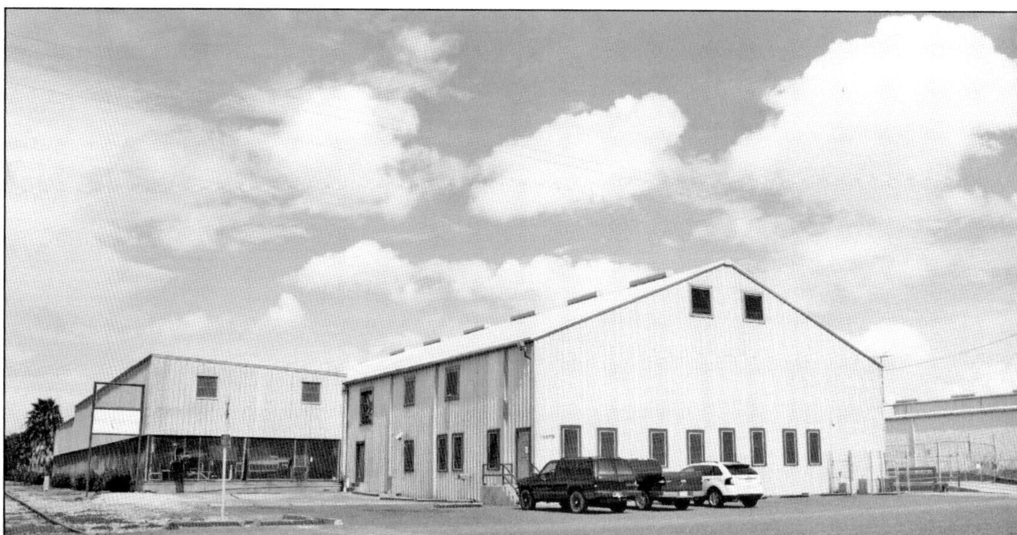
Pictured here from the south side of the railroad tracks on Business 83 is Progreso Produce. The company was founded by Dale DeBerry over 40 years ago in Progreso, Texas. It originally specialized in the growing and selling of onions but branched out to grow and sell watermelons, Mexican strawberries, Roma tomatoes, and cucumbers. Today, Pharr is now home to one of the company's headquarters. It is at 11 North Birch Street, which is where the old Elmore and Stahl packing warehouse was located. This has been a site for packing produce since the 1920s. (Courtesy of Julio Enriquez.)

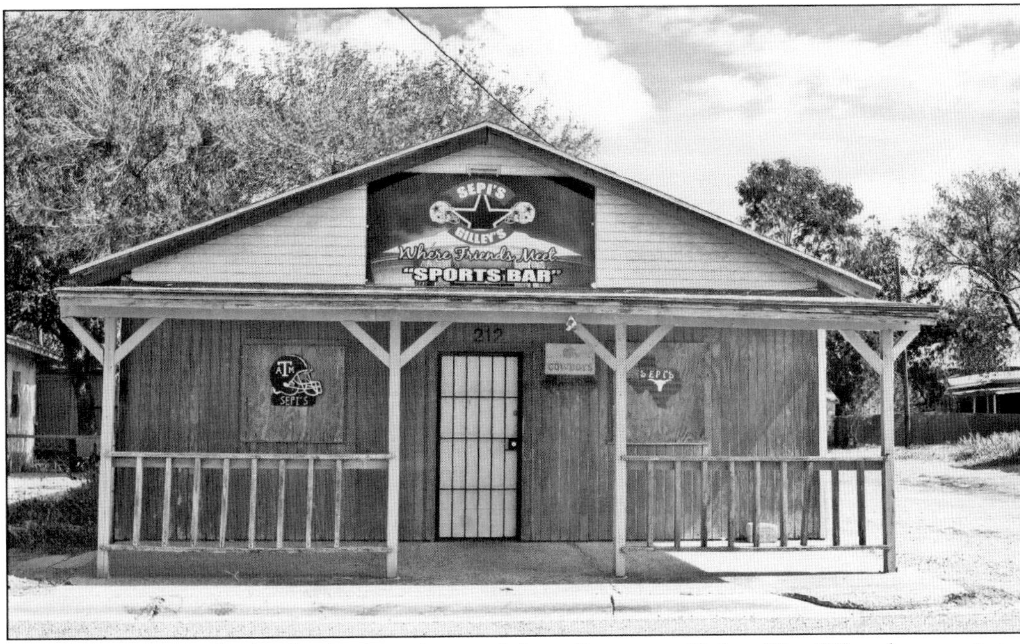

Sepi's Cantina was the last bar built in the city. Mayor Bowe gave Ruben "Sepi" Rosales permission to construct it in 1971. When A.C. Jaime became mayor, he did not issue permits to build bars. Rosales recently retired in 2006 but still owns the cantina. He is a very well liked and respected man in the city. Sepi's is a very well-known establishment where friends meet. (Courtesy of Julio Enriquez.)

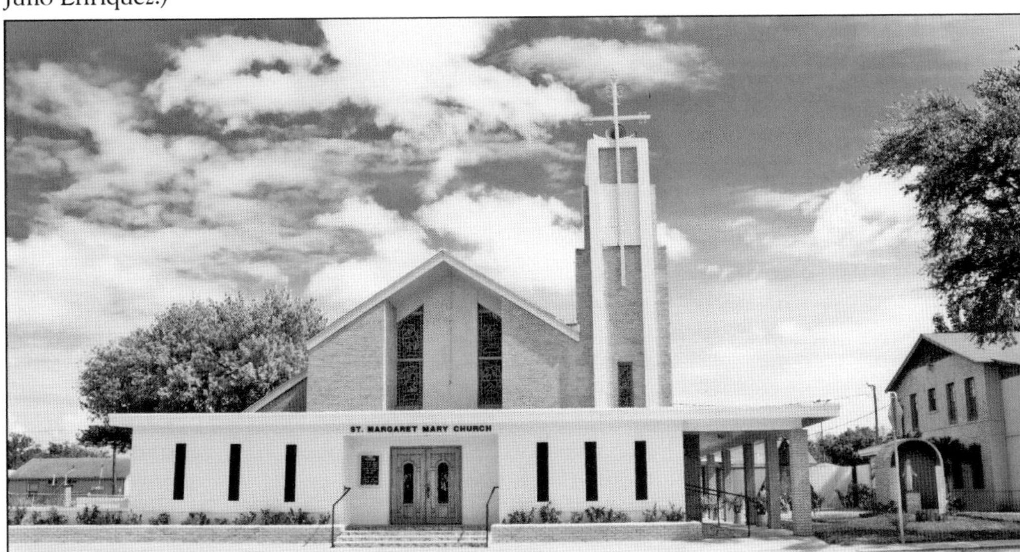

This is St. Margaret Mary Catholic Church as it looks today. The church recently underwent some renovations under Father Genaro's direction. This picture was taken from across Hawk Avenue, where the church's parish hall is located. The parish hall has numerous classrooms that are used during the school year for catechism. St. Margaret Mary Church has been around for a very long time and will continue to serve the community for a long time to come. (Courtesy of Julio Enriquez.)

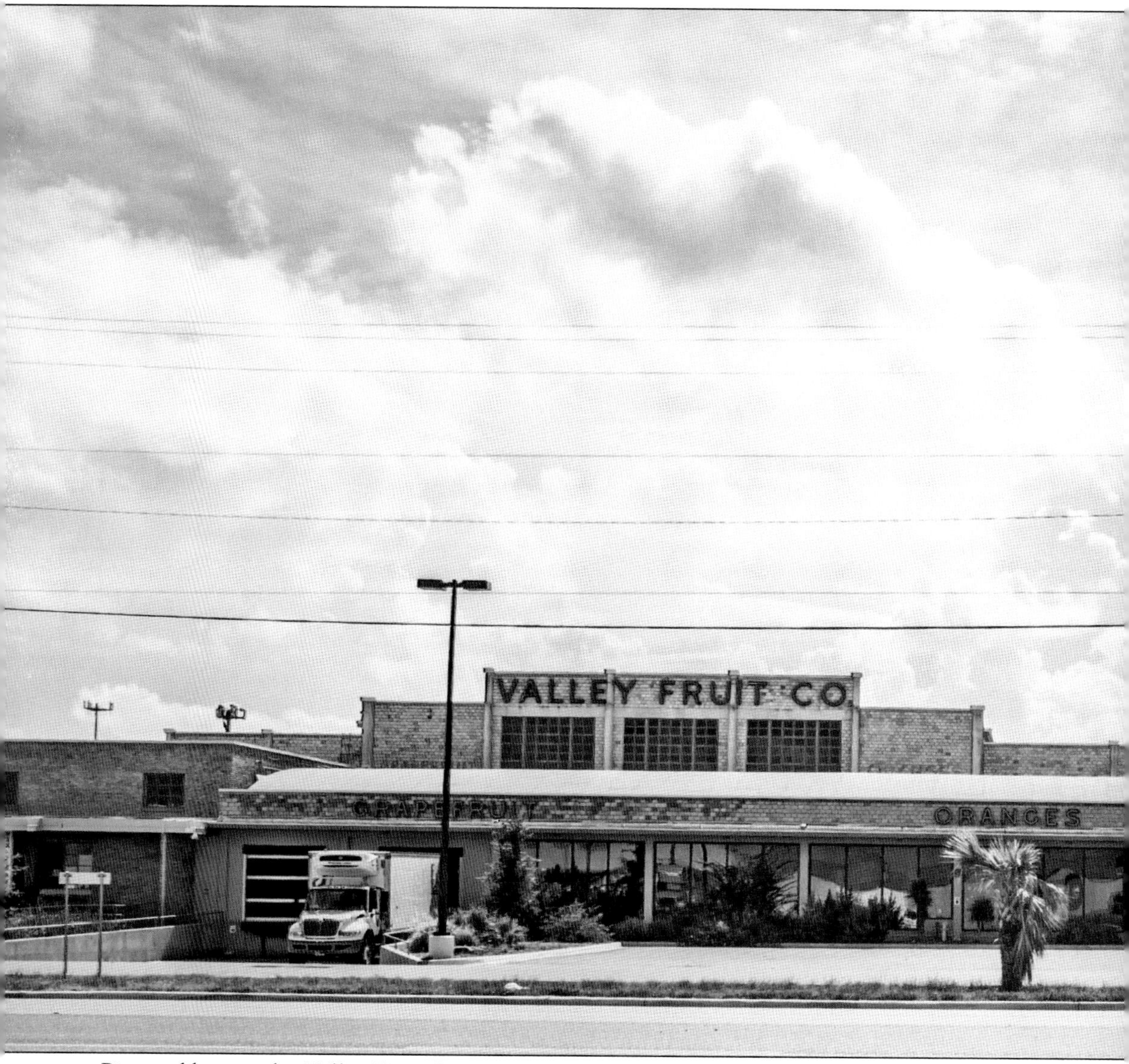

Pictured here is the Valley Fruit Company in its current state. This historic building is situated on Cage Boulevard but is no longer in operation as a fruit packing warehouse. The Valley Fruit Company building now serves as the headquarters of the Food Bank of the Rio Grande Valley. In its heyday in the 1940s, it was the hub of the Rio Grande Valley produce market, employing some 1,500 people, making it one of the world's largest packing companies and the biggest employer

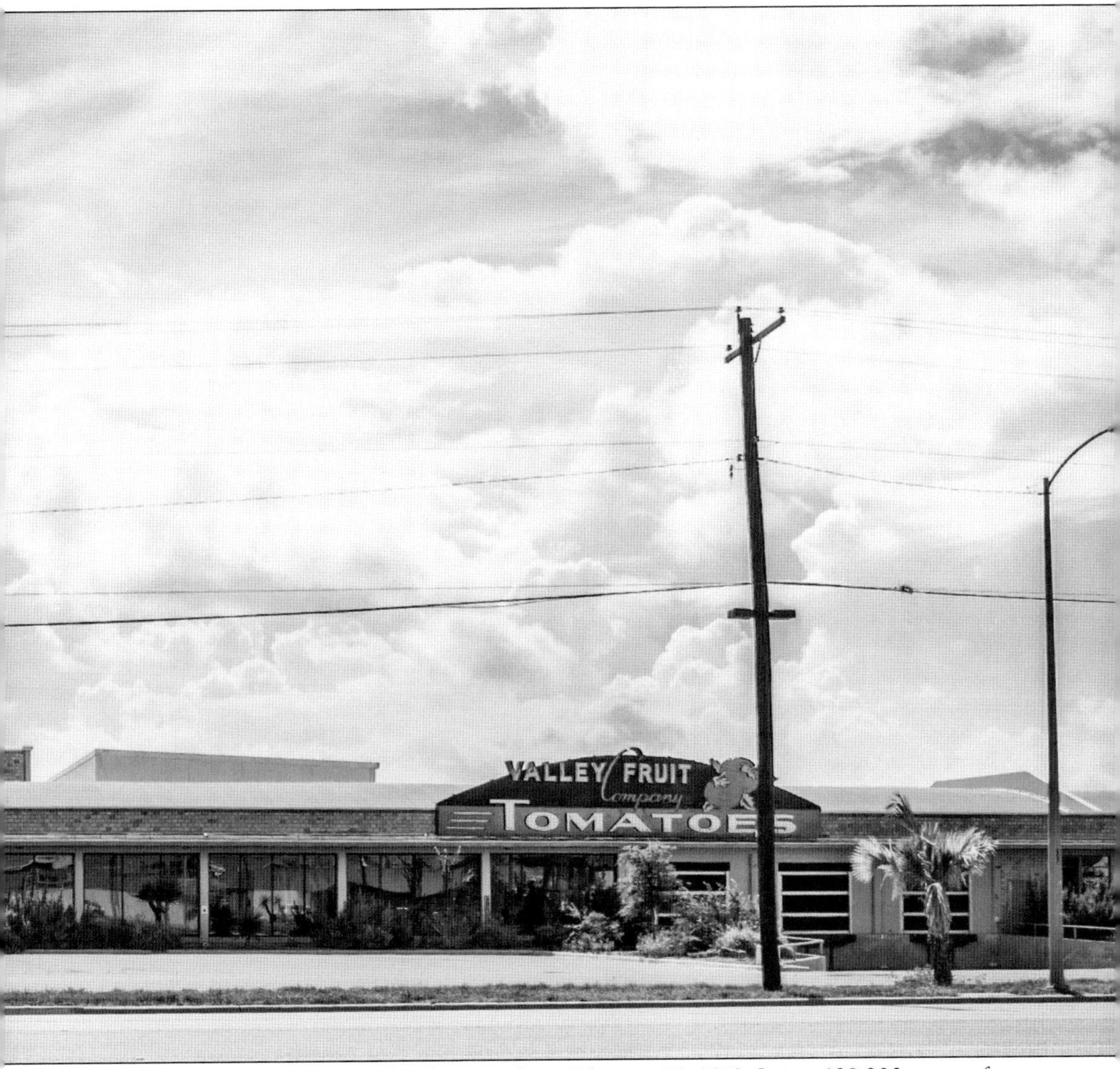

in Deep South Texas. The food bank opened on February 29, 2012. It is a 108,000-square-foot facility that holds a special place in the hearts of many Pharr natives. The building's location near the intersection of US Route 281 and US Route 83 is ideal for food distribution in Hidalgo, Willacy, and Cameron Counties. The structure is listed in the National Register of Historic Places. (Courtesy of Julio Enriquez.)

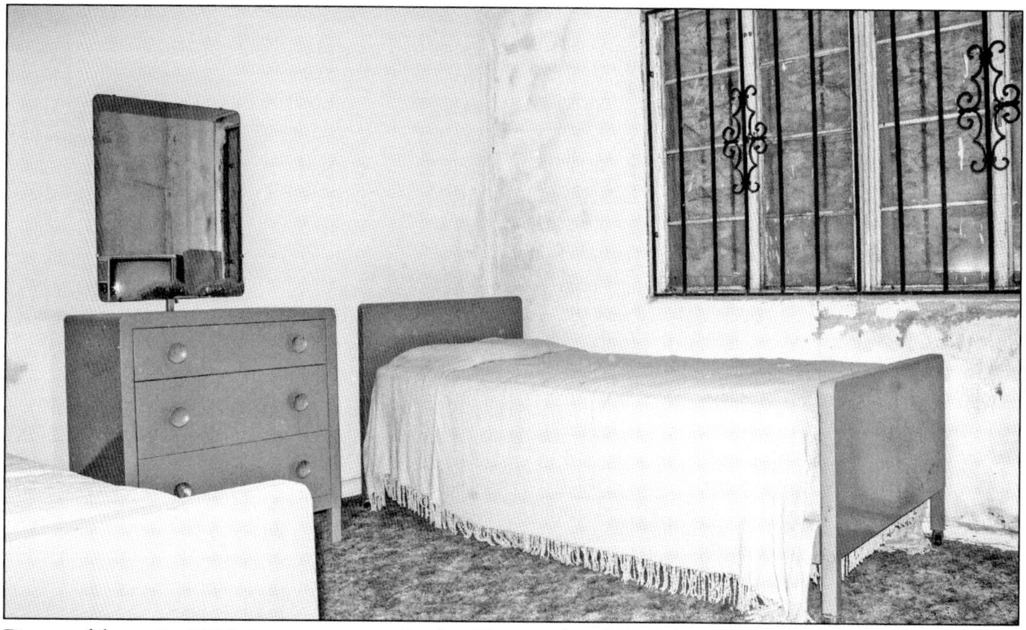

Pictured here in 2013 is a room inside the Texan Hotel that has the window boarded up but strangely has two beds perfectly made with a dresser that is in immaculate condition. It is as if time stood still in the hotel. Many local residents claim that the hotel is haunted. There is no proof of these claims, but it is an interesting story that comes up when the Texan Hotel is mentioned. (Courtesy of Julio Enriquez.)

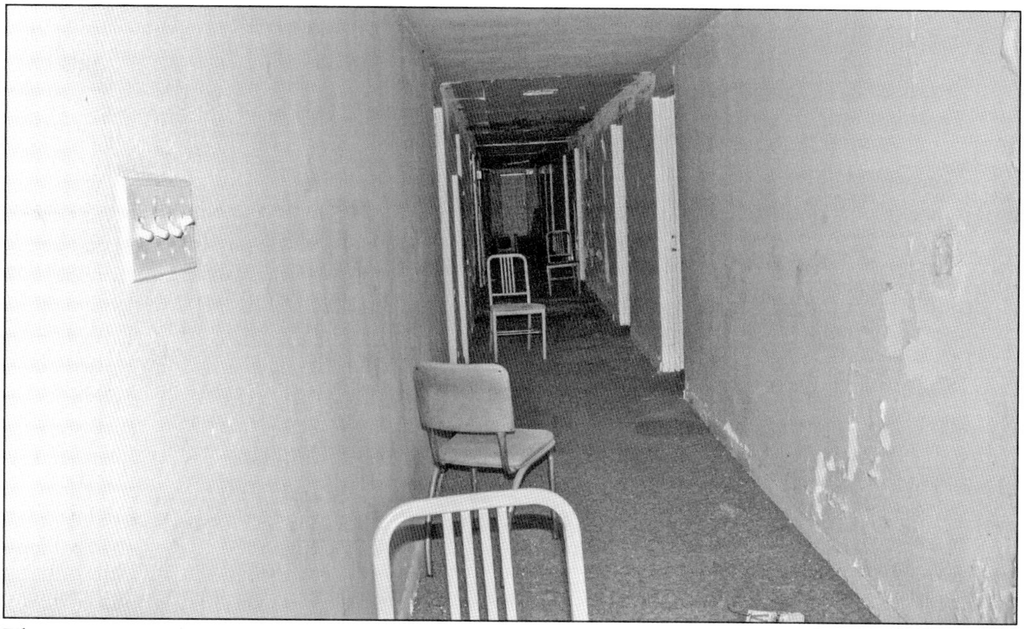

This eerie 2013 photograph was taken from the inside of the Texan Hotel, which ceased operations in 1987. These days, most Pharr natives can say that they have never been inside the Texan Hotel so this is a rare look at the interior. Randomly placed in this very dark hallway are several chairs that belonged to the hotel. The building has two long hallways that make an L shape where a number of rooms can be found. (Courtesy of Julio Enriquez.)

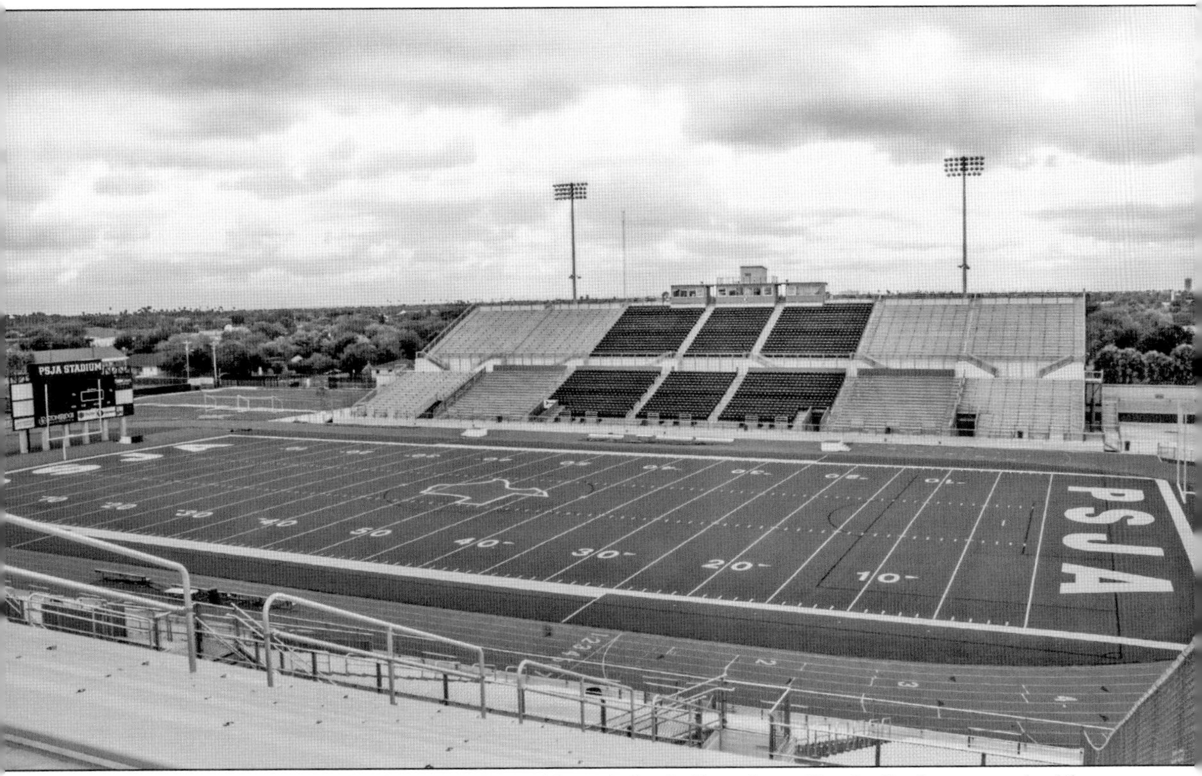

Pictured here is a look inside Pharr-San Juan-Alamo's football stadium. Football is known to be like a religion in the state of Texas, and this stadium gets packed for Friday night games. It is located in Pharr but is home to teams from four high schools in the Pharr-San Juan-Alamo area. The Pharr-San Juan-Alamo Bears, Pharr-San Juan-Alamo Raiders, Pharr-San Juan-Alamo Wolverines, and Pharr-San Juan-Alamo Javelinas all share this field. (Courtesy of Julio Enriquez.)

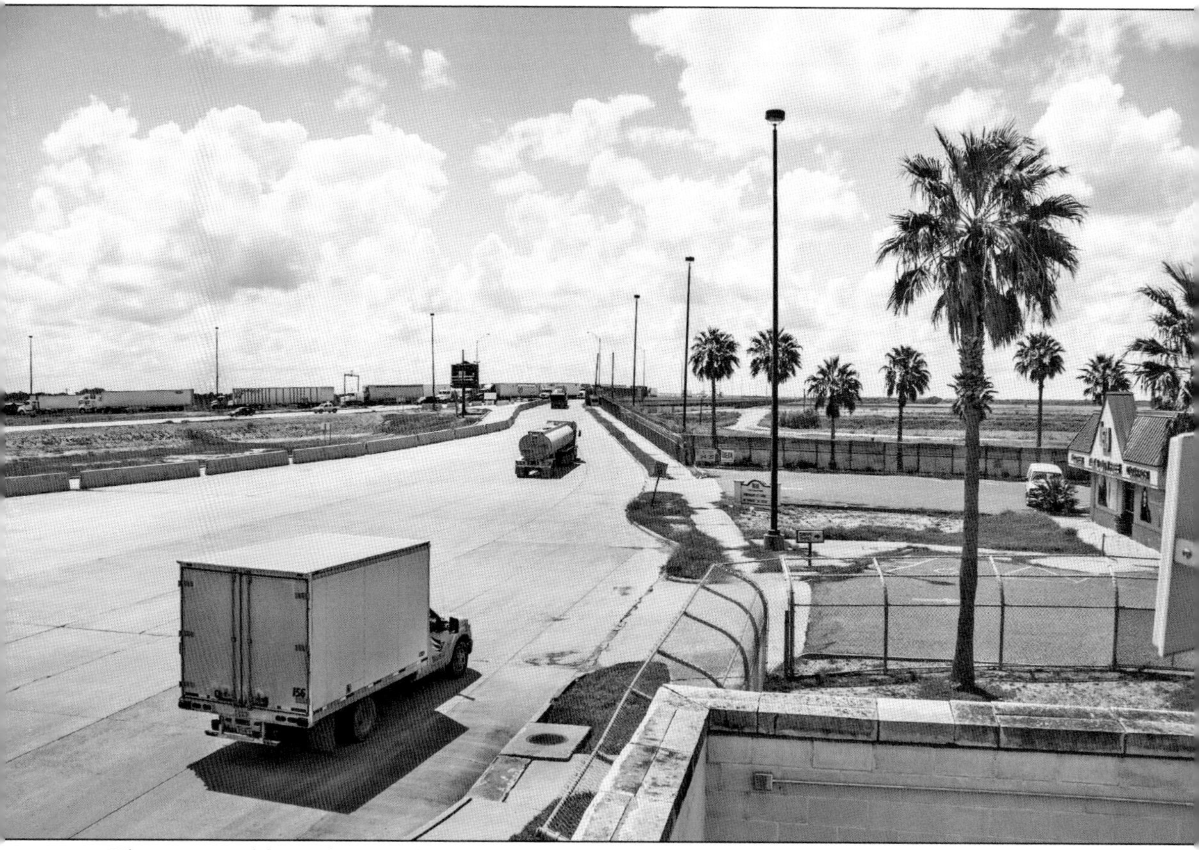

This is a southbound view of the Pharr-Reynosa International Bridge, connecting Interstate 69 to the city of Reynosa, Tamaulipas, in Mexico. This bridge, the longest connecting the United States and Mexico, serves as one of the most important ports of entry along the border and handles commercial vehicles as well as passenger-operated vehicles. This photograph was taken atop the roof of the Pharr-Reynosa International Bridge Department. Lines of trailers can be seen making their way to the US port of entry. Just a few feet north of where this photograph was taken is the country of Mexico. (Courtesy of Julio Enriquez.)

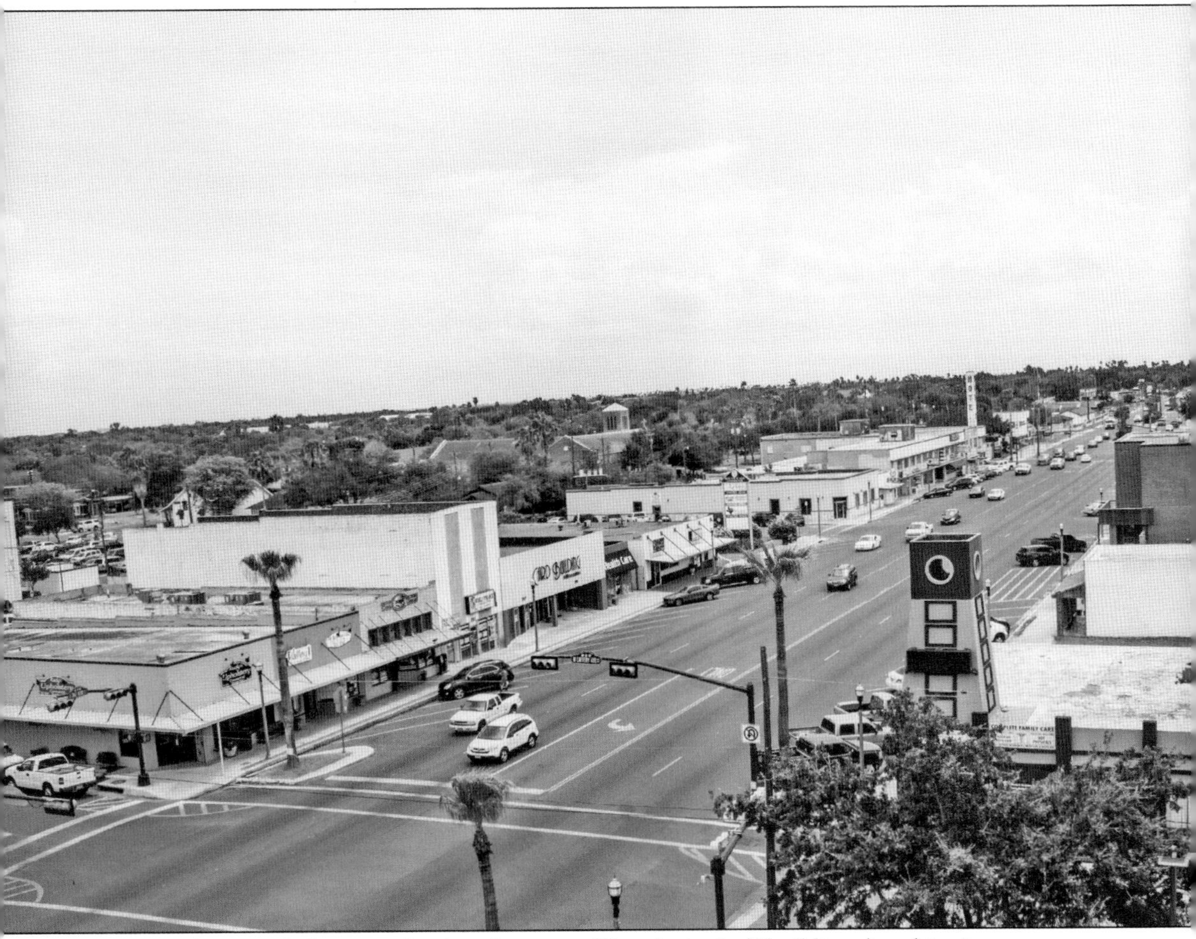

Here is another aerial photograph taken from atop Pharr's city hall building, but this view captures Cage Boulevard facing south. Pictured are several businesses that make up part of the downtown of the city. This area has also seen tremendous growth over the years and is the heart of Pharr. In the distance is the Texan Hotel, without its familiar Texan Cowboy up on top. (Courtesy of Julio Enriquez.)

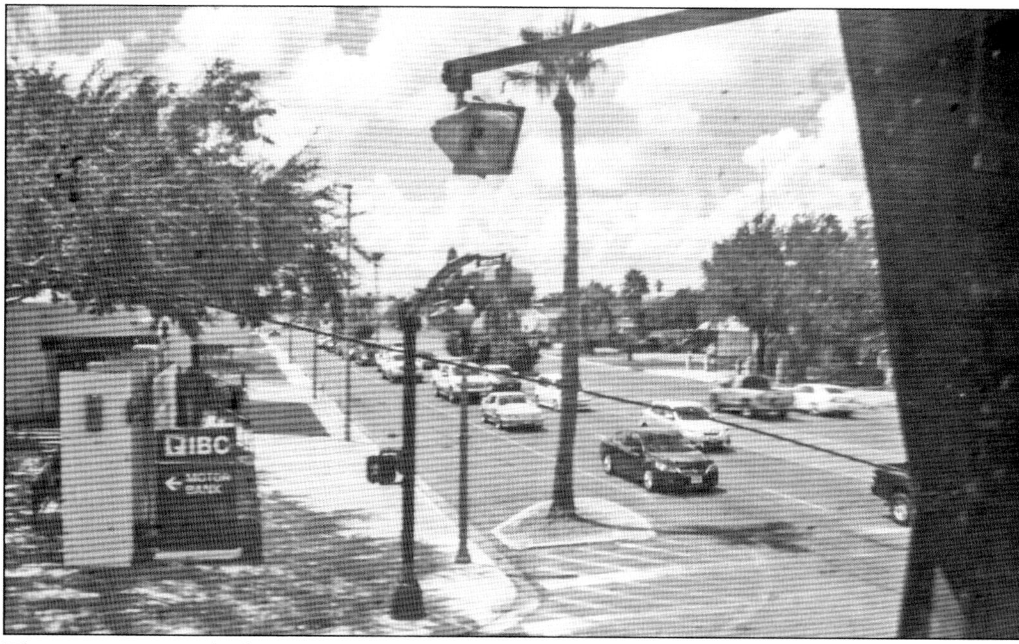

This image was made through a window screen in the Texan Hotel's suite room, located right on the corner of Cage Boulevard and Kelly Avenue. This photograph captures a view facing south on Cage Boulevard. It is a wonderful look at the city's main street. (Courtesy of Julio Enriquez.)

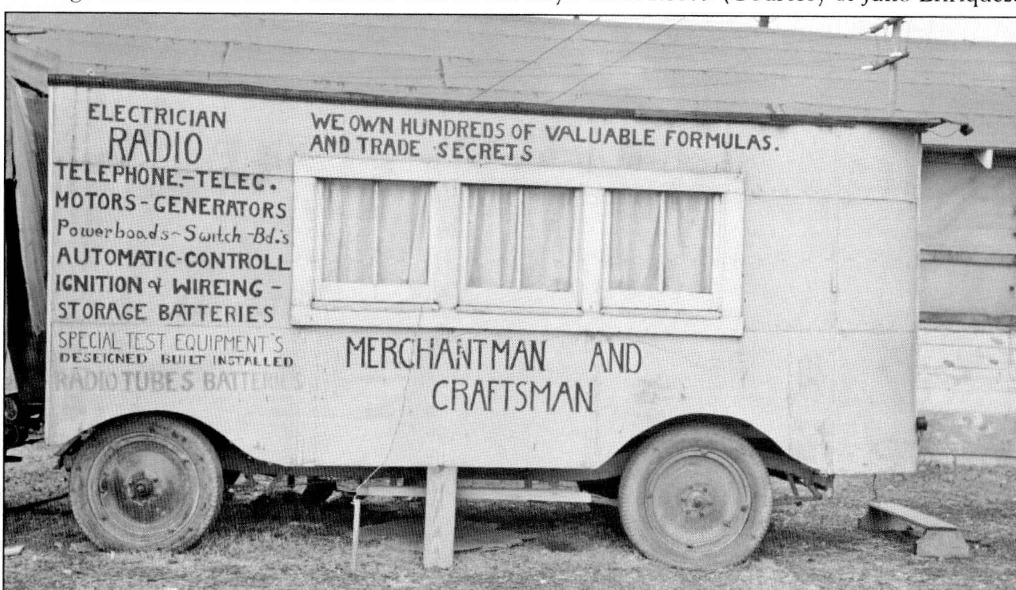

The city of Pharr has enjoyed a rich history since its incorporation in 1916. This final photograph of a merchantman's work truck was taken in the late 1930s. This image reminds all Pharr natives that the city has come a long way and has enjoyed many changes and tremendous growth in its 100-plus years. Pharr has progressed from being a settlement founded as a center for sugarcane and other agriculture to becoming a beautiful city that has amassed wealth and history and attracts various businesses as it grows into the 21st century. Pharr will forever be linked to the amazing history that has occurred in South Texas. (Courtesy of the Library of Congress.)

BIBLIOGRAPHY

Chambers, Henry E. *A History of Louisiana: Wilderness, Colony, Province, Territory, State, People.* Chicago: American Historical Society, 1925.

Congdon, Capt. H.W., "Twenty-third Infantry." *New York Division National Guard War Record* (1917): 16–17.

Congdon, Herbert. *Herbert Congdon Collection.* New York State Military Museum.

Grain and Farm Service Centers, Vol. 38. Chicago: University of Chicago Press, 1917.

Herbert W. Congdon Papers Collection. cdi.uvm.edu/findingaids/collection/congdon.ead.xml

O'Ryan, Maj. Gen. John F. *The Story of the 27th Division.* NY: Wynkoop Hallenbeck Crawford Co., 1921.

www.rgvsugar.com/history

www.tn.gov/tsla/history/state/recordgroups/findingaids/rg216.pdf

www.tshaonline.org/handbook/online/articles/afc01

www.tshaonline.org/handbook/online/articles/ama01

www.tshaonline.org/handbook/online/articles/hep05

www.window.state.tx.us/specialrpt/tif/southtexas/sidebars/agriculture.html

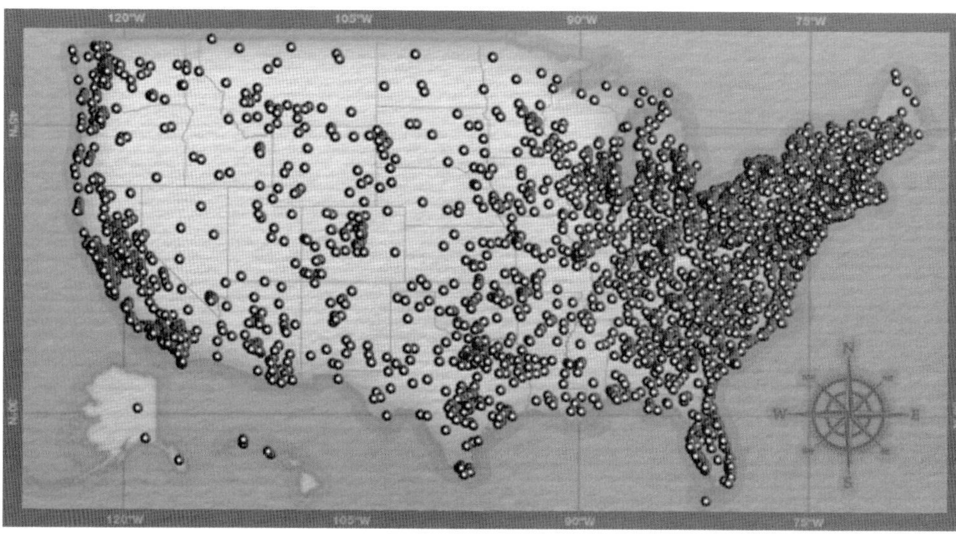